W9-CHV-003

Literacy for the New Millennium

I dedicate this series of books to all those who center their professional lives on fostering the development and practice of literacy.

LITERACY FOR THE NEW MILLENNIUM

Volume 1

Early Literacy

Edited by Barbara J. Guzzetti

Praeger Perspectives

Westport, Connecticut
London

Library of Congress Cataloging-in-Publication Data

Literacy for the new millennium / edited by Barbara J. Guzzetti.
v. cm.
Includes bibliographical references and indexes.
Contents: v. 1. Early literacy — v. 2 Childhood literacy — v. 3 Adolescent literacy — v. 4 Adult literacy.
ISBN-13: 978–0–275–98969–9 (set : alk. paper)
ISBN-10: 0–275–98969–0 (set : alk. paper)
ISBN-13: 978–0–275–98992–7 (v.1 : alk. paper)
ISBN-10: 0–275–98992–5 (v.1 : alk. paper)
[etc.]
1. Literacy. 2. Language arts. I. Guzzetti, Barbara J.
LC149.L4987 2007
302.2'244—dc22 2007018116

British Library Cataloguing in Publication Data is available.

Library of Congress Catalog Card Number: 2007018116
ISBN-13: 978–0-275–98969–9 (set) ISBN-10: 0–275–98969–0
ISBN-13: 978–0-275–98992–7 (vol. 1) ISBN-10: 0–275–98992–5
ISBN-13: 978–0-275–98993–4 (vol. 2) ISBN-10: 0–275–98993–3
ISBN-13: 978–0-275–98994–1 (vol. 3) ISBN-10: 0–275–98994–1
ISBN-13: 978–0-275–98995–8 (vol. 4) ISBN-10: 0–275–98995-X

First published in 2007

Praeger Publishers, 88 Post Road West, Westport, CT 06881
An imprint of Greenwood Publishing Group, Inc.
www.praeger.com

Printed in the United States of America

The paper used in this book complies with the Permanent Paper Standard issued by the National Information Standards Organization (Z39.48–1984).

10 9 8 7 6 5 4 3 2 1

CONTENTS

SET PREFACE

This set of four volumes—*Literacy for the New Millennium: Early Literacy; Literacy for the New Millennium: Childhood Literacy; Literacy for the New Millennium: Adolescent Literacy;* and *Literacy for the New Millennium: Adult Literacy*—presents a current and comprehensive overview of literacy assessment, instruction, practice, and issues across the life span. Each volume presents contemporary issues and trends, as well as classic topics associated with the ages and stages of literacy development and practice represented in that text. The chapters in each volume provide the reader with insights into policies and issues that influence literacy development and practice. Together, these volumes represent an informative and timely discussion of the broad field of literacy.

The definition of literacy on which each of these volumes is grounded is a current and expanded one. Literacy is defined in this set in a broad way by encompassing both traditional notions of literacy, such as reading, writing, listening, and speaking, and the consumption and production of nonprint texts, such as media and computer texts. Chapters on technology and popular culture in particular reflect this expanded definition of literacy to literacies that represents current trends in the field. This emphasis sets this set apart from other more traditional texts on literacy.

The authors who contributed to this set represent a combination of well-known researchers and educators in literacy, as well as those relatively new to the profession of literacy education and scholarship. Contributors to the set represent university professors, senior scientists at research institutions, practitioners or consultants in the field, teacher educators, and researchers in literacy. Although the authors are experts in the field of literacy, they have written their chapters to be reader friendly by defining and explaining any professional jargon and by writing in an unpretentious and comprehensible style.

Each of the four volumes shaped by these authors has common features. Each of the texts is divided into three parts, with the first part devoted to recent trends and issues affecting the field of literacy for that age range. The second part addresses issues in assessment and instruction. The final part presents issues beyond the classroom that affect literacy development and practice at that level. Each of the texts concludes with a chapter on literacy resources appropriate for the age group that the volume addresses. These include resources and materials from professional organizations, and a brief bibliography for further reading.

Each of the volumes has common topics, as well as a common structure. All the volumes address issues of federal legislation, funding, and policies that affect literacy assessment instruction and practice. Each volume addresses assessment issues in literacy for each age range represented in that text. As a result of the growing importance of technology for instruction, recreation, information acquisition, communication, and participation in a global economy, each book addresses some aspect of literacy in the digital age. Because of the importance of motivating students in literacy and bridging the gap between students' in-school literacy instruction and their out-of-school literacy practices, each text that addresses literacy for school-age children discusses the influence and incorporation of youth and popular culture in literacy instruction.

In short, these volumes are crafted to address the salient issues, polices, practices, and procedures in literacy that affect literacy development and practice. These texts provide a succinct yet inclusive overview of the field of literacy in a way that is easily accessible to readers with little or no prior knowledge of the field. Preservice teachers, educators, teacher trainers, librarians, policy makers, researchers, and the public will find a useful resource and reference guide in this set.

In conclusion, I would like to acknowledge the many people who have contributed to the creation of this set. First, I recognize the outstanding contributions of the authors. Their writings not only reflect the most informative current trends and classic topics in the field but also present their subjects in ways that take bold stances. In doing so, they provide exciting future directions for the field.

Second, I acknowledge the contributions to the production of this set by staff at Arizona State University in the College of Education. My appreciation goes to Don Hutchins, director of computer support, for his organizational skills and assistance in the electronic production of this set. In addition, I extend my appreciation to my research assistant, Thomas Leyba, for his help in organizing the clerical aspects of the project.

Finally, I would like to thank the staff and editors at Praeger Publishers, who have provided guidance and support throughout the process of producing this set. In particular, I would like to thank Marie Ellen Larcada, who has since left the project but shared the conception of the set with me and supported me through the initial stages of production. My appreciation also goes to Elizabeth Potenza, who has guided this set into its final production, and without whose support this set would not have been possible. My kudos extend to you all.

Barbara J. Guzzetti

PREFACE

LITERACY FOR THE NEW MILLENNIUM: EARLY LITERACY

This book, the first in the set of four, is crafted around the recent reconceptualization of early literacy as including the ages from birth to age three, as well as children in preschool or kindergarten and the primary grades (grades K–3). The term "early literacy" recently replaced the term emergent literacy. It is now recognized that just as there is no ending point of literacy, there is also no turning point or single boundary that signifies literacy.

This book reflects this shift in terminology. The text is based on the premise that even very young children, in their awareness of environmental print, exhibit literacy. Experts in the field recommend that even infants can benefit from being read to and young children are stimulated by their environment as they learn to speak and read language. Early literacy development is crucial to students' success in school and life.

To provide insight into the problems, issues, and topics associated with early literacy, this text is organized into three main parts. These parts range from three to eight chapters per part and provide an overview of topics related to the field of early literacy. These topics were chosen to reflect and address the concerns of a variety of readers, including undergraduates considering a career in education, teachers, researchers, librarians, policy makers, parents, and interested members of the public.

The first part of *Literacy for the New Millennium: Early Literacy* addresses current problems, policies, and legislation in the field of early literacy. This part, "Recent Issues in the Field of Early Literacy," begins with a chapter by

Susan Neuman, who describes federal funding and legislation for early literacy instruction. She discusses redistribution of federal funds so that more funding is targeted at the younger ages to prevent reading difficulties in later school years, and the need to fund approaches and programs that work. The next chapter, by S. Jay Samuels, Terri Fautsch Partridge, and Caroline Hilk, provides an overview of the impetus for and the findings of the National Reading Panel, a committee of literacy educators and scholars that was charged with synthesizing instructional studies from the extant research to identify the most effective approaches to reading instruction. This chapter is an overview of the work and findings of the panel. The third and final chapter in this part, by Mario Castro, discusses the political, social, economic, cultural, and environmental issues that impact early literacy, and in doing so, summarizes some popular methods to manage that impact. To illustrate his points, Castro presents a case study that provides an example of how political and economic issues affect literacy learning among young children of Mexican origin in the state of Arizona.

The second part, "Best Practices in Early Literacy Instruction and Assessment," presents both classic and new topics in early literacy. Traditional topics include methods of assessing early literacy, oral language development, phonics and phonemic awareness, and fostering early literacy. Relatively new topics are reflected in chapters that discuss using informational books with young readers, computer technologies in young children's literacy development, and the role of media and popular culture in fostering and practicing early literacy.

This part begins with a chapter by Terry Salinger on early reading assessment. Salinger provides a summary of the major approaches available to assess students' progress as they learn to read. The author also discusses the decisions that teachers make as they develop their own tools for screening students at entry into their classes and develop measures for monitoring students' progress in reading throughout the school year.

The next chapter in this part focuses on oral language by comparing oral and written language with regard to modalities that rely on the same base of linguistic knowledge. Lynn Hebert Remson discusses five components of language—morphology, phonology, syntax, semantics, and pragmatics. She traces oral language development from the infant's random sound through intentional, nonverbal communication, and then through various stages of oral language in each of the five areas.

In the following chapter, Benita Blachman reviews the importance of phonological awareness and decoding for early literacy instruction. She provides suggestions for simple activities that foster phonological awareness and describes the core features of effective phonics instruction. She describes an instructional model that demonstrates how instruction in phonemic awareness, decoding, fluency, text-based reading, and spelling can be incorporated into a systematic lesson.

Next, Diane Tracey and Leslie Mandel Morrow summarize key information regarding early literacy development and the ways that literacy can be fostered in schools. The authors highlight the importance of oral language, vocabulary, phonemic awareness, word identification skills, comprehension, fluency, texts, motivation, writing, technology, and home-school connections. The authors conclude with a case study that illustrates the application of these elements in instruction.

The chapter by Lee Galda and Lauren Aimonette Liang presents recommended literature and read alouds for young children by detailing some of the ways that reading aloud to young children influences their knowledge of and attitudes toward reading. The authors emphasize the importance of the discourse surrounding the read alouds before, during, and after reading. They conclude their chapter by providing guidelines for evaluating and selecting quality children's literature appropriate for reading aloud to young children.

The next chapter, by Barbara Marinak and Linda Gambrell, defines informational books and makes a case for the inclusion of informational books along with narrative story structures for early readers. In doing so, the authors offer several reasons for including more informational texts for primary children. The authors conclude the chapter with a description of the predictable elements of informational text and examples of how those elements can be incorporated into read alouds, discussion, and writing.

The next two chapters in this part address children with special needs. The chapter by Carmen Martinez-Roldán and Jeanne Fain provides an overview of literacy and culture in various American communities. The authors move on to consider how a curriculum that enables literacy/biliteracy development might look. Martinez-Roldán and Fain highlight the role of inquiry in children's learning and discuss such instructional practices as literature discussions, drama, poetry, writing workshops, and writers' notebooks with English language learners. The chapter concludes with some considerations regarding assessment of literacy learning for English Language Learners.

The final chapter in this part discusses the needs of and appropriate instruction for students with learning disabilities. Kathleen McCoy explains that most often children with neurological or perceptual disabilities perform like early readers. Frequently, there is a poor fit between the students' information-processing skills and the approach to reading instruction. The author makes a case for differentiated instruction that accounts for the impact of a child's disability across cognitive, affective, and sensory abilities.

The third and final part of the book, "Foundations for Early Literacy Development," includes other topics that are just now gaining attention but have not typically been explored in other texts on early literacy. These topics are represented in chapters on the role of popular culture, technology, and media in early literacy development, practice, and instruction. These chapters are balanced by classic topics, including the role of play in literacy development and how parents and family literacy practices support early literacy.

The first chapter in this part, by Christine Walsh, is written from the perspective of a woman who is both a professor of English/Language Arts and a mother of an early literacy learner. In challenging readiness theories about early stages of literacy development, Walsh relates interesting and sometimes humorous stories about her own son's journey as a language learner. The author argues that reading, writing, speaking, and listening are language processes that develop recursively rather than in a linear fashion and that parents and teachers can learn about their children's literacy development mainly by watching them, listening to them, and supporting them.

The next chapter in this part, "Play and Early Literacy in These Times," describes the role of children's play in early childhood education. The authors look back and look ahead both by revisiting studies reported in earlier reviews and by introducing new inquiries into the role of play in early literacy development and learning, especially studies that shed light on school readiness. Kathleen Roskos and James Christie relate the role of play in developing the child's mind, describe how play contributes to the literacy learning environment, and explain the role of play as social activity that scaffolds literacy performances and mediates literacy practices.

In the following chapter, Donna Grace argues for the inclusion of media and popular culture in the school lives of children. She demonstrates how the results of a study that integrated video production into the literacy curriculum contribute to the growing body of research that validates the importance of students' interests in television, movies, video games, and comics. Grace contends that connecting children's out-of-school and in-school literacies holds potential to provide pathways into classroom literacy practices for reluctant readers and writers; offers opportunities for transfer of children's knowledge of the media and popular culture to school literacies; provides spaces for children to rework some of the messages of the media; and provides sites for the exploration of identities and contexts for developing the critical literacy skills necessary for analyzing and evaluating media texts.

The next chapter in this part, by Linda Labbo, explores the role of computer technologies in facilitating young children's early literacy development. Labbo provides a brief historical perspective to frame the current definition of digital literacy. She offers guidelines for computer technology use, including selecting developmentally appropriate software and Internet sites. The chapter offers examples of effective computer technology and integration into the curriculum, including the use of digital cameras and guided Internet explorations.

This part and this volume conclude with a final chapter that offers resources for early literacy development. Ruth Jurey presents resources for parents and teachers to enhance the critical aspects of children's language on which literacy is built—communication processes, auditory skills, and comprehension. This chapter includes a range of authoritative resources on learning to read, from an introductory overview to detailed suggestions.

Part One

RECENT ISSUES IN EARLY LITERACY

Chapter One

POLICY AND LEGISLATION IN EARLY LITERACY

Susan B. Neuman

For most of our nation's history, education has been a local issue. Funds for education have traditionally relied on local property taxes. Early attempts to get the federal government involved largely fell on deaf ears in Congress, foundering according to historian Diane Ravitch on the three deadly, controversial sins of race, religion, and fear of federal control (Cross, 2004). Whether or not to provide federal funds to racially segregated schools in the South and to private schools were sticking points that could not be easily resolved.

This logjam was permanently broken by Lyndon Johnson's Great Society programs and his War on Poverty. During his administration, federal spending immediately shot up by 1,400 percent in the 1960s and 1970s, followed by increases in state and local government spending as well. Much of the new money came in categorical programs targeted to disadvantaged children, most notably by the Elementary and Secondary Education Act of 1965, and for children with disabilities. Since then, federal spending has risen rapidly, going from 4.4 percent of total education spending in 1960 to about 8 to 9 percent in 2005 (McCluskey, 2004). Today, the federal government spends about $53 billion; states and local taxes provide the rest, bringing the total up to about $500 billion a year on education.

When you ask the average citizen, however, 76 percent of Americans, according to a recent poll by the Educational Testing Service (Barton, 2003), believe that at least a fair to a great deal of this money on education is wasted. It turns out that the public has a remarkable lack of confidence in educational reform.

It is time to step back and take a fresh look at how to make the most of both time and resources. Policy makers must decide what programs to fund among the bewildering array of choices and the multitude of pet projects. These decisions can no longer rely on good intentions, however. Rather, a results-based approach is needed that essentially clears the decks and employs a simple set of questions to determine if programs are worthy of funding. They are as follows:

- Does it work?
- Is it cost-effective?
- Does it target children's needs?
- Is it equitable?

This chapter describes how policy makers might adopt a results-based accountability approach to grant-making for highly disadvantaged children. I will start by addressing these questions. Then I will provide three examples of how these principles might be implemented. Finally, I will suggest the ways in which these principles might lead to the achievement of better results for our at-risk children.

ESTABLISHING A RESULTS-BASED APPROACH FOR POLICY IN EARLY LITERACY

Policy makers must address the following issues:

Question 1: Does It Work?

Evidence is needed to determine whether programs are improving children's outcomes: Which children are faring well and not so well? Are gaps are increasing or shrinking? Are there data that contain valuable clues for reaching families and children? Without measurement, it is impossible to determine what programs are most plausibly helping to shrink the gap. Further, how can educators legitimately know how to improve the quality of programs?

To do this well, policy makers can provide a rich set of clues and indicators from programs on both processes and outcomes. This information helps to identify the attributes that are essential to a program's success and the infrastructure required to support and sustain them.

Consider the example of a massive effort to bring books to over eighteen thousand children in child care centers in Philadelphia, known as the Books Aloud project (Neuman, 1999). The project called for child care workers to attend regular workshops at regional libraries on learning the techniques of storybook reading. It also involved setting up libraries in centers to help support good reading habits. Evaluators following the program efforts, however, soon discovered that child care workers rarely attended the workshops, largely due to concerns about safety late in the evening in the neighborhoods. Based on the evidence, program leaders brought the workshops to the centers, resulting in major improvements for children in literacy outcomes.

Progress-monitoring strategies provided formative information that was crucial to improving the project. It saved a $2 million program. It solved a problem by looking at the evidence of attendance and retention.

Good evaluations of literacy programs look at a rich array of indicators. They make a case for multiple methods to examine outcomes. They draw on a large body of evidence, including evidence from practice, systematically analyzed, and sensitive to the multiple components of programs in the context in which they occur. Achievement scores, for example, may be important indicators of program effectiveness, but so are increased motivation to learn, better school attendance, and greater parent involvement. In judging what works, then, policy makers need to take a careful look at what constitutes credible evidence, remembering that social and behavioral skills, although often hard to measure, also play an important role in equipping children for a productive life.

Question 2: Is There a Return on Investment?

Programs should represent quality investments, and the best programs should provide the largest social returns. For example, a program might be considered a smart investment if its benefits to children exceed its costs. Economists use the term "economically efficient," meaning that at a minimum, a good investment should have greater payoffs than its costs (Barnett, 1995). Basically, this requires policy makers to develop a list of all the ingredients and the amounts of each that are needed by the program, determine the cost of each ingredient, and look at the benefits in terms of long-range costs to society, including such negative markers as remediation and incarceration costs, as well as positive markers of increased employment and productivity.

Perhaps the most widely known and researched investment is the Perry Preschool Project in Ypsilanti, Michigan (Weikart, Bond, & McNeil, 1978). Following their preschool experience, children were followed over their life cycle. The evidence (Schweinhart, 2004), which is now about 40 years old, indicates that those enrolled in the program had higher earnings and lower levels of criminal behavior in their late twenties than did comparable children randomized out of the program. Reported benefit-cost ratios for the program suggested a rate of return about $5.70 for every dollar spent. When returns are projected for the remainder of the children's lives, the returns rise to $8.70, with a substantial fraction (65 percent) of the return attributed to reductions in crime.

Surely some literacy programs will have better returns than others. At the very least, however, it is hoped that savings generated by programs (in terms of fewer children retained in grade, special education, remediation) would be greater than the program costs.

Question 3: Is the Program Targeted to Those Who Need It the Most?

Programs designed for poor children should serve the poor and help bring them up to par. Too often, programs have become diluted by increasing eligibility way beyond the target audience. As a result, poor children lose out.

Looking at the demographic makeup of the United States, we can see that over 6.7 percent of the population live in the poorest and most vulnerable census tracts, with a disproportionately high number of these tracts in the nation's largest cities (Wertheimer & Croan, 2003). Compared to the nation as a whole, these census tracts will have the largest proportion of triple-at-risk children: They will have much higher proportions of very young children between the ages of zero and five, higher rates of single parenting, and a less-educated adult population, with fewer working adults to support the children. These children are likely to have the most problems as they climb the education ladder.

Yet, in a startling recent analysis by Education Trust (2004), an advocacy group that supports high academic achievement for all, many of our states provide the lowest level of financial support to those in the highest-poverty school tracts—children who depend on public support for their academic development are getting the absolute least. In fact, the top 25 percent of school districts in terms of child poverty were receiving less funding than the bottom 25 percent! Coming from families with limited social capital, poor children get less of everything.

Programs aimed at improving economically disadvantaged children's odds should be targeted to their needs and challenges and help them achieve the gains that only the highest quality intervention can provide.

Question 4: Is It Equitable?

Programs should support the same high expectations for all children, recognizing that what poor children lack is the opportunity to learn, not the ability to learn. We know, for example, that obstacles caused by poverty are not insurmountable, yet it is striking how many believe that all poor children need is the "basics," depriving them of the very quality of help and instruction that would enable them to thrive.

People might be literally stunned by how little is expected in some programs specially designed for poor children. Visiting a school in the heart of a high-poverty neighborhood in Philadelphia, for example, my colleagues found children watching a two-hour movie, *Space Monkeys,* while teachers were taking a long coffee break, a treat according to these teachers for all the "work" they had accomplished in the morning. Others have written about other time wasters. After touring about 300 high-poverty schools in several states during children's reading period, one freelance writer found what was actually going on: in these classrooms, children weren't reading, they weren't writing, they weren't learning the alphabet or its corresponding sounds or how to read short texts. They were coloring—coloring on a scale unimaginable to most of us. Dubbing it a "crayola" curriculum, Schmoker (2001) was stunned that children were given more coloring assignments than mathematics and writing.

The logic is pretty plain: children, especially those from high-poverty settings, don't have a chance unless teachers teach. Poverty is no excuse for dumbing down requirements, curriculum, and standards. Instead, what these children need are intellectually rich programs of learning that engage their minds and spark their interests and imaginations. This is the truest and fairest definition of equity.

The bottom line is that funding decisions must move to a more evidence-based strategy to serve more poor children more effectively. In light of these criteria, I will now look at the evidence, using three well-known programs specifically targeted to educating poor children: Head Start; Title I, and Even Start. I'll focus just a bit on services, and more particularly on outcomes.

APPLYING A RESULTS-BASED APPROACH: THREE EXAMPLES

Head Start

My first example is the easiest. Head Start is probably the best-known preschool program for economically disadvantaged children. Created during the heady, idealistic days of the mid-1960s, the program was designed to counteract the corrosive influences of turbulent neighborhoods, shoddy healthy care, and undereducated parents. Serving about 900,000 children, with a budget now in the $6.8 billion range, the federally funded grant program was designed to improve preschoolers' skills so that they can begin schooling on a more equal footing with their more advantaged peers. Despite some modest efforts to serve a larger age range, Head Start is still basically a half-day, five-day-a-week, nine-month program for poor four-year-olds.

Studies (Currie & Duncan, 1995) agree that Head Start produces an initial boost in children's achievement. Most studies, however, also show that these effects begin to fade within a year or two after children enter school (Currie & Neidell, 2003). This is not to say that programs are not effective. For its size, the program has plainly exceeded all expectations. It's a bargain. Head Start's children, according to many studies, begin school healthier and better prepared for school. The program helps children transition to school, reduces their placement in special education, and limits retention in grade, essentially providing a huge savings compared to its costs. The strongest evidence comes from studies published in 1995 and 2000 by economist Janet Currie and her colleagues at UCLA (Currie & Neidell, 2003). Using data from surveys of representative samples of families that included information on whether children had or had not participated in Head Start, Currie found that children who attended Head Start were less often held back in school than siblings who did not participate, had higher tests scores, which persisted into adolescence, and higher high school graduation rates.

Despite all these successes, however, the achievement gap persists. Data on school readiness for children entering Head Start 1997 and 2001, for example, show that children start the program with test scores far below average. While their performance improves, it's not nearly enough to make a real difference in the achievement gap. These sobering facts have led to a number of efforts by the Bush administration to try and retool the program toward a greater academic focus through training and accountability.

In contrast to its small size, however, Head Start has been a giant in the field, basically putting preschool on the educational map, creating rigorous standards, reviewing programs for quality performance, using research to inform practice, and taking an enormous step toward helping poor children and their parents to progress. It has been less successful in providing the intensity of help that may address children's already cumulative deficits in background knowledge and vocabulary (U.S. Department of Health and Human Services, 2005). For children to catch up, programs will have to up the ante, starting earlier, with better-trained professionals, and more intensive learning experiences.

Nevertheless, as the centerpiece of federal early childhood programs, Head Start provides a tremendous return for investment. It targets poor children's school readiness, and builds social capital through family and community involvement. It is by far the most highly rated program for economically disadvantaged children.

Title I

Title I is a more complicated story. Established as the Elementary and Secondary Education Act (ESEA) in 1965, during the euphoric days of the War on Poverty and at about the same time as the beginning of Head Start, Title I was designed to help schools meet the needs of economically disadvantaged students. Unlike Head Start, however, the Title I program has never really been a "program" per se. Rather, it's a funding stream, distributing financial resources from the federal coffers to the state, which in turn, distribute resources to high-poverty school districts. The actual amounts school districts receive are based on complex formulas, fiddled with over the course of seven reauthorizations of the law, to incorporate, among other items, average per-pupil expenditure in the state, number of children in poverty, and previous allocations to the state and the district.

Whereas Head Start bases its compensatory efforts on highly detailed comprehensive services, Title I is more about equating resources. Comparability is a key concept in Title I: schoolchool districts must demonstrate that they are spending as much per pupil in Title I schools as in schools not receiving Title I funds. From its outset, this approach showed deference both to local control (an answer to critics who feared federal control of the curriculum) and to the prevailing belief that the main shortcoming of high-poverty school districts is a lack of funding, not a lack of knowledge about better ways to educate the economically disadvantaged.

Dashing cold water on this very supposition, ironically, the government's monumental study, *Equality of Educational Opportunity,* commonly known as the Coleman report, arrived about a year after Title I was first enacted (Coleman et al., 1966). This report was the U.S. Office of Education's response to a requirement of the Civil Rights Act of 1964 to investigate the extent of inequality in the nation's schools. Surveying and testing six hundred thousand students in some three thousand schools across the country, James Coleman, a sociologist from the University of Chicago measured on a grand scale for the very first time the inputs—differences in resources—against the outputs—student performances in schools.

The report captured people's attention not only because it provided an unparalleled description of schools and students, but because its conclusions seemed so totally counterintuitive to what we might expect. School resources, it turned out, did not seem to have very much to do with student achievement. Instead it was families and their widely different social and economic conditions that seemed to account for more of the differences.

Since then, a cottage industry has emerged attempting to refute Coleman's methods, statistical analyses, and conclusions (Fischer et al., 1996). More articles have been written about this controversial finding probably than about any other single issue in education aside from the *Brown v. Board of Education* decision, which essentially denied the argument that separate schools for children of different races were constitutional if regarded as "equal." Nevertheless, after detailed research on the impact of resources on achievement spanning more than four decades, observing performance in many different educational settings, studies have confirmed Coleman's initial findings that expenditures are not systematically related to students' achievement. No wonder, then, that an evaluation using a nationally representative sample known as the Sustaining Effects Study, found Title I to have modest to little effect on achievement or on closing the gap for poor children (Cross, 2004).

Rather than question the assumptions underlying the premise of Title I, policy makers tried to adjust some of the anomalies of the allocation system that led some low-poverty schools to receive more Title I funds than high-poverty schools. By the 1990s, Title I contained four different allocation formulas designed to help channel more funding to high-poverty districts.

Yet, at the same time, believing that the needs of poor children would best be served through a school-wide reform policy, it retreated from singling out Title I students for instructional intervention. Instead, by 1994, rather than targeting, it expanded its focus by increasing the number of schools eligible to use their Title I funds to improve the school as a whole by raising standards and assessments. Unfortunately, it introduced new problems and exacerbated old ones. Funds that had been directed specifically to the early grades now were to be expanded to 4th through 12th grades. What was once an almost exclusive focus on poor children now included every student enrolled in more than sixteen thousand schools with school-wide Title I programs. Diluting what was already a weak intervention for low-performing low-income children, Title I now reached more than 90 percent of all school districts in the country. Not surprisingly, a second evaluation, known as the Prospects Study confirmed the results of the first: on average, Title I assistance failed to improve students' achievement. This congressionally authorized, three-year longitudinal study involving a sample of 40,000 found that students receiving Title I services performed no better than those not receiving Title I services. Harkening back to Coleman's report, findings indicated that the characteristics of the individual student and his or her family accounted for a large share of variation in student achievement (Cohen & Hill, 2001).

That Title I had been far from a homogenous treatment from school to school, however, did not figure prominently in the national evaluation. Or the fact that most school districts did not seem to know how to use program monies strategically, centering their efforts on broad coverage and local control. Or that school-wide programs had little experience with school improvement, often flailing in one direction or another, demonstrating that improving instruction was far more complicated than simple fiscal transfers. Rather, these studies seemed to close the book on the belief that resources alone could improve educational outcomes. Money for poor children was not likely to raise educational proficiencies.

Despite these dismal evaluations, the No Child Left Behind Act of 2001, the latest reauthorization of the Elementary and Secondary Education Act, represented the most significant expansion of Title I, now at $12.7 billion. Along with its sizable increase in funding came new mandates: a deadline for *all* public schools to bring *all* children up to proficiency, a minimum set of qualifications for teachers in *all* the nation's public schools whether or not they receive federal funding, and a voucher-like program of extra tutoring for children in the most troubled Title I schools. What was once a compensatory education program for poor children now became a national reform effort to improve educational excellence for all children.

The law also required states and local school districts for the first time to use "scientifically based research" techniques—curriculum-based materials that had been proven to work effectively for achievement. Nevertheless, schools had tremendous latitude in how they used resources. Instruction being a difficult lever to control, traditionally Title I had not devoted much attention to it, using its money on salaries for instructional personnel and aides with little attention to the results produced. Even today with more sophisticated accounting practices, it is still surprisingly hard to get a clear picture of how schools spend money on instructional programs and services for poor children.

To its credit, the No Child Left Behind Act has redirected the national conversation from focusing strictly on inputs to looking at outputs and outcomes. Districts and schools today are being held specifically accountable for helping at-risk students learn. Further, despite rumblings from more affluent districts, the law concentrates more funding on fewer school districts, helping to serve the neediest students. Still, given the federal government's expanded role, and states' and school districts' penchant for spreading dollars rather than solving problems, it is highly questionable whether funds will be adequately targeted to address poor children's instructional needs. More likely than not, it will depend on the vagaries of school leadership, budgeting, and knowledge about school improvement. Raising a skeptical voice, some suggest that too often, additional resources allotted for helping poor children are used to maximize the status and employment of educational personnel while being packaged in the rhetoric of helping children.

In short, the failure of additional funding to improve educational outcomes is not a failure of the theory of action as much as it is a technical by-product of the failure ever to reach its intended audience. Providing compensatory education through additional funding to poor children has not failed; it has never been tried. Despite the enormous amount of resources provided over the years, there is strikingly little to no evidence that Title I works, that it is cost-effective, that it is targeted to poor children, or that it ensures an equitable education. Title I has rarely delivered on any of its promises. As a result, even today, children who depend the most on public education services for their academic achievement are getting the very least.

Even Start

Even Start may be the nation's largest family literacy program at $250 million a year, but it is small in comparison to Head Start or Title I. Recognizing poverty's multigenerational, multidimensional aspects, it attacks these problems by providing early childhood education and parenting programs for parents and children up to age eight. Even Start typically works with the most multirisk families, even those harder to reach than Head Start—parents who have dropped out of high school, immigrant families who have not yet learned English, and teenage parents living at or significantly below the federal poverty line.

Originally championed by Pennsylvania Congressman Bill Goodling in 1990, Even Start began as a small family literacy demonstration program modeled after a highly successful program run in Kentucky, called Parent and Child Education. or PACE/Kenan, later the National Center for Family Literacy (Darling, 1989). It has grown throughout the past 15 years, now serving approximately thirty-two thousand families in 50 states. Federal funds are given to the states to award to local projects, the average amount being about $100,000 to $200,000. Even though state agencies are given considerable discretion with regard to where to house the program, how to run it, how to use resources, and the approach to instruction, the legislation still requires programs to follow the largely untested PACE/Kenan model. Eligible families receive each of four core instructional components: early childhood education, parenting education, adult literacy education, and parent-child joint literacy activities, creating what is described as a unified literacy program for children and their parents.

It may sound ideal, but in reality, it is hard to accomplish. Mandated by law to collaborate with local service agencies and build on existing services to avoid duplication, Even Start programs often cobble together services from other agencies. Some early childhood centers, for example, may offer a sound preschool program, but not infant or toddler services; others may have parenting education facilities, but no provision for adult literacy classes. Projects borrow from or adapt existing materials, or subcontract for these services from other programs, resulting in collaborations that are nightmarish for quality control. Add in the difficulties of trying to run literacy-based programs for infants through primary grades, programs for adults including high school completion courses (GED), and English as a second language programs, and one can see that instructional intensity inevitably shortchanges some groups of children and adults.

Some Even Start programs are remarkably effective, demonstrating what good leadership, a good curriculum, and sound adult literacy programs can do to bring literacy to life for families. I visited such a program in Brooklyn, targeted to immigrant families, where three-year-olds were engaged in a Japanese tea ceremony while the parents looked on with an adult instructor who was teaching them the importance of play in early literacy development. The program had all the attributes of an effective intervention, involving highly trained professionals engaging respectfully with the community. Other programs lack stable leadership, and end up serving neither parents nor children well. In some cases, states have provided too much autonomy to programs and too little accountability, with poor quality services and poorly trained staff.

Unfortunately, it shows. Three large-scale national evaluations (St. Pierre, Ricciuti, Tao, & Creps, 2001) report only minimal to no effects on gains for children's school readiness skills. By the end of the program, these studies reported that children scored on vocabulary no better than at the sixth percentile, at the bottom of the testing distribution . There were no substantive improvements in the quality of the home environment, or parent-child interactions during book reading, or parental expectations for their children. There were no effects of program participation on employment, or income, or adult literacy improvements. Even more revealing, 46 percent of Even Start mothers, classified as having high levels of depressive symptoms at the outset, were no better off by the end of the program. Concluding from one of the evaluations, St. Pierre and his colleagues from Abt Associates found that "the gains were not greater than those that similarly motivated families obtained for themselves using locally available services" (2001, p. 18).

Looking at the details of the evaluation, it is noticeable that participation rates in all the parts of the program were strikingly low. In 2000–2001, for example, parents and children participated in only a small fraction of the hours offered: 30 percent of adult education, 24 percent of parenting education, and 25 percent of parent-child activities. The average number of hours in adult literacy courses hovered around 95 hours a year, with hours ranging from 68 to 107 hours, not nearly enough to significantly improve literacy skills for adults. The average estimate is that it takes about 100 hours to move up one grade level alone. Parents participated in programs about 35 hours a year, less than an hour per week. Further, surprisingly few hours of early childhood education were received by children. Although offered an average of 591 hours, they attended an average of 220 hours, which is small compared to the amount of time that children would spend in an excellent early childhood program. Even programs using the soundest research-based practices to teach instructional content could not be expected to impact lives if parents and children did not attend sufficiently long or intensively.

According to the evaluators, at least 14 percent of the families leave Even Start because of a "general lack of interest." To retain families, programs have had to resort to rewards for participating in programs, rewards such as books, toys, fans, T-shirts, and food. Asked the reasons for the low participation, one leader suggested that parent education sessions were hardly "a drawing card" for parents who might be depressed, living in poverty, with no job prospects and a fairly bleak future.

Despite 15 years of trying and billions of federal dollars, the Even Start program has not delivered on its promises to boost children's achievement and adult literacy. Services do not come close to the intensity of the child-focused services delivered by programs such as Head Start or to the services of adult literacy programs, with the consequences that most programs have yielded only very small effects.

HOLDING PROGRAMS ACCOUNTABLE FOR RESULTS

Demanding results through evidence provides a tool to make big changes at a time when they are absolutely necessary. It roots decisions in results, helping policy makers deliver the outcomes that citizens value, even when there may be no increases in budgets.

How might this work in the case of our three examples? It works very directly: if a program achieves outcomes, or shows promising evidence of effects, it receives funding. If a program performs poorly, it can find its funds rerouted to its competitors.

Given that many programs are still underresearched, this process should not be automatic, however. If the program is not achieving all of its goals, it might need to rethink its theory of action, it might need to adopt more successful practices, or it might need more money. Each program should be analyzed to examine why it may be underperforming and what the most effective remedies might be.

Take, for example, Head Start. Clearly, the program delivers, giving poor children and their families access to an array of nutritional, health, and school benefits. Yet the achievement gap persists, despite the program's commitment to school readiness and high standards. Now compare per-pupil spending in Head Start, averaging about $7,170 in 2002, to studies of other programs that have shown remarkable long-term improvements in academic achievement, like Abecedarian, at about $15,000 per child (in 1968), and one can note that Head Start is seriously underfunded for what its intended to accomplish.

If programs are going to deliver the highest quality of education that appears to reduce placement in special education and remediation, they will need to demand more funding.

The case of Title I is a bit more complicated. It is clear that the program has not demonstrated results. Rather than relentlessly focus on educational outcomes for poor children, Title I works rather like the old parlor game, telephone. The federal government sends funds to the states, the states send funds to the school districts, and the school districts send funds to the schools. As the game progresses, the funds get smaller and smaller due to the percentage cuts for "administration." The program ends up delivering relatively modest sums to schools, which they can use with wide discretion. Children in high-poverty schools often end up with top-heavy administration, and personnel rather than instructional programs. It has become a jobs program, employing thousands of unskilled workers and administrative staff. This program is in need of draconian structural reform to reduce inefficiencies and wasteful spending.

Even Start has not delivered. Compare, for example, the long waiting lines for entry into Head Start to the no-show participation rates of Even Start. People are telling us that the program does not meet their needs. Policy makers should listen and reroute funds to programs that do meet needs. Several efforts by policy makers have been made to cut Even Start over the last four years. One wonders why it has taken so long. Funds should be redistributed to programs that work.

In short, when policy makers examine programs by outcomes, they may review programs against targets using data on results to make improvements, changes in strategies, outcomes, and work processes. This allows public leaders to do some big-picture, creative thinking that essentially entails the following:

- Reduction of inefficiencies and wasteful spending on ineffective programs
- Redistribution of funds from other, less effective, interventions
- Addition of new dollars when needed

GETTING BETTER RESULTS

Seeking more resources, particularly higher expenditures, has been the single most common educational policy for improving poor children's achievement. How these funds might be used to pursue programs and activities that achieve better outcomes has often been an afterthought. This equation needs to be turned around.

A results-based approach demands that. for every dollar spent, there should be a decent return. Good returns mean putting funds into programs where they are likely to matter the most. To get results, priorities must be reexamined, efforts must be concentrated, funding approaches must be adjusted and, finally, funds must be rerouted from failing programs to programs that work. This means taking no existing program or organization as a given.

The paradigm of a results-based approach shifts the equation toward prevention of problems rather than remediation of learning difficulties. To achieve this, however, the funding equation must begin to change. Instead of spending nearly seven times more during the school-age years, policy makers should redistribute funds toward the early years to achieve the greatest impact. Estimates of cost-savings for quality, well-implemented programs (Bruner, 2002) have been reported to exceed 10 percent and go as high as 17–20 percent in mean rate of return.

Even after redistributing funds, however, there is still a missing critical ingredient, which could be the hardest to achieve. Traditionally, policy makers have used discrete and isolated strategies for solving problems. In the long run, this approach has inherent dangers. Program leaders have had to promise to ameliorate all sorts of problems to gain attention and financial commitment. Unrealistic expectations have often undermined good services. All this has resulted in a growing pessimism about the ability to solve problems.

Rather than succumb to a single strategy for helping poor children, policy makers must adopt a 360-degree surround that embraces every aspect of children's development.

A 360-degree surround recognizes that no single isolated strategy, no matter how good it is, will solve the problems associated with growing up poor. Quality child care is vital for stimulating children's cognitive and social development right from the start. It is not sufficient, however. Neither is home-based intervention to promote healthy development. Nor is good school teachers who demand high standards and get high-quality performance, or charismatic mentors in after-school enrichment programs. Each of these interventions, by themselves, is critically important. Yet each alone will be insufficiently powerful to address the deeply rooted problems that result from persistent poverty and the social exclusion and inequality that accompanies it.

What this realistically means is that the more children can be surrounded with quality home-based programs, child care, community enrichment, good schools, and after-school and summer programs, the greater will be the effect. Each program will make an independent contribution, but it is the synergy among quality programs that will produce the most powerful long-term and life-changing effects. This means that agencies traditionally associated with health and early child care must begin to communicate with agencies that address education, to support children's comprehensive needs related to early learning and school readiness. These agencies deal with the same children and families, yet historically they have had a rocky relationship. This needs to change. States like Massachusetts and Georgia, recognizing the comprehensive needs of children, have come to establish important connections between offices that other states may wish to emulate.

It also means that in contrast to spreading the funds, spreading programs to different groups of children who are at less risk of failure, services should be concentrated on the most vulnerable children. Too often, these children have lurked in the shadows of classrooms, overwhelmed by those with greater social capital who demand that funds be diverted toward their own interests. Federal programs funded for poor children must serve poor children, putting resources in their hands. There also needs to be greater transparency in tracking funds to stop the abuses.

These funding reforms can be initiated right now, putting millions perhaps billions of dollars to better taxpayer use, preventing problems before they overwhelm the school systems in costly remedial interventions that have shown only marginal results. Nevertheless, funding, while important, is only the first step in reforming policies that benefit children from low-income, multirisk families. Simply placing more resources in funding streams has not been a reliable measure of the improvement of children's outcomes. It just gets to the starting gate. Programs will need to be well implemented to achieve significant cost benefits and improve the lives of at-risk children.

REFERENCES

Barnett, W. S. (1995). Long-term effects of early childhood programs on cognitive and school outcomes. *The Future of Children, 5,* 25–50.

Barton, P. (2003). *Parsing the achievement gap.* Princeton, NJ: Educational Testing Services.

Bruner, C. (2002). *A stitch in time: Calculating the costs of unreadiness.* Washington DC: The Finance Project.

Cohen, D., & Hill, H. (2001). *Learning policy.* New Haven, CT: Yale University Press.

Coleman, J., Campbell, E., Hobson, C., McPartland, J., Mood, A. M., Weinfeld, F., & York, R. (1966). *Equality of educational opportunity* (Vols. 1–2). Washington, DC: U.S. Department of Health, Education, and Welfare, Office of Education.

Cross, C. (2004). *Political education.* New York: Teacher's College Press.

Currie, J., & Duncan, T. (1995). Does Head Start make a difference? *American Economic Review, 85*(5), 341–364.

Currie, J., & Neidell, M. (2003). *Getting inside the "black box" of Head Start quality: What matters and what doesn't?* Cambridge, MA: National Bureau of Economic Research.

Darling, S. (1989). *Kenan Trust family literacy project and program model.* Louisville, KY: Kenan Trust Family Literacy Project.

Education Trust. (2004). The real value of teachers. *Thinking K–16, 8*(1).

Fischer, C., Hout, M., Jankowski, M. S., Lucas, S., Swidler, & Vos, K. (1996). *Inequality by design: Cracking the bell curve myth.* Princeton, NJ: Princeton University Press.

McCluskey, N. (2004). *A lesson in waste: Where does all the federal education money go?* Washington, DC: Cato Institute.

Neuman, S. B. (1999). Books make a difference: A study of access to literacy. *Reading Research Quarterly, 34,* 286–312.

Neuman, S. B. (in press). *Changing the odds: Overcoming disadvantage for at-risk children.* New York: Guilford Press.

Schmoker, M. (2001, October 24). The crayola curriculum. *Education Week.*

Schweinhart, L. (2004). *The High/Scope Perry Preschool Study through age 40: Summary, conclusions, and frequently asked questions.* Ypsilanti, MI: High/Scope Educational Research Foundation.

St. Pierre, R., Ricciuti, A., Tao, F., & Creps, C. (2001). *Third National Even Start Evaluation: Description of projects and participants.* Washington, DC: Planning and Evaluation Services.

U.S. Department of Health and Human Services, Administration for Children, Youth, and Families (2005). *Head Start impact study: First year findings.* Washington, DC: Office of Planning, Research and Evaluation: Administration on Children, Youth, and Families. Head Start Bureau.

Weikart, D. P., Bond, J. T., & McNeil, J. T. (1978). *The Ypsilanti Perry Preschool Project.* Ypsilanti, MI: High/Scope.

Wertheimer, R., & Croan, T. (2003). *Attending kindergarten and already behind: A statistical portrait of vulnerable young children.* Washington, DC: Child Trends.

Chapter Two

THE NATIONAL READING PANEL

S. Jay Samuels, Terri Fautsch-Patridge, and Caroline L. Hilk

FORMATION OF THE NATIONAL READING PANEL

Imagine the following: as a member of a United States congressional committee with millions of dollars that your committee wishes to award to school districts for reading improvement, you, together with other members of your committee, are concerned that the money may not be used in the most judicious and efficient manner possible. Members of your committee are aware that there are as many different opinions about the best way to teach beginning reading to children as there are colors, and shades of colors, in the rainbow. This dilemma is not new, and attempts to find solutions to this problem go back long before Jean Chall wrote her pivotal book, *Learning to Read: The Great Debate,* in 1967.

To provide a solution to this problem, Congress, in 1997, in collaboration with the secretary of education, asked the director of the National Institute of Child Health and Human Development (NICHD) to convene a national panel that would have the responsibility of examining the research-based knowledge of what works in reading instruction. The panel would be required to accomplish three goals. First, the panel would be asked to synthesize from the research base what they considered to be the most effective approaches to reading instruction. Second, the panel would be asked to indicate the applicability of the different effective approaches. Third, the panel would provide, if appropriate, a strategy for disseminating these findings to the schools.

The panel of 14 people who were selected included some of the leading scientists in reading research, reading teachers, school administrators, and parents. The panel was named the National Reading Panel (NRP). Although the original plan was to have a final report by November 1998, it quickly became obvious that this deadline was unrealistic and could not be met because of the large number of studies that had to be reviewed. Consequently, the panel was granted permission to delay its final report, and Congress received the *National Reading Panel Interim Report* in February of 1999.

HOW THE PANEL DID ITS WORK

The NRP search of the public databases found that there were approximately 100,000 studies on reading that had been published between 1966 and 1999 and about 15,000 studies that had been published before 1966. It was obvious that the sheer volume of studies was more than the NRP could examine critically in the time that had been allocated. Consequently, the panel decided to form topic subgroups based upon the National Research Council Committee on Preventing Reading Difficulties in Young Children (NRC) designation of topics considered to be central to learning to read—alphabetics, fluency, and comprehension (Snow, Burns & Griffin, 1998).

Because of the sheer volume of research in reading instruction that the panel had to review in the relatively short time period before the report was due, the panel had to make decisions about how the literature search could be reduced in scope. The panel decided that in the time available they would review only experimental or quasi-experimental studies. An experimental study is one in which one can logically determine cause and effect because there is a control group and an experimental group. In a quasi-experimental study, one is forced to use intact groups rather than randomly assigned groups. Correlational studies would not be included in the literature search because correlation does not imply causation. The studies that were selected for critical analysis were to address the age range of students from preschool to grade 12. Furthermore, the studies had to be published in a peer-reviewed journal and had to be in English. Each of the panel subgroups focused on those studies that were relevant exclusively to their domains.

Another important decision was made by the panel. All of the literature reviews would follow a common structure, including questions related to 61 variables such as the use of control and experimental groups, the random assignment of participants to groups, or the use of preexisting intact groups. To maintain fidelity of coding, 10 percent of the studies were randomly chosen for reexamination to test for interrater reliability or consistency among coders. If coding agreement fell below 90 percent in any category, the subgroup took action to improve agreement.

DATA ANALYSIS

A meta-analysis is a statistical technique whereby the results of many studies on a topic are combined to allow a general conclusion about the efficacy of a treatment. Many of the studies under review reported only probability values. All that probability values do is simply state the likelihood that differences between the means of the experimental and control groups could only occur by chance, for example, five times out of a hundred (e.g., $p < .05$) or one time in a hundred (e.g., $p < .01$). The problem with probability values is that by themselves they do not inform the scholar as to how much of a difference there was between the mean of the experimental condition and the mean of the control condition. Consequently, when possible, the NRP computed effect sizes for the studies. An effect size shows in standard deviation units how much larger the experimental treatment effect is than the control condition effect, or vice versa. Effect sizes were weighted by the number of subjects in the study under review to prevent small studies from overwhelming the effects of the much larger studies.

ALPHABETICS: PHONOLOGICAL AND PHONEMIC AWARENESS

Phonemes may be thought of as the separate sound components of words; they are sounds in the speech stream that serve to distinguish meaning; changing a single phoneme in a word can change its meaning. A single letter can represent a phoneme; for example, the three letters in the word "tip" represent three phonemes (i.e., /t/ /i/ /p/). The four letters in the word "ship," on the other hand, represent three phonemes, because "sh" is considered one phoneme. The ability to perceive and manipulate the 42 phonemes of the English language, or "phonemic awareness," is generally achieved by most children by age eight; however, it is thought that a significant number of children fail to develop this ability; this failure is highly correlated with reading difficulties (Snow, Burns & Griffin, 1998).

It is this correlation with reading disabilities that interested the NRP in phonemic awareness. The NRP sought to determine whether research demonstrated that phoneme awareness could be successfully taught, and further, whether the interventions, if successful, would also affect reading and spelling ability. This was a particular concern for the NRP, because the teaching of phonemic awareness was fast becoming a best practice in beginning reading instruction and a required component in the curricula of states such as California and Texas.

PHONEME AWARENESS INSTRUCTION IN THE STUDIES REVIEWED

Phonemic awareness is often addressed as the final segment of instructional programs that begin with larger units of language. While the NRP reviewed studies addressing these larger units of language, a study was included in the review only if it also specifically addressed phonemic awareness. The phonemic awareness skills taught in the 58 studies the NRP reviewed involved a variety of skills, including having students identify phonemes (e.g., "What sound is the same in these thee words: sub, sad, sit?"), categorizing phonemes (e.g., for initial phoneme: "Which word doesn't belong: dog, dip, sun?"), blending phonemes (e.g., the teacher may elongate each phoneme and asks the child what is the word: "/mmmm/ /aaaa/ /pppp/" The child responds, "map"), segmenting phonemes (e.g., "Tell me the sounds you hear in "bus"), and deleting phonemes ("Say 'cat' without the /c/"). The NRP also included studies that taught students to manipulate onset/rhyme units (e.g., changing the initial onset, keeping the rhyme /b/-at, /c/-at, /r/-at, /s/-at) and to phonetically spell words. Some of these interventions included the physical manipulation of magnetic letters, or the manipulation of letters on a computer, the use of pictures, and the use of mirrors to allow children to attend to their mouths when articulating phonemes; others were confined solely to an auditory mode. Some studies also included a metacognitive component that called attention to the purpose of the phonemic awareness skills, as well as requiring the student to practice the skill in the context of reading.

The 58 studies included interventions that addressed one, two, or a multitude of phonemic awareness skills, lasted from as little as an hour to as many as 75 hours, were conducted via computer, researchers, or teachers who taught students individually, in small groups, or as a whole class. Studies involved students as young as preschoolers and as old as 6th graders, included normal, at risk children, and/or children with documented reading disabilities.

FINDINGS ON ALPHABETICS AND IMPLICATIONS FOR INSTRUCTION

The NRP concluded that phonemic awareness could very successfully be taught, that becoming aware of phonemes resulted in increased reading and spelling skills for most students, and that the effects were maintained over time. Because a variety of approaches proved to be effective, prescriptions for teaching a specific set of phonemic awareness skills were not advocated by the NRP. The NRP concluded, however, that teaching one or two skills did result in more powerful effects than focusing on a multitude of skills, and receiving instruction on these skills while simultaneously manipulating letters was also more effective than the auditory mode alone.

It is not surprising that results showed that teaching students about sounds would be more successful in small groups than in large groups. That small-group instruction was better than individualized instruction, however, is not so intuitive. This result may have been due to the fact that students receiving individualized instruction were likely to have more significant deficits. Because of the inclusion of students with a range of deficits, and a range of ages, the NRP did not come to any conclusions about the most successful instructional length of phonemic awareness (PA) sessions. Clearly, the length of successful instructional sessions is likely associated with the ability level of the students.

PHONICS

While instruction in phonemic awareness is concerned with the child's ability to hear and manipulate the sounds in spoken language, instruction in phonics is concerned with the child's ability to recognize and use the sounds of letters in written language. Once children learn letter-sound correspondences, they are taught to blend the sounds represented by the letters into words (synthetic phonics) or use larger units, such as rimes or phonograms (e.g., ack, ain, eat) contained in unknown words to compare to words they can read (phonics by analogy), thus allowing them to decode words they cannot recognize. There are many variations of phonics, including techniques that combine synthetic and phonics by analogy.

One purpose of the NRP review was to address this controversy from the perspective of purely scientific evidence. The NRP conducted a comprehensive review of all studies published since 1970 in peer-reviewed professional journals that compared the use of systematic phonics, unsystematic phonics, and no phonics. Studies had to meet specific criteria including the use of control groups and the use of interventions consisting of phonics techniques typically used in schools. Using these criteria, the panel examined 38 published studies that contained 66 comparisons. The NRP's meta-analysis revealed that the effect size for systematic phonics instruction demonstrated important differences, proving to be more successful than either incidental phonics or no phonics treatments. This finding was in keeping with prior work (e.g., Adams, 1990; Bond & Dykstra, 1967; Chall, 1967) that had found systematic phonics was better than no phonics. These findings were based on outcome measures such as the ability to read words, to read pseudo words, and to read and comprehend text. Generally, findings across studies indicated growth in all these outcome measures, but growth in reading comprehension as a result of systematic phonics instruction is less definitive.

Beyond the central question of whether systematic phonics instruction was effective, the NRP sought to determine whether there were some phonics programs that proved more effective than others. The results indicated that synthetic phonics programs, in which students were taught all letter-sound correspondences and then taught to blend them, were not significantly better than analytic or analogy phonics programs that taught children to use larger units such as rhymes. The kind of phonics program was not critical, but the use of a systematic approach for phonics instruction was critical.

Further questions on how phonics programs were implemented included whether phonics was best taught in small or large groups, or whether a one-on-one approach would be most beneficial. One might assume that small groups or tutoring situations would naturally be better than whole-class instruction because of the ability of the teacher to attend to individual students. Surprisingly, the NRP found that all three strategies were effective, and the effect sizes for each type of instructional strategy did not differ significantly from one another.

In addition to questions concerning how phonics was implemented, questions regarding when phonics could best be used were also considered. For example, the NRP asked whether phonics is best introduced before students begin to read, or whether introduction in higher grades could also be beneficial. The NRP concluded that phonics was best introduced in early grades (kindergarten and 1st grade) before children had learned to read independently. In a related question, they asked whether phonics could be used as an effective preventative measure for students identified as being at risk for reading problems based on their family's socioeconomic status. The panel concluded that intervention in early grades, before students learned to read, produced significant growth in these students.

The review also included studies providing phonics treatment to students who showed problems in learning to read. Moderate effect sizes were achieved in studies with younger students (kindergarten and 1st grade) identified as low achievers who had average IQs. Older low-achieving students (2nd through 6th grade) did not show significant benefits from phonics instruction. The panel cautioned, however, that the eight studies reviewed may have been too small a number from which to draw firm conclusions about this group of students.

IMPLICATIONS FOR PHONICS INSTRUCTION

There is a long history of support for the use of phonics in teaching young children to read. The NRP findings added yet another source of support for the inclusion of phonics as one component in a balanced program of reading instruction. One important caution noted by the panel, however, was that phonics will not be an effective strategy unless children have developed phonemic awareness. Without phonemic awareness, children are unable to perceive the sounds in spoken words, and so will be unable to apply letter-sound correspondences learned in a rote manner to decode the printed word into a spoken word and create representation of the print. The NRP cautions that it is this application of phonics to daily reading and writing activities that is most important if children are to effectively use phonics instruction.

In addressing the application of the findings on phonics, the NRP also noted the importance of the teacher's expertise in the application of systematic phonics instruction. Teachers must understand the individual needs of students in their classroom regarding phonics skills, and provide not only systematic instruction but instruction that matches each student's needs. Most importantly, however, teachers must not make phonics the dominant component of their reading program, but rather integrate it as part of a complete, balanced reading program.

FLUENCY

In many ways, phonics and fluency have shared similar fates over the years, at least as measured by interest in these topics is concerned. Both topics have experienced fluctuating periods of high and low status, but not necessarily at the same time. Presently, reading fluency is a very hot topic within the educational community. We believe that the *NRP Interim Report* is partly responsible for the high popularity and status that fluency currently enjoys, because the report gave fluency the same position of importance as comprehension and alphabetics. While most teachers agree that fluency is an important milestone in reading, it seems to be an elusive goal for many students. The National Assessment of Educational Progress did a large-scale study of the status of fluency achievement in American schools and found, for example, that 44 percent of the fourth graders were disfluent with grade level materials that they had read under supportive testing conditions (Donahue, 2001).

CHANGING CONCEPTS OF FLUENCY

The *NRP Interim Report* acknowledges that as the social sciences, such as psychology, make advances, these increases in knowledge may transfer to improved instructional methods, as well as refined definitions of fluency that can be used to discuss the research. Changes in definitions that are based on improved theory are not trivial, since they can lead to important advances in the development and assessment of fluency. Presently, there is far greater agreement about how to develop fluency than there is about how to measure and assess it. Fluency assessment has become a contentious issue. How one defines a construct such as fluency can help in deciding if a measurement tool is an appropriate and valid tool. Specifically, the *NRP Interim Report* states, "The purpose of this report is to review the changing concepts of fluency as an essential aspect of reading, and to consider the effectiveness of two major instructional approaches to fluency development and the readiness of these approaches for wide use by the schools" (pp. 3–5). LaBerge and Samuels' (1974) theoretical article on automatic information processing in reading generated considerable interest in reading fluency. At the time the article was written, the authors' attention was focused primarily on the automatic decoding of text. Although they clearly recognized that when decoding was performed automatically (i.e., with little attention or effort) it enabled comprehension to take place at the same time, they made no attempt to define fluency. The fact that fluent readers could perform two tasks at the same time, such as decode and comprehend a text, was implicit in their work, however. The emphasis on the automatic aspects of decoding is reflected in *The Literacy Dictionary* (Harris & Hodges, 1995). The authors' definition of fluency states that fluency is "freedom from word identification problems" (p. 85). While the early emphasis by LaBerge and Samuels focused on how the automatic decoding of words facilitated comprehension, Schreiber (1980, 1987) took a linguistic approach. He reasoned that the route to fluency was brought about as the student learned how to automatically parse a text into its linguistic units, such as a noun phrase and a verb phrase. According to Schreiber, fluent readers were able to use punctuation and were able to rapidly determine where to place emphasis and how to separate the text into grammatical units. When this activity of breaking a text into linguistic units took place almost effortlessly, it freed up the cognitive resources for comprehension.

Others have extended the idea that as reading skill increases, more and more of the subskills become automatic, and recent conceptualizations of what can become automatic in reading have extended well beyond word identification. Thurlow and van den Broek (1997), for example, have stated that several components of comprehension can become automatic. Thus, the concept of automatic information processing, which started with the automatic decoding of words in texts, has been extended to include certain components of the comprehension process as well. One of the reasons there is so much interest in fluency is the finding that the development of efficient word recognition skills is usually associated with improved comprehension (Calfee and Piontkowski, 1981). Despite the finding that good word recognition skills are positively correlated with good comprehension, it is still possible, however, to find many instances where a student's word recognition skills outstrip his or her comprehension skills because of poor vocabulary knowledge, as is the case with some English language learners.

Another avenue that has led to changes in how fluency is described has been the work of cognitive psychologists, such as Posner and Snyder (1975), Schneider and Shiffrin (1977), Ackerman (1987), and Logan (1997). They have described the characteristics of highly skilled and complex activity. What most of them seem to agree on is that the seemingly effortless automatic text-processing skills are acquired gradually over an extended period of time as the result of extended practice. Ackerman (1987), for example, has stated: "Automatic processes are characterized as fast, effortless (from a standpoint of allocation of cognitive resources), and unitized (or proceduralized) such that they may not be easily altered by a subject's conscious control, *and they may allow for parallel operation with other information processing within and between tasks. These processes may be developed only through extensive practice under consistent conditions, which are typical of many skill acquisition situations*" (p. 4, emphasis added). The underscored portions of Ackerman's text emphasize two important characteristics of automaticity and fluency. First, when a person is automatic at decoding, it allows for parallel processing. Parallel processing means that a person is able to perform several tasks at the same time, such as decoding the words in a text, breaking sentences in the text into proper grammatical units, and understanding the text. This concept of the ability to perform several tasks at the same time is extremely important to our definition of fluency and to the valid measurement of fluency. The second concept that is underscored in the selection by Ackerman emphasizes the importance of practice that is consistent in developing automaticity.

DEFINITION OF FLUENCY

The theoretical work that has been done on the characteristics of readers' highly skilled and automatic behaviors shows that these behaviors share several characteristics:

- They are fast.
- They are accurate.
- They are performed with little attention and effort.
- Two complex tasks can be done at the same time. Before the automatic level of performance was reached on the primary task (in the case of reading it would be decoding), a secondary task (such as comprehension) could not be performed at the same time. The critical characteristic of a skill that is at the automatic level is that two complex tasks can be performed simultaneously.

The *NRP Interim Report* defines fluency as follows: "The fluent reader is one who can perform multiple tasks—such as word recognition and comprehension—at the same time. The non-fluent reader, on the other hand, can perform only one task at a time. The multitask functioning of the fluent reader is made possible by the reduced cognitive demands needed for word recognition and other reading processes, thus freeing cognitive resources for other functions, such as drawing inferences" (pp. 3–8). For the nonfluent reader, the word recognition task might require all of his or her cognitive resources. Consequently, comprehension cannot get done at that moment. Having completed the word recognition–decoding task, the beginning reader switches attention to comprehension and all the cognitive resources are used for that task. By switching attention back and forth from decoding to comprehension, the nonfluent reader can work through a text, but it is slow and hard work, and it places a heavy load on short-term memory. If the beginning reader cannot work his or her way through a sentence in 18 seconds or less, what has been put into short-term memory is lost, and the student must start the sentence over again. After a long period of practice, the student becomes automatic at the decoding tasks, and the bulk of the available attention can be directed at the task of understanding the sentence. When the lower-level decoding tasks can be done automatically, the student can be considered to be fluent, and is characterized by the ability to get decoding and comprehension tasks done at the same time.

The ability to decode text and comprehend a text at the same time is the essential characteristic of the fluent reader. There are other characteristics of the fluent reader, such as the ability to read a text orally with expression, with accuracy, and with speed. These characteristics of fluency—oral reading speed, word recognition accuracy, and expression—are secondary to the critical characteristic of fluency that is the ability to simultaneously decode and understand the text. For example, there are some students who can read orally with sufficient speed and accuracy but their comprehension may be poor, due to vocabulary or other language-related deficits. Thus, attempts to assess fluency using one of its secondary indicators, such as reading speed, can lead to incorrect judgments.

DEVELOPING READING FLUENCY

How does a reader become so fluent that when asked to read orally, he or she can read the words in the text with accuracy, speed, expression, and comprehension? Analysis of studies that used repeated reading (Samuels, 1979) showed that repeated reading had a consistent and positive impact on word recognition, fluency, and comprehension. Conventional wisdom dictates that it is only through extended practice spent in reading that one develops high levels of skill. Allington (1977), for example, in his article titled "If They Don't Read Much, How Are They Ever Going to Get Good?" found that the students who needed the most practice in reading spent the least amount of time in actual reading. The *NRP Interim Report* states, "What is surprising is that most of the evidence linking input variables, such as amount read and output variables such as reading ability is correlational" (pp. 3–10).

There are a host of correlational studies linking independent reading and reading outcomes, and these all have found positive correlations, indicating that those who read more have higher achievement in reading. Stanovich (1986), in his classic article, "Matthew Effects in Reading," has taken a phrase from the Bible, "The rich get richer and the poor get poorer," and has shown how it applies to reading outcomes. In essence, Stanovich claims that reading more is associated with higher levels of reading achievement, while reading less is associated with lower levels. Stanovich speculated that the gap in reading achievement between the good and the poor readers would increase over time because of differences in the amount of practice each group would get.

The reading research literature contained abundant information from correlational studies showing the positive linkage between time spent reading and reading achievement. It has long been accepted as a given that practice at any skill leads to improvement. The fact that there was a lack of experimental studies showing a cause and effect relationship between amount of time spent reading and reading achievement was not surprising, because researchers usually avoid doing studies where the outcome seems obvious. The lack of evidence from an experimental study published in a peer-reviewed journal posed a problem for the NRP, however. Since the rules the panel adopted for evidence-based conclusions restricted the members f looking at correlational data showing that students who read more had higher reading achievement, the panel, after much heated discussion, decided to make a cautionary statement about independent reading and achievement. In the "Executive Summary" of the *NRP Interim Report* one finds the caveat: "With regard to the efficacy of having students engage in independent silent reading with minimal guidance or feedback, the Panel was unable to find a positive relationship between programs and instruction that encourage large amounts of independent reading and improvements in reading achievements, including fluency. In other words, even though encouraging students to read more is intuitively appealing, there is still not sufficient research evidence obtained from studies of high methodological quality to support the idea that such efforts reliably . . . result in improved reading skills" (p. 13). This statement has led to considerable criticism, because it violates conventional wisdom and the experience of teachers everywhere.

THE RED FLAG OF CAUTION: DOES INDEPENDENT READING LEAD TO FLUENCY?

The NRP statement indicating that the panel could not support the practice of encouraging students to read independently, because of the lack of experimental evidence showing that this practice led to improved reading achievement, led to considerable criticism by all segments of the educational community. As stated above, while experimental researchers have valid reasons for not doing studies where the outcome seems obvious, given the importance of the NRP statement, the need to do a an experimental study showing how the amount of time spent in independent reading affects reading achievement seemed warranted. Consequently, Samuels and Wu (2006) did an experimental study in which 3rd graders and 5th graders in an inner-city St. Paul school were randomly assigned to either a 15-minute independent reading group or to a 40-minute independent reading group. Data analysis showed that while more time spent reading led to significant positive achievement outcomes on a variety of measures, such as word recognition and comprehension, there was an interesting additional finding that made sense. The study indicated that the higher-achieving readers seemed to gain more with longer time spent in independent reading, while less able readers seemed to gain more with the shorter periods. In conclusion, the results of this experiment strongly support the importance of encouraging students to read independently. The only factor that should be kept in mind in deciding how much time to allocate to independent reading is that students who are skilled in reading have longer attention spans than less-skilled readers, who may not be automatic at decoding.

A FINAL CAVEAT—POST *NRP INTERIM REPORT*

With the growing importance of the No Child Left Behind legislation, how schools test students has become as important as the methods used to teach them. School staff may be providing effective instruction, but if the evaluation instruments are less than adequate, the tests may give faulty results and lead to incorrect decisions regarding curriculum or instruction. As might be expected, the growing emphasis on fluency has led to widespread use of testing and evaluation instruments that have the term "fluency" in their titles. It is time for the federal government to support studies that reevaluate the adequacy of the validity claims for these testing instruments, using validation procedures that are in harmony with the latest theoretical constructs supporting definitions of fluency.

COMPREHENSION

When the NRP reviewed the literature on comprehension, they addressed three major themes: vocabulary, reading comprehension strategies employed as the reader is actively engaged in reading, and how teachers are prepared to teach these comprehension strategies.

Vocabulary

The NRP focused its review of vocabulary research on those studies that attempted to teach the meanings of words to improve reading comprehension. The importance of vocabulary to reading comprehension is widely documented and is crucial from beginning reading instruction to advanced levels. In beginning reading, as students decode letters into sounds, they come to understand that these sounds can be blended into words that match their oral vocabulary. In this way, they are able to make sense of what they are reading. Clearly, words that are not in the student's listening and/or speaking vocabulary cannot contribute to the meaningful representation or comprehension of what was read. Just as with speaking vocabulary, in which the meanings of new words are learned as a natural consequence of engaging in conversation, the meanings of words are learned incidentally while reading. This indirect learning of vocabulary can come from students engaging in reading or listening to stories being read to them. Often, this indirect method is engineered by the teacher or by the nature of the material (e.g., new vocabulary words are repeated often in the text). In direct vocabulary strategies, student are explicitly introduced to new vocabulary words via their definitions, via other attributes (e.g., calling attention to root words or affixes), or via given algorithms for discovering meanings. The NRP concluded from its review of the literature that many of these studies revealed gains as a result of vocabulary interventions.

Comprehension Instruction

A review of the research on text comprehension instruction resulted in identifying 16 distinct categories of instruction, of which 7 appeared to have sufficient evidence to conclude that they improved comprehension in nonimpaired readers. These strategies with proven effectiveness included comprehension monitoring, cooperative learning, use of graphic and semantic organizers, including story structure, question answering, question generation, and summarization. All of these comprehension strategies were found useful to varying degrees when taught alone, but they have also been found to be beneficial when used as part of a multiple-strategy approach.

Comprehension Monitoring instruction encourages readers to be aware of how well they understand the material as they read. Although the research does not provide strong evidence for using this strategy in isolation, it has been shown to be an effective component of multiple-strategy instruction.

Cooperative Learning allows readers to work together in pairs or small groups to discuss text and instruct one another. This type of engaged interaction has been demonstrated to increase learning of other strategies, and to encourage intellectual discussion and improved comprehension of reading material.

Graphic Organizers are visual diagrams that represent relationships among concepts from the text. These pictorial graphs allow readers to construct a text structure, summarize main ideas, and remember what has been read. Although graphic organizers are most often used in expository texts, they are also applied to narratives as story maps. Teaching students to organize content graphically may lead to improved comprehension and general achievement.

Question Answering is a cognitive strategy often taught to students to facilitate reasoning during the reading of a text. Instruction in this approach is intended to teach students procedures for finding answers within the text and to focus on specific content during reading to learn more from the text.

Question Generation is encouraged during reading to make readers more active and engaged with a text. The goal is to encourage readers to self-question their understanding of the material and construct integrative memory representations. Research indicates that question generation benefits reading comprehension in terms of summarizing main points and answering questions about the text (Rosenshine, Meister, & Chapman, 1996). Teachers often use this approach along with other methods such as reciprocal teaching as part of a multistrategy instructional approach.

Story Structure allows readers to organize episodes presented in the plot structure of a story. Students are instructed to identify the who, what, where, when, and why of a narrative to better understand the sequence of events and construct a coherent memory representation of the story.

Summarization requires a reader to identify the main ideas presented in the text and succinctly communicate this recall in spoken or written form. Research has concluded that summarization is an important component of comprehension instruction, as it helps students improve their memory of the material and generalize ideas from the reading content (Bean & Steenwyk, 1984; Rinehart, Stahl, & Erickson, 1986).

Multiple Strategy Instruction has been shown to be more effective than any one strategy alone. Empirical evidence supports the use of a flexible combination of reading strategies that can be used according to the situation. Teachers often model strategies such as questioning, monitoring, and summarizing, followed by an opportunity for students to engage in reciprocal teaching or collaborative learning to scaffold independent reading. Mental imagery and mnemonic (keyword) strategies are often used with students to help them visualize and comprehend what they are reading; these strategies also aid memory and can be effectively used as an alternative means of representing text.

Implementation of Instruction in Reading Comprehension

Various conditions in the classroom may interfere with effective comprehension instruction. Factors such as classroom management, monitoring behavior, instructional techniques, and degree of student involvement vary from teacher to teacher. Teachers are often more effective when they remain flexible and adjust instruction to students' needs. Research suggests that an emphasis on developing metacognitive awareness and the use of modeling during instruction can have positive results for readers of varying abilities, even when instructional strategies are only partially implemented (Duffy, 1993).

The panel called for future research in the area of reading comprehension that could transfer to the classroom. To accomplish this goal, researchers should attempt the following: use of experimental methods when possible, use of consistent training materials, analysis of intervening factors such as teacher characteristics, and assessment of the long-term impact of the intervention. The NRP suggests several directions for future research, including an examination of whether specific strategies are more effective in certain content areas, or are more useful with different ages, reading abilities, and text genres. Further evidence is needed to determine effective approaches for preparing teachers in comprehension strategies instruction.

Teacher Preparation and Comprehension Strategies Instruction

The NRP identified two primary approaches to comprehension strategies instruction: direct explanation (DE) and transactional strategy instruction (TSI). Both of these approaches are a shift away from the early direct instruction approach, which did not place emphasis on students' understanding of the reasons for using a particular reading strategy.

The direct explanation (DE) approach advocates a problem-solving framework in which students learn to think strategically about reading comprehension. Research on the DE approach conducted by Duffy et al. (1986, 1987) suggests that students who received reading instruction from teachers trained in the DE method were significantly more aware of the specific comprehension strategies they had learned and score higher on word skills posttests than students taught by an untrained teacher, but mixed results on standardized measures of comprehension do not indicate significant differences in reading comprehension ability between the two groups.

Transactional strategy instruction (TSI) and the direct explanation approach share similar components, such as scaffolding and systematic practice, but view the role of the teacher quite differently. Whereas the DE approach emphasizes the teacher's ability to articulate explanations, TSI advocates an interactive exchange among students and instructor. Teacher preparation in TSI emphasizes facilitating discussion and collaboration among students. The studies published on TSI seem to indicate that instructional methods allowing for high levels of student participation and active involvement can have significant positive effects on reading comprehension.

Although research does not provide evidence in favor of one specific set of instructional procedures, previous studies have shown that instruction of teachers in teaching reading comprehension strategically can lead to increased student awareness and engagement. The general guidelines provided by the panel's investigation of comprehension instruction suggest that teachers should explain fully what they are teaching, model proper use of strategies, and encourage student participation through discussion and question-asking.

Teacher Education and Reading Instruction

Because there were too few studies on preservice teachers, and because there were no student measures taken in these studies, the NRP made no conclusions about the effectiveness of preservice teacher training in reading. The evidence for inservice teachers, however, was quite encouraging. The NRP concluded that teachers could be taught to improve their teaching of reading, and, most importantly, this improvement leads to corresponding improvement of their students' reading achievement.

Computer Technology and Reading Instruction

The NRP found little systematic research on the use of computers for reading instruction. The panel concluded that computers are useful tools for motivating children to read, and tools that can provide hypertext and hypermedia. As teachers know, reading and writing are closely linked in a symbiotic relationship, and the computer has proven its usefulness as a reading tool and as a writing tool. The general conclusion of the NRP is that computer technology can be used to deliver a variety of different kinds of reading instruction, and with the ongoing development of computerized speech recognition, the future of computers in reading instruction seems secure.

REFERENCES

Accelerated Reader [Computer software]. (1993). Wisconsin Rapids, WI: Renaissance Learning.

Ackerman, P. (1987). Individual differences in skill reading: An integration of psychometric and information processing perspectives. *Psychological Bulletin, 102,* 3–27.

Adams, M. J. (1990). *Beginning to read: Thinking and learning about print.* Cambridge, MA: Massachusetts Institute of Technology Press.

Allington, R. (1977). If they don't read much, how they ever going to get good? *Journal of Reading, 21,* 57–61.

Bean, T. W., & Steenwyk, F. L. (1984). The effect of three forms of summarization instruction on sixth graders' summary writing and comprehension. *Journal of Reading Behavior, 16*(4), 297–306.

Bond, G. L., & Dykstra, R. (1967). The cooperative research program in first-grade reading instruction. *Reading Research Quarterly, 2,* 10–141.

Calfee, R. C., & Piaotkowski, D. C. (1981). The reading diary: Acquisition of decoding. *Reading Research Quarterly, 16,* 346–373.

Chall, J. S. (1967). *Learning to read: The great debate.* New York: McGraw-Hill.

Donahue, P. (2001). The nation's report card: Fourth-grade reading 2000. *The nation's report card.* Washington, DC: National Center for Education Statistics. Available at http://purl.access.gpo.gov/GPO/LPS15978

Duffy, G. G. (1993). Rethinking strategy instruction: Four teachers' development and their low achievers' understanding. *Elementary School Journal, 93*(3), 231–247.

Duffy, G. G., Roehler, L. R., Meloth, M. S., Vavrus, L. G., Book, C., Putnam, J., & Wesselman, R. (1986). The relationship between explicit verbal explanations during reading skill instruction and student awareness and achievement: A study of reading teacher effects. *Reading Research Quarterly, 21*(3), 237–252.

Duffy, G. G., Roehler, L. R., Sivan, E., Rackliffe, G., Book, C., Meloth, M. S., et al. (1987). Effects of explaining the reasoning associated with using reading strategies. *Reading Research Quarterly, 23*(3), 347–268.

Goodman, K. 1976. Reading: A psycholinguistic guessing game. In H. Singer and R. B. Ruddel (Eds.), *Theoretical models and process of reading* (2nd ed.). Newark, DE.: International Reading Association.

Harris, T. L., & Hodges, R. E. (1995). *The Literacy Dictionary.* Newark, DE: International Reading Association.

LaBerge, D., & Samuels, S. J. (1974). Toward a theory of automatic information processing in reading. *Cognitive Psychology, 6,* 293–323.

Logan, G. D. (1997). Automaticity and reading: Perspectives from the instance theory of automatization. *Reading and Writing Quarterly, 13,* 123–146.

National Institute of Child Health and Human Development. (2000). *Report of the National Reading Panel: Teaching children to read: An evidence-based assessment of the scientific research literature on reading and its implications for reading instruction: Reports of the subgroups* (NIH Publication No. 00–4754). Washington, DC: U.S. Government Printing Office.

Posner, M. I., & Snyder, R. R. (1975). Attention and cognitive control. In R. L. Solso (Ed.), *Information Processing and Cognition: The Loyola Symposium.* (pp. 55–85). Mahwah, NJ: Erlbaum.

Rinehart, S. D., Stahl, S. A., & Erickson, L. G. (1986). Some effects of summarization training on reading and studying. *Reading Research Quarterly, 21*(4), 422–438.

Rosenshine, B., Meister, C., & Chapman, S. (1996). Teaching students to generate questions: A review of the intervention studies. *Review of Educational Research, 66*(2), 181–221.

Samuels, S. J. (1979). The method of repeated reading. *The Reading Teacher, 32,* 403–408.

Samuels, S. J., & Wu, Y. C. (2006). *How the amount of time spent on independent reading affects reading achievement: A response to the National Reading Panel.* Unpublished manuscript, University of Minnesota, Twin Cites.

Schneider, W., & Shiffrin, R. M. (1977). Controlled and automatic information processing: Perceptual learning, automatic attending, and general theory. *Psychological Review, 84*(1), 127–190.

Schreiber, P. A. (1980). On the acquisition of reading fluency. *Journal of Reading Behavior, 12,* 177–186.

Schreiber, P. A. (1987). Prosody and structure in children's syntactic processing. In R. Horowitz & S. J. Samuels (Eds.), *Comprehending Oral and Written Language.* New York: Academic Press.

Snow, C., Burns, M., & Griffin, P. (Eds.). (1998). *Preventing reading difficulties in young children.* Washington, DC: National Academy Press.

Stanovich, K. (1986). Matthew effects in reading: Some consequences of individual differences in the acquisition of literacy. *Reading Research Quarterly, 22,* 360–406.

Thurlow, R., & van den Broek, P. (1997). Automaticity and inference generation. *Reading and Writing Quarterly, 13,* 16.

Chapter Three

POLITICAL, SOCIAL, ECONOMIC, CULTURAL, AND ENVIRONMENTAL ISSUES IMPACTING EARLY LITERACY

Mario Castro

Early childhood literacy is a function of much more than individual ability. Broader issues, such as political, social, economic, cultural, and environmental issues, deeply impact early childhood literacy. These broader factors intersect with educational policy and practice to impact early childhood literacy. Moreover, because children in the United States are especially reliant on other persons for care and well-being from birth to grade 3, how these broader factors impact their caretakers is vital to children's literate futures.

In this chapter, I examine the impact of the broader context on early childhood literacy. Because discrete populations are affected distinctly and react in their own way to any given policy or practice, the chapter avoids blanket declarations about how broader issues impact early childhood literacy among all populations. Instead, I analyze the Mexican-origin population in one state to illustrate how unique factors affect this population's early childhood literacy. I present a case study of language attributes focused on early childhood literacy among Arizona's Mexican-origin population and find that economic and political issues are more salient than social or cultural issues at this point in time for this specific population. I note that Arizona education policy, aimed at improving the educational success of students who come to school speaking little or no English, is currently misdirected toward only increasing English proficiency. I further contend that students who are classified as English language learners are not the only ones who are harmed by the state's highly politicized early language and literacy policies. As detailed below, a high portion of other persons in the state is also negatively impacted by these policies. I conclude that Arizona's policy should be redirected toward eliminating obstacles to schooling—more than toward the promotion of English—because educational attainment far exceeds English ability as a predictor of economic opportunity for the Mexican-origin population in the state.

Before presenting the case study, I briefly consider what recent early childhood literacy research says about how broader issues impact early childhood literacy. I include methods to manage the ever-increasing diversity encountered in classrooms in many parts of the United States. I include two popular methods that early childhood literacy researchers recommend to early literacy educators to manage the impact of broader issues on early childhood literacy.

EARLY LITERACY EFFORTS: THE BROADER CONTEXT

According to Jones Diaz and Makin, "In recent years, there has been increasing dissatisfaction with developmental theories. The main criticism is that there has been too much focus on the individual and not enough on the [broader] context, with a corresponding undervaluing of the importance of interaction with other people" (2002, p. 4). The importance of the social context in determining literacy is recognized by these early childhood literacy authors. They recognize that school literacy often clashes with literacy in regular life activities. In the classroom, literacy is framed at the individual level; in social situations, however, literacy is community wide, as when a person requests feedback from neighbors on a document (Heath, 1998). When considering the broader context of early literacy promotion, other factors affecting literacy and schooling, such as economic, political, cultural, and environmental factors, also come more into focus depending on the population under examination.

A review of early childhood literacy research reflects a reluctance to address this larger "big picture" of sociocultural and sociopolitical influences on literacy and schooling. Without addressing underlying factors that can affect literacy and education, educators and the public may come to believe that young children's social problems will be solved through literacy, early intervention, or proper schooling, and thus disregard lived experience. In this regard, Collins contends that "the idea of mobility through literacy and education remains persuasive, despite . . . the historical experience of most people" (1991, p. 235). In a similar way, Wiley (2005) argues that the connection between literacy and socioeconomics needs to be reversed. Collins and Wiley are among a large number of scholars who conclude that rather than literacy levels *causing* socioeconomic conditions, literacy levels *result* from socioeconomic conditions. Socioeconomic forces affecting literacy should be contended with when focusing on the broader context of literacy, as should, for example, applicable political, cultural, and environmental forces.

In recent years, early childhood literacy researchers focusing on how sociocultural and political issues impact early childhood literacy commonly recommended to early literacy educators that they should either (1) accept diverse literacies or (2) bring critical literacy into the classroom. These recommendations are presented as methods for managing the impact of broader issues, such as political, social, economic, cultural, and environmental issues, on early childhood literacy. A brief description of each method follows.

Accepting Diverse Literacies

Researchers calling for an acceptance of diverse literacies recommend that early childhood educators recognize and value the diverse literacies young children bring from home, community, and culture. "An awareness of the many dimensions of literacy learning and of the diversity in children's literacy experiences will equip early childhood educators to adopt inclusive literacy practices that strengthen the pathways into literacy for all children" (Martello, 2002, p. 48). This research calls for accepting all students regardless of their situation and appreciating and working with their varied literacy experiences. For example, a language minority child's literacy skills are appreciated and built upon as are a poor child's literacy skills, and both sets of literacy skills are valued as much as any other child's literacy skills.

The early childhood years not only encompass the key years of brain development but also encompass the age of transition from home to school and school to home. Accepting diverse literacies implies recognizing the impact of forces on early childhood literacy, such as sociocultural, political, and economic forces, by offering a way to avoid the stratification of children at the start of their formal schooling based on their situation, whatever it may be. "Achieving continuity between home and early childhood literacy practices is a prime responsibility of early childhood educators" (Martello, 2002, p. 48).

Critical Literacy in the Classroom

A second method that researchers subscribe to for managing broader issue influences on early childhood literacy is bringing critical literacy into the classroom. Although less common as an approach to handle the broader context of literacy, this method has seen an increase in popularity. This increase mirrors the increased popularity of critical thinking and critical applied linguistics, which view knowledge, including knowledge related to schooling, literacy, and language learning, as political. Pennycook argues that

> Everything in the classroom, from how we teach, what we teach, how we respond to students, to the materials we use and the way we assess the student, needs to be seen as social and cultural practices that have broader implications than just pieces

> of classroom interaction. . . . In any educational domain, therefore, we need to focus on the cultural politics of what we do and understand the implications of our own and our students' pedagogical choices as both particular to the context and related to broader domains. (2001, p. 139)

Critical literacy likewise aims to understand literacy as a social practice linked to broader political, social, cultural, and economic interests. In early childhood literacy, critical literacy involves challenging "power structures and social practices that privilege some groups over others" and encourages young children to dive "beneath the surface of the text to critique ways in which dominant world views, discourses and ideologies are valued, and minority views suppressed" (Jones Diaz, Beecher, & Arthur, 2002, pp. 308–309).

In *Negotiating Critical Literacies with Young Children,* Vasquez (2004) describes how she implemented critical literacy in an early childhood education setting. Vasquez objects to teachers' attempts to engage in critical literacy by treating social issues as variables to be added to an existing curriculum rather than by using the issues to build a curriculum. In Vasquez's critical literacy classroom, social issues or topics are looked at in different ways, analyzed, and possible changes or improvements are suggested. For example, Vasquez's class considered the topic of vegetarianism following the school barbecue, when it became known that one of the students in the class was a vegetarian and was not able to suitably eat at the barbecue. In considering vegetarianism, the class was "learning a different way of being and acting in the world" (p. 110). Looking at this topic led the class to question who else may be marginalized in some way at their school. Following social action in the form of a letter-writing campaign, the status of vegetarians in their school improved with the offering of a vegetarian option at subsequent events. Vasquez writes that the class members enjoyed their studies because the topics they dealt with were socially significant to them. This implies that, if she implemented a critical literacy curriculum with a different set of students, the issues that the class would look at and analyze might well be very different.

Summary

Bringing critical literacy to schoolrooms of children in their early childhood years and urging an acceptance of diverse literacies respond to Jones Diaz and Makin's criticism of developmental theory, that there has been too much attention paid to the individual and not enough focus on the broader context. Accepting diverse literacies implies dealing with sociocultural and economic differences, such as differences in students' culture and families' financial situations, and not ignoring differences in the experiences and situations of young children. Rather, educators acknowledge that differences exist and capitalize on them rather than allowing them to create obstacles to literacy. With critical literacy, teachers work on increasing students' literacy skills by becoming aware of how the children's situations position them.

Since both methods rely on recognizing the effects of the broader context on early childhood literacy, the effectiveness of the methods improve with a deeper understanding of how factors such as environmental, sociocultural, political, and economic factors impact literacy. In looking at early literacy for persons classified as English language learners, Xu advises teachers to examine their own beliefs about the culture of their students:

> Just as English language learners bring to the classrooms their unique cultures, teachers' own cultures color the way they teach. It is important to discover how learner's cultures differ from those of their teachers, to constantly examine the way in which teachers react to such differences, and to pay special attention to the differences. (2003, p. 67)

Besides recognizing differences in young children's literacy experiences in order to build diverse literacies, early childhood literacy educators must recognize their own differences from their students. While teachers are part of the school domain, they are also influenced by the broader context; that is, teachers are not exempt from misconceptions about such contextual conditions as race, languages, income levels, and gender. A deeper understanding of how they too are influenced by these conditions improves teachers' effectiveness as early childhood literacy educators.

Educators occasionally are not aware of their own role in sustaining existing power structures. Sometimes even a critical literacy educator fails to see his or her own role in marginalizing others. For example, when taking on environmental issues, Vasquez (2004) led her early childhood class into an inquiry about rain forests. The class's efforts to learn and inform others about the need to preserve rain forests and to send a message regarding what happens when rain forests are harvested for profit included sending a poster and a letter to all places selling wood, asking them not to sell wood that has been harvested from rain forests and also mailing the letter to different lumberyards in the city. Vasquez reported that the creation of the poster and the letter resulted from conversations in the classroom about the economics involved in producing goods made from using *wood from rain forests*—that is, conversations about buyers, sellers, and producers.

The class members' concern for rain forest animals and the rain forest environment did not transfer to concern for animals or the environment endangered by their own community's actions, however. The hidden political, social, and economic lesson being taught was that it is not acceptable for faraway persons to take down trees for profit, while it is perfectly acceptable for the local community to do so, because the local community is not situated in a rain forest, because local trees do not sustain animals or provide oxygen, because local people know how to manage the environment, and because local people are not greedy.

Another example of how even critical literacy educators are themselves victims of existing power structures surfaces with the class's analysis of McDonald's Happy Meal toys. Rather than criticizing consumerism, the angle taken by Vasquez was that the Happy Meal toys increased her students' cultural capital. In other words, students who had whole collections of Happy Meal toys, or at least were knowledgeable about a popular collection, were esteemed by their peers and increased their cultural value in their peers' eyes. One of the criticisms that the class came up with is that this collection of McDonald's toys is not accessible to poor children. This example shows that recognizing broader contextual influences on literacy and education (in this case, capitalism and consumerism) is often not an easy task.

There are studies available that provide a deeper understanding of the impact of broader issues, such as political, social, economic, cultural, and environmental issues, on early childhood literacy and education. Because different populations are affected uniquely, early literacy educators and interested others are advised to seek out works covering specific population types that address the broader context, such as *Contemporary Perspectives on Language Policy and Literacy Instruction in Early Childhood,* a volume edited by Saracho and Spodek (2004), which focuses on the early childhood literacy of persons classified as English language learners.

In the next section, I present a case study showing how the broader context impacts the literacy levels of an important segment of early childhood children in the state of Arizona.

MEXICAN-ORIGIN STUDENTS' EARLY LITERACY: A CASE STUDY

To assist in demonstrating how political, social, economic, and cultural issues impact literacy learning among young children of Mexican origin in the state of Arizona, I first present some key demographics, including statistics about language speakers. I follow the demographic figures with a description of the political climate in the state and describe the effects of this on the early childhood population of students of Mexican origin. I interject literacy and schooling data specifically related to persons in their early childhood years, and I demonstrate how social and economic policies affect their literacy and schooling.

The Mexican-ancestry population is Arizona's largest ancestry group. Most people of Mexican origin in the state are citizens of the United States (Hunnicutt & Castro, 2005). The 2000 Census (U.S. Census Bureau, 2000) data for Arizona indicate that the size and rate of U.S. citizenship are even greater for the early childhood population of Mexican origin. Using the Arizona 5 percent Public Use Microdata Sample, or PUMS (U.S. Census Bureau, 2003) from the 2000 Census, I estimate that people whose first ancestry was Mexican made up 25 percent of those nine years old and under. (The Arizona 5 percent PUMS file contains individual records of responses to census questionnaires representing a 5 percent sample of the occupied and vacant housing units and the persons in the occupied units.) PUMS data show people whose first ancestry was Mexican comprised 17 percent of the total population in the year 2000. The important point here is that, while the Mexican-ancestry population was 1.5 times larger than the second most frequently cited ancestry choice for people responding to the census survey, the Mexican-ancestry population was than 3.5 times larger than the second most frequently cited ancestry group in the early childhood years (German is the second most frequently cited choice in Arizona). In addition, I estimate from PUMS data that, while 70 percent of persons from the overall Mexican-origin population in Arizona were U.S. citizens in 2000, 89 percent of Mexican-origin persons nine years old and under were U.S. citizens.

Moreover, PUMS data show that Arizona's Mexican-origin population overwhelmingly speaks Spanish, but the rates are lower for school-aged children in their early childhood years. Whereas 76 percent of the Mexican-origin population five years and older speak Spanish at home and 24 percent speak only English, 67 percent of those between the ages of five years and nine years speak Spanish at home and fully one-third speak only English (see Table 3.1).

Table 3.1
Arizona Mexican-Origin Population by Proportional Share of Language Spoken at Home and Ability to Speak English

Language spoken at home		How well English is spoken by those who speak Spanish at home			
Population 5 years of age and over	Share	Very well	Well	Not well	Not at all
Spanish	76%	38%	15%	14%	10%
English-only	24%	–	–	–	–
Total	100%				
Population between 5 and 9 years of age					
Spanish	67%	32%	19%	12%	4%
English-only	33%	–	–	–	–
Total	100%				

Note. The percentage of Spanish speakers falls below the percentage speaking very well, well, not well, and not at all due to rounding.

Because statistics about language are collected by the census only for persons five years old and over, children less than five years old are not included in the analyses presented in Table 3.1. PUMS data show, however, that 84 percent of Mexican-origin children less than five years old reside in Arizona households where the household language is Spanish. This figure of 84 percent is also the same for the five- to nine-year-old Mexican-origin population, as well as for the Mexican-origin population as a whole.

Although Arizona's Mexican-origin population overwhelmingly speaks Spanish, although Mexican ancestry represents the modal (most frequent) category in the state, and although persons of Mexican origin are overwhelmingly U.S. citizens, especially those in their early childhood years, there are statewide political efforts to depress the use of Spanish through language planning policy, masked as education policy. Wiley (1992) stated that "Schools have been the principal instruments in promoting a consensus regarding the alleged superiority of standardized languages" (p. 113). Wiley's quote holds for the alleged superiority of any specific standard language; in Arizona, it is the version of English spoken by the state's English monolingual speakers.

Arizona education policy as mandated by Proposition 203 severely restricts Spanish language use and requires the teaching of students English only through so-called structured English immersion. The Arizona State Constitution dictates that all public school instruction should be conducted in English: "Provisions shall be made by law for the establishment and maintenance of a system of public schools which shall be open to all the children of the State and be free from sectarian control, and said schools shall always be conducted in English" (Art. 20, § 8, 2004). Following Arizona voters' approval of Proposition 203, the Arizona legislature enacted a measure requiring students classified as English language learners to "be taught English by being taught in English and all children shall be placed in English-language classrooms" (English Language Education for Children in Public Schools, A.R.S. § 15-751–§ 15-756, 2004).

Arizona education policy is framed as if it is tailored to assist those whose native or familial language is not English. Wright and Choi (2005) dispute the idea that using only English in the classroom benefits persons labeled English language learners. What policy makers and voters ignore is that Arizona's English monolingual students are the beneficiaries of the advantages, privileges, and prestige bestowed by a politically instigated education policy that suppresses Spanish, advocates the falsity that Spanish is foreign to the United States, and promotes English monolingualism. Also ignored is the point that language standards are very important in creating distance in literacy levels and schooling success between Spanish speakers and English monolinguals.

In *Subtractive Schooling: U.S.-Mexican Youth and the Politics of Caring,* Valenzuela (1999) shows how the abilities, skills, and culture that students bring to school are given value, and that the Spanish language is typically seen as inferior. Perceived inferiorities are communicated by ridicule, by ignoring the additive properties of traits, and by other many other means. Those with undesirable traits, like a speaking ability in Spanish, are encouraged and expected to drop out or become poor performers. School is shown to *subtract* from students, who attempt to shed the undesirable traits and become resistant to schooling. Valenzuela writes that "Unassessed in current scholarship are the academic consequences to many Mexican youth who 'learn' perhaps no stronger lesson in school than to devalue the Spanish language, Mexico, Mexican culture, and things Mexican" (p. 19).

A popular, but erroneous, belief assumes that the lack of native English skills among Mexican-origin persons is to blame for their lower literacy levels, social status, and schooling and economic success compared to non-Mexican-origin persons. So, inevitably, English proficiency often becomes the misdirected goal of sociopolitical and economic policies and practices. Examples of Arizona sociopolitical policies and practices with the goal of English proficiency include "Official English" (which voters once again approved in 2006, although the 1988 measure was stuck down *a decade later* by the Arizona Supreme Court in *Ruiz v. Hull*) and "English-Only in the Schools," the practice of providing Mexican-origin persons with English instruction instead of subject instruction, and the practice of Spanish-speaking households withholding bilingualism from school-aged children because of the false belief that speaking only English will result in greater school success. Examples of Arizona economic policies and practices with the goal of English proficiency include college admission policies, hiring practices, and other policies and practices requiring a strong command of the English language prior to delivery of educational services and jobs. While policies such as these may not be conclusive about their effects on language use (that is, the policies are not conclusive on whether or not they increase or decrease use of a language), the effects on access to educational services and workforce training are noticeable. Thus, it is not the lack of English skills that has a reducing effect on Spanish speakers' literacy levels, social status, and schooling and economic success; it is the lack of access to quality education and workforce training services that has a reducing effect.

As mentioned earlier, the great majority of Mexican-origin people in Arizona are U.S. citizens. The increasing number of Mexican-origin people has been met with a voter backlash through additional propositions that burden and are hostile to the state's large Mexican-origin population. In the mid-term elections in November 2006, four propositions were passed, each with more than a 70 percent voter approval rate, and these propositions further highlight the current political climate in the state. Proposition 100 adds to the list of nonbailable felony offenses that of being in the U.S. illegally. Proposition 102 denies punitive damages in any civil action to persons who are in the U.S. illegally. Proposition 103 makes English the official language of the state of Arizona, although the legality of this proposition will be tested in the courts. Finally, Proposition 300 provides that only citizens or legal residents are entitled to in-state classification for education purposes, tuition and fee wavers, financial assistance, and child care assistance. In addition, only citizens or legal residents may participate in family literacy programs and immigrant and adult education classes.

Current Arizona education policy rejects what education policy analysts and education academics have known for over 40 years. In early 1967, at the hearings for the Bilingual American Education Act, the precursor to the Bilingual Education Act that provided federal assistance to local education agencies for the development of bilingual education programs, testimony by several witnesses revealed that it was already well acknowledged that the best way to teach children is through their mother tongue. Literacy in one language facilitates literacy in another, and the debasing or rejecting of a student's native tongue, not the language itself, works negatively on a student's self-esteem and promotes dropping out and low educational attainment (see U.S. Congress, Senate, Committee on Labor and Public Welfare, Hearings before the Special Subcommittee on Bilingual Education, 1967).

Unfortunately, because of the persistent belief that a lack of native English skills is to blame, the solution to lower levels of literacy and education is habitually to increase English oral proficiency. Castro and Wiley (in press) state that overemphasizing oral English-language skills at the expense of literacy and job skills that can be mediated in non-English languages overtly delimits the workplace and educational policy options that would better accommodate our linguistically diverse society. English proficiency is the misdirected goal of Arizona education policy for the improvement of the educational success of students who come to school speaking little or no English, and this goal is actually a large part of the problem. Current Arizona education policy implies a preference for changing the Spanish-speaking Mexican-origin student into an English language speaker rather than providing the non-English-speaking student the greatest possible number of years of schooling and the best possible education and literacy services. Speakers of non-English languages are damaged by ill-informed education policies focusing on the acquisition of English rather than on, for example, subject matter.

The following statistics from the National Assessment of Educational Progress, or NAEP (U.S. Department of Education, 2006), further highlight the reasons why English proficiency is a misguided goal. In testing reading and writing achievement levels for students in grade 4, or just beyond our early childhood focus from birth to grade 3, the latest NAEP data show Mexican-origin students who only speak English at home in Arizona are (at a statistically significant level) just as likely to be below basic reading and writing levels as Mexican-origin students who speak a non-English language at home once in a while, half of the time, or all of the time (see Table 3.2) (U.S. Department of Education, 2002; U.S. Department of Education, 2005). In other words, speaking only English does nothing to support Mexican-origin students' literacy success.

PUMS data might provide plausible insight into why Arizona's school-aged Mexican-origin children in their early childhood years who speak only English at home are just as likely to be below basic reading and writing levels. Table 3.1 shows that 33 percent of Mexican-origin children between five and nine years of age speak only English in the home. Of these children, less than half (46 percent) reside in households where the household language is English, creating a possible literacy disconnection between child and home. This implies that some Mexican-origin Spanish-speaking households are drawn to the social practice of withholding bilingualism from young children because of the false belief that speaking only English will result in greater school success. These households may actually be coconspirators with governments and schools in hurting their children's literate future. This also highlights the reason why, as Jones Diaz and Makin (2002) noted, there is growing dissatisfaction with developmental theories focusing on the individual learner. The importance of interaction with other people in early childhood literacy development must not be undervalued. Ill-informed social practices and policies, like Arizona's English Language Education for Children in Public Schools, that spur beliefs such as speaking only English will translate to educational success, need to be stamped out. Data may help inform, but only early childhood educators and families can put suggestions into practice.

Concluding Suggestions Based on the Case Study

In summary, the data do not support current Arizona education policies and practices that focus on English oral proficiency in an attempt to improve

Table 3.2
Percentages of Mexican-Origin Students Who Are below Basic Reading and Writing 4th-Grade Levels by Frequency of Language Other Than English Spoken at Home

Speak a language other than English at home	Below basic reading level, 2005 (standard error)	Below basic writing level, 2002 (standard error)
Never	62% (4.5)	35% (5.8)
Once in a while	54% (3.5)	28% (3.5)
Half of the time	59% (5.6)	32% (6.5)
All of the time	64% (2.6)	32% (3.4)

the literacy outcomes of Spanish speakers in the state, of whom a great many are Americans of Mexican ancestry. In their attempt to pose some important questions in the hope that those questions may lead to policy improvement in the state, Hunnicutt and Castro (2005) ask,

> Since Spanish is so prevalent among Mexican-origin persons, with the vast majority not enrolled in school, are efforts to stamp Spanish out of schools masked efforts to deny education services to Mexican-origin persons and garner [educational] resources for English monolinguals? (p. 123)

To improve the literacy and the educational outcomes of Spanish speakers, the state of Arizona should instead concentrate on removing barriers to literacy and education, including removing policies and practices requiring a strong command of the English language prior to delivery of educational services, jobs, or workforce and job-skills training. Eradicating poverty (not turning everyone into English monolinguals) should be the goal. Castro and Wiley (in press) demonstrate that U.S.-born persons who have had the opportunity for schooling are likely to acquire English-speaking skills. Rather than educational attainment being seen as a function of English ability, English ability is a function of educational attainment obtained under English or bilingual instruction.

The data related to early childhood literacy support the path of redirecting efforts from English acquisition to the provision of quality literacy experiences. For example, Mexican-origin students who speak only English but who are National School Lunch program eligible are more likely to be below basic 4th-grade reading levels than Mexican-origin students who speak a non-English language once in a while and who are not National School Lunch program eligible (see Table 3.3) (U.S. Department of Education, 2005). Perhaps even more surprising, Mexican-origin students *who speak only English but who are National School Lunch program eligible* are more likely to be below basic 4th-grade reading levels (at a statistically significant level) than Mexican-origin students *who are not eligible for the National School Lunch program and who speak a non-English language all or most of time!* Observably, English proficiency is not the solution for the improvement of Spanish speakers' literacy outcomes.

Comparing students who have similar language use patterns, Mexican-origin students who speak a non-English language once in a while are more likely to be below basic 4th-grade reading and writing levels (at statistically significant levels) if they are eligible for the National School Lunch program than if they are not eligible for the National School Lunch program (U.S. Department of Education, 2002; U.S. Department of Education, 2005). These figures offer testament to Wiley's (1995) contention that rather than literacy

Table 3.3
Percentages of Mexican-Origin Students Who Are below Basic Reading and Writing 4th-Grade Levels by Frequency of Language Other Than English Spoken at Home and National School Lunch Program Eligibility

Speak a language other than English at home	Eligible for National School Lunch program	Below basic reading level, 2005 (standard error)	Below basic writing level, 2002 (standard error)
Never	Yes	73 (6.4)	48 (9.0)
	No	*	*
Once in a while	Yes	61 (3.6)	35 (4.2)
	No	40 (7.1)	18 (4.9)
Half of the time	Yes	69 (8.0)	33 (7.5)
	No	*	*
All of the time	Yes	66 (2.8)	35 (3.4)
	No	48 (7.1)	*

* Reporting standards not met.

levels causing socioeconomic conditions, literacy levels result from socioeconomic conditions.

Early childhood educators should note that it is not a lack of English proficiency but primarily political and economic interests that impact the literacy of young Mexican-origin students in their early childhood years. This chapter has aimed to assist in recognizing and valuing the diverse literacies that young children bring from home and community to school, to strengthen the pathways into literacy for all children. Likewise, this chapter has aimed to provide ammunition to early childhood educators who practice the art of critical literacy in their quest to challenge the power structures and social practices that privilege some groups over others. While I have mainly addressed language standards, I encourage a look at other areas, such as discriminatory practices in housing and lending, that are supported by industry, government, and individuals, resulting in much of the discrepancy in wealth between groups in the United States (Lipsitz, 1998).

REFERENCES

Arizona Constitution, Art. 20, § 8 (2004).

Castro, M., & Wiley, T. G. (in press). Adult literacy and language diversity: How well do national data inform policy? In K. M. Rivera and A. Huerta-Macías (Eds.), Adult *biliteracy: Sociocultural and programmatic responses.* Mahwah, NJ: Lawrence Erlbaum Associates.

Collins, J. (1991). Hegemonic practice: Literacy and standard language in public education. In C. Mitchell & K. Weiler (Eds.), *Rewriting literacy: Culture and discourse of the other* (pp. 229–253). New York: Bergin & Garvey.

English Language Education for Children in Public Schools, Arizona Revised Statutes § 15-751–§ 15-756 (2004).

Heath, S. B. (1998). Protean shapes in literacy events: Ever-shifting oral and literate traditions. In E. R. Kintgen, B. M. Kroll, & M. Rose (Eds.), *Perspectives on literacy* (pp. 348–370). Carbondale: Southern Illinois University Press.

Hunnicutt, K., & Castro, M. (2005, Spring). How Census 2000 data suggest hostility towards Mexican-origin Arizonians. *Bilingual Research Journal, 29*(1), 79–95.

Jones Diaz, C., Beecher, B., & Arthur, L. (2002). Children's worlds and critical literacy. In L. Makin & C. Jones Diaz (Eds.), *Literacies in early childhood: Changing views challenging practice* (pp. 305–322). Philadelphia: MacLennan & Petty.

Jones Diaz, C., & Makin, L. (2002). Literacy as social practice. In L. Makin & C. Jones Diaz (Eds.), *Literacies in early childhood: Changing views challenging practice* (pp. 3–14). Philadelphia: MacLennan & Petty.

Lipsitz, G. (1998). *The possessive investment in whiteness: How white people profit from identity politics.* Philadelphia: Temple University Press.

Martello, J. (2002). Many roads through many modes: Becoming literate in early childhood. In L. Makin & C. Jones Diaz (Eds.), *Literacies in early childhood: Changing views challenging practice* (pp. 35–52). Philadelphia: MacLennan & Petty.

Pennycook, A. (2001). *Critical applied linguistics: A critical introduction.* Mahwah, NJ: Lawrence Erlbaum Associates.

Proposition 100, House Concurrent Resolution 2028, Proposing an amendment to the Constitution of Arizona; Amending article II, section 22, Constitution of Arizona; Relating to bailable offenses (2006).

Proposition 102, Senate Concurrent Resolution 1001, Proposing an amendment to the Constitution of Arizona; Amending article II, Constitution of Arizona, by adding section 35; Relating to standing in civil actions (2006).

Proposition 103, House Concurrent Resolution 2036, Proposing an amendment to the Constitution of Arizona; Repealing article XXVIII, Constitution of Arizona; Amending the Constitution of Arizona by adding a new article XXVIII; Relating to English as the official language (2006).

Proposition 300, Senate Concurrent Resolution 1031, Enacting and ordering the submission to the people of a measure relating to public program eligibility (2006).

Ruiz v. Hull, 191 Ariz. 441 (Ariz. 1998).

Saracho, O. N., & Spodek, B. (Eds.). (2004). *Contemporary perspectives on language policy and literacy instruction in early childhood.* Greenwich, CT: Information Age Publishing.

U.S. Census Bureau. (2000). *Census 2000.* Retrieved February 7, 2005, from http://www.census.gov.

U.S. Census Bureau. (2003). *Census 2000,* public use microdata sample, United States. Washington, DC: Author.

U.S. Congress, Senate Committee on Labor and Public Welfare, Hearings before the Special Subcommittee on Bilingual Education. (1967). A bill to amend the Elementary and Secondary Education Act of 1965 in order to provide assistance to local education agencies in establishing bilingual American education programs, and to provide certain other assistance to promote such programs, Part 1 & Part 2, Pub. 81–367, 90th Cong., 1st sess., May 18, 19, 26, 29, and 31, 1967, & June 24 and July 21, 1967, S. 428. Washington, DC: U.S. Government Printing Office.

U.S. Department of Education. (2002). *National Assessment of Educational Progress.* Washington, DC: Author.

U.S. Department of Education. (2005). *National Assessment of Educational Progress.* Washington, DC: Author.

U.S. Department of Education, Institute of Education Services, National Center for Education Statistics (2006). *National Assessment of Educational Progress.* Retrieved November 23, 2006, from http://nces.ed.gov/nationsreportcard.

Valenzuela, A. (1999). *Subtractive Schooling: U.S.-Mexican Youth and the Politics of Caring.* New York: State University of New York Press.

Vasquez, V. M. (2004). *Negotiating critical literacies with young children.* Mahwah, NJ: Lawrence Erlbaum Associates.

Wiley, T. G. (1992). Language planning and policy. In S. McKay & N. Hornberger (Eds.), *Sociolinguistics and language teaching* (pp. 103–147). Cambridge, UK: Cambridge University Press.

Wiley, T. G. (2005). *Literacy and language diversity in the United States* (2nd ed.). Washington, DC: Center for Applied Linguistics and Delta Systems.

Wright, W. E., & Choi, D. (2005, December). *Voices from the classroom: A statewide survey of experienced third-grade English language learner teachers on the impact of language and high-stakes testing policies in Arizona.* Tempe, AZ: Education Policy Studies Laboratory, Language Policy Research Unit, EPSL-0512–104-LPRU.

Xu, S. H. (2003). The learner, the teacher, the text, and the context: Sociocultural approaches to early literacy instruction for English language learners. In D. M. Barone & L. M. Morrow (Eds.), *Literacy and young children: Research-based practices* (pp. 23–44). New York: Guilford Press.

Part Two

BEST PRACTICES IN EARLY LITERACY INSTRUCTION AND ASSESSMENT

Chapter Four

ASSESSMENT OF EARLY READING DEVELOPMENT

Terry Salinger

For years, early childhood reading assessment has drawn intense criticism and generated many cautious words. Criticisms have frequently concerned the overuse of tests in the early childhood years, and the cautions have alerted educators, policy makers, and parents about the relative lack of measurement precision, validity, and reliability of instruments designed for use with young learners. For example, the National Association for the Education of Young Children (NAEYC) published an edited volume in 1990 with the provocative title of *Achievement Testing in the Early Grades: The Games Grown-ups Play* (Kamii, 1990). The author contended that the rush to test is motivated by various political and social purposes that can be categorized as "the vote-getting game, the looking good game, the keep-my-job game, or the buck-passing game" (p. 3). The insight provided by the book is certainly relevant today.

More recent critics question the supposed link between increased testing, teacher and school accountability, and improved student achievement (Nichols, Glass, & Berliner, 2005). The crux of the questioning is whether the imposition of more testing will bring about the kinds of instructional changes needed to improve the chances for all students, especially those at risk for failure, to become strong readers and writers. Time spent on testing, critics claim, is time taken from instruction; and many of the tests currently in use do not provide teachers with the kinds of information that can improve their instruction (Manning, Chumly, & Underbakke, 2006).

Critics' concerns have only intensified because of the No Child Left Behind (NCLB) legislation and Reading First. Reading First is a massive, federally funded program that focuses on improving reading instruction and student achievement in kindergarten to 3rd-grade classes. Reading First schools must use core reading programs that contain periodic theme tests. They must also screen students upon entry into each grade, provide diagnostic testing and intervention for students found to be at risk for reading difficulties, and document students' development with frequent progress monitoring assessments. The Dynamic Indicators of Basic Early Literacy Skills or DIBELS (http://reading@uoregon.edu; www.dibels@uoregon.edu) has become the most widely used instrument to measure early reading, and in many ways, DIBELS has narrowed the definition of what early reading development is all about (Tierney & Thome, 2006).

This chapter discusses some of the methods used in early childhood classes to assess young learners' development of reading, including DIBELS. It takes the stance that gathering assessment data about early reading is important; in fact, teachers should gather multiple forms of evidence about their young students' reading acquisition . It is important, however, that the assessment data are valid and reliable, that collection procedures are not intrusive and make sense to children, and that the data are useful for instructional decision making. Therefore, this chapter begins with a summary of some of the negative aspects of early reading testing, continues with a more positive picture of how several forms of assessment can help teachers improve their early literacy instruction, and ends with a discussion of DIBELS.

THE CURRENT MODEL FOR EARLY LITERACY ASSESSMENT

A three-part model of assessment is currently advocated and is required in Reading First schools. The model consists of three specific levels of testing: initial screening of all students; diagnostic assessment for students whom the screening test identifies as potentially at risk; and ongoing progress monitoring for all children. Children found to be at risk are supposed to be given extra help, at first by their teachers and then if needed by specialists. In 3rd grade, students take a standardized, paper-and-pencil reading test requiring them to bubble in their answers to multiple-choice questions. The 3rd-grade data contribute to schools' annual yearly progress (AYP) rating.

On the surface, this is an excellent model because it provides children with ample opportunities to show what they know and can do and to demonstrate those areas where they need some level of intervention before being confronted with a high-stakes test at grade 3. The plan, in and of itself, is a strong one, at least so long as what is being advocated makes sense conceptually and practically and will not result in unintended negative consequences.

WHY EARLY TESTING OF READING MAY BE INAPPROPRIATE

No matter whether reading will be tested by a standardized reading test or by a more informal method, many variables can influence how children perform on any given day. These include children's health or mental state on the testing day; capacity to attend to the test or assessment tasks; ability to sit still and hold a pencil; familiarity with testing routines, including bubbling in responses if necessary; or even the teacher's demonstrated attitudes toward the test. Bad vibes from teachers who are stressed about giving students a test or about how the test results may be used can easily be communicated as frustration to students. Standardized tests, unlike many classroom-based assessments, capture performance at one moment in time. Learning to read is a dynamic process; and as children learn, they progress along a developmental continuum that includes both the acquisition of knowledge about literacy and also numerous skills and strategies. The most valuable information for teachers is where children are on that continuum and how they are orchestrating what they are learning, not how they are able to read at one particular point.

Many classroom-based assessment approaches fall victim to some of the same difficulties as standardized tests. If the tasks that students are asked to perform seem as unfamiliar as filling in bubbles for answer choices on a reading test, then the measurement of reading may be seriously flawed. An example of such a situation would be asking students to read as many nonsense words as possible in one minute. There is nothing inherently wrong with the use of nonsense words; in fact, students' ability to read nonsense words is a good measure of their decoding. If students' reading instruction has centered primarily on making meaning from text, however, the nonsense-word activity may be so confusing that its measurement value is lost.

The example of the nonsense-word assessment activity illustrates another reason why early reading assessment may be inappropriate. Some informal classroom-based assessments and most standardized measures conceptualize reading acquisition as an accumulation of discrete skills and strategies (Pearson, 2006) that can be measured discretely. The current attention to the five essential components of reading discussed in the *Report of the National Reading Panel* (National Institute of Child Health and Human Development, 2000) perpetrates this view of early reading, and misinterpretation of the recommendations of the report often inappropriately merges discussion of instructional emphases with students' own orchestration of the different cognitive activities involved in learning to read. Assessment reports that offer only information on discrete skills or clusters of skills are often used primarily to identify what students have not learned, that is, to highlight the aspects of reading that are not developed up to a particular criterion for mastery at different grade levels. Teachers may then focus instruction on these deficit areas in which students need to improve. If Stanovich's (1984) contention that it is impossible to find single elements or subsets of elements that are the definitive cause of children's potential reading difficulties is to be trusted, viewing reading achievement as the accumulation of a set of scores on an assessment makes even less sense.

A final reason for concern about much early reading assessment is that teachers often feel pressure to teach to the test, whether it is a standardized measure or an assessment such as DIBELS that is administered individually. Teaching to the test occurs when teachers know the content that will be covered on a test and make that the core of their curriculum. For example, if kindergarten students will be tested on their understanding of phonemic awareness and beginning consonant sounds, teachers may provide a steady diet of drill on these two components of early reading, often skipping other instructional foci such as knowledge of text structure or beginning comprehension strategies. Sometimes, the nature of the tasks included on an assessment drive the instruction. Teachers might, for example, make sure that students know how to select from a series of pictures "the picture whose name begins with the letter I will say," or they may provide extensive practice reading lists of words quickly and accurately. Such practice may increase students' phonics knowledge or oral reading fluency, but again, these are only aspects of the entire range of cognitive behaviors that students need to master as they begin to read. Further, this kind of instruction totally ignores the affective aspects of learning to read—the satisfaction students gain from listening to and then reading stories themselves.

Letting the content of a test or assessment tasks determine what teachers emphasize limits the curriculum and shortchanges students in a very vulnerable phase of early reading development. From the teachers' perspective, this content and these tasks constitute beginning reading instruction; and from the students' perspective, the repetitive drill and practice may simply not be worth the cognitive and affective effort needed to stay engaged and motivated. Pearson (2006) has sagely pointed out that "assessments should reflect, not lead, curriculum and instruction. We need instructionally sensitive assessments, not assessment-sensitive curriculum" (p. xvii).

Teachers may engage in this practice because tests are part of the accountability system in place in their school or district and they want their students to do well. In addition, when students do well, teachers themselves will be viewed as effective. This practice is what Kamii (1990) referred to as the "looking good game" that adults play. From a measurement perspective, teaching to the test ultimately decreases the meaningfulness of the test data, because students' deeper knowledge of the content is not assessed.

WHAT EFFECTIVE ASSESSMENT OF EARLY READING *CAN* DO

Being trained on and then using an effective classroom-based assessment system can have far-reaching and positive effects on the early childhood instructional program. It matters less whether teachers use a commercial product or a locally developed system than that their approach to gathering, interpreting, and acting on assessment data is systematic. Classroom-based assessments should yield huge quantities of rich, descriptive data about what students do as they learn to read, and the process of collecting these data give teachers tremendous opportunities to get to know their students' strengths and weaknesses and to evaluate the effectiveness of their instruction. As they use the assessment and get to know their students, teachers expand their ability to make sense of what they see and to act on the information they gather through instructional decision making. The process also gives teachers new insight into the complexity of reading development.

SOME BACKGROUND ON CLASSROOM-BASED ASSESSMENTS

Classroom-based assessment of early reading that teachers administer themselves is not a new idea. In fact, there is a long history of reading researchers working to find the best forms of classroom-based assessments to give teachers the information they need to help young students learn to read. The research and theoretical work of Clay (1985), Holdaway (1979), and Teale and Sulzby (1986) has been highly influential in shaping assessment approaches that are very similar to common activities in early childhood classes. This similarity to business as usual gives high levels of face validity to assessment tasks, like running records, story retellings, or invented spelling tests (Clay, 1985). Anecdotal records, oral reading of vocabulary or sight word lists, fluency checks (Rasinski. 2003, 2004; Zutell & Rasinski, 1991), self-assessments (McKenna & Kear, 1999), motivation inventories (Gambrell, Palmer, Codling, & Mazzoni, 1999), use of *Concepts about Print* exercises (see Clay, 2000), and other tasks or inventories (Parker et al., 1999) are also common. In most systems, data are collected throughout the year for teachers to document and chart the range of skills and strategies their students are acquiring.

The common underlying feature of comprehensive approaches to classroom-based assessments is that various facets of reading are measured accurately, efficiently, and without undue stress to teacher or students. Approaches to classroom-based assessment seem to be divided into two distinct categories. In the first, the assessment system consists of distinct tasks that are administered either at scheduled times throughout the year or in an on-demand manner dictated by students' seeming mastery of content. Teachers administer and score tasks and use data to monitor students' progress and to make decisions about instruction. Individual tasks have integrity within an underlying theoretical perspective about how reading develops, but each task exists as a stand-alone instrument that gathers data on specific aspects of reading (e.g., fluency, invented spelling, knowledge of letter-sound correspondences). The scores from the distinct tasks cumulatively yield an accurate picture of how students are developing as readers.

In the second model, tasks are administered and work is collected at specific points throughout the year to document progress along a theoretically grounded developmental trajectory. For example, a teacher may administer the tasks at the beginning, middle, and end of the year. Work is kept together, may be shared at parent conferences, and usually travels as a whole or in summary with children from grade to grade to familiarize receiving teachers with the progress that students have made in the previous year. Often such data allow teachers to place students on a developmental continuum with behavioral anchors at each point to describe how students orchestrate knowledge, skills, and abilities at different stages in literacy learning

WHAT EFFECTIVE EARLY READING ASSESSMENT LOOKS LIKE

Next, let us consider the positive aspects of assessing early reading development, and let us do so from the perspective of a group of teachers in kindergarten to grade 2 and their reading coach, who want to improve their approach to assessing the reading development of the students they teach. Twenty years ago, Johnston (1987) wrote that teachers in early grades need to become "evaluation experts" who can make sense of what they see their students doing and trying to do as they learn to reading and write. This is what teachers want to be. They know that collecting classroom-based data will be time-consuming if they are going to do it well, but they are convinced that doing so will improve their teaching and their students' learning. With full support from their principal, they set out to learn more about assessment in general, to find alternatives to DIBELS that their school might adopt, and to make plans to improve early literacy instruction in their school.

The teachers want especially to improve their ability to screen students' strengths and weaknesses when they enter their classes and to monitor their progress throughout the year. They recognize that good screening assessments may suggest that some students need further testing to diagnose cognitive or language deficits, so they ask the school guidance counselor to begin to identify individually administered diagnostic tests for use with beginning readers.

The teachers find that there are many models of instructionally sensitive, age appropriate assessment procedures that can make them true evaluation experts. Some are comprehensive systems like the *Work Sampling System* (Meisels, Jablon, *Fox in a Box*, and the *New Standards Portfolio System*, all of which are available commercially, or the *Texas Primary Reading Inventory,* which was developed by university researchers for use in Texas. Others models have been developed at the district or state level (see Harrison & Salinger, 1998, and Valencia, Hiebert, & Afflerbach, 1994, for summaries of locally developed systems). Although a comprehensive classroom-based assessment system may take many forms, it should demonstrate adherence to three important principles:

1. The system must facilitate the collection and use of multiple forms of evidence of reading development;
2. It must have a high degree of face validity, in that it includes assessment tasks that make sense to teachers and students; and
3. It must include procedures to help teachers become knowledgeable about gathering and using data.

The concept of multiple forms of evidence means that data should be collected in different reading situations with different kinds of text and should tap different aspects of young learners' reading. These data reflect the complex, dynamic nature of learning to read. A comprehensive system may even factor in results from a standardized, paper-and-pencil assessment of reading or from the administration of tests like DIBELS.

At the same time, the tasks should make sense to teachers and students and be as similar as possible to normal classroom activities. When teachers use routine activities for assessment purposes—for example, analyzing errors that students make when they read orally—the assessment event is less stressful than administration of a formal test. Even when assessment tasks are administered according to a set schedule, tasks that are similar to what students normally do are more likely to yield accurate information about developing reading skills.

To be true evaluation experts, teachers need to learn to collect, understand, use, and respect data. The skills needed to do this successfully are not usually taught in teacher preparation programs, and they need to be part of the professional development opportunities that teachers receive. Comprehensive assessment systems often include training programs, but as discussed below, teachers can—and should—learn to incorporate assessment methods into their everyday teaching routines. One of the most important roles that reading coaches can play is to help teachers feel more comfortable as data users.

After several months of reading articles and books about early reading assessment and reviews of commercial packages, the members of the assessment development committee report to their principal that they want an assessment system that will allow them to gather data on children's development by taking advantage of the activities that engage students as part of high-quality literacy instruction. They have decided against recommending a commercial product, because they want to work together to create and try out an assessment system that aligns to their understanding of reading development, will be appropriate for their diverse student population, and will not impose extra burdens on their already busy instructional day. They have learned that the most common data sources are students' oral reading, students' written products, and teachers' observations and interactions with students. Further, they have read about and seen examples of assessment tasks for kindergarten to grade 2 that work together to provide teachers with rich data to guide instruction and to use to keep parents informed about students' progress.

THE DATA SOURCES

Their plan is to concentrate first on their data sources: oral reading, written products, and teacher observations, and then to find, adapt, or design assessment tools to capture the data they need.

Oral reading is a dependable source of data on children's developing reading skills because it provides evidence of how they are making sense of the written word. In keeping with the goal of collecting multiple forms of evidence, teachers ask students to read different kinds of materials: lists of words, continuous text in familiar books, and informational and narrative texts developed for assessment purposes. Some of the texts used for assessment may have illustrations to help students make sense of what they are reading, but is it always wise to get a sense of how well students can read unillustrated text as well.

Finding out what students know about books, book handling, and language is an important screening procedure that has particular value in kindergarten and grade 1. The *Concepts about Print* test (see Clay, 2000) is a formalized approach to this assessment with its own printed materials. For example, some of the print in one of the little test booklets is written upside down to measure children's sensitivity to print orientation. Teachers can simulate the test on their own by handing student a small book with minimal print per page and ample illustrations. Even noticing whether the child immediately turns the book to the front and orients it so that the text is upright is an important piece of screening information. Teachers can then ask students to perform simple tasks, such as identifying the title, pointing out where the text begins and ends on a page, where the words are (as distinct from the pictures), and what the punctuation is for. Teachers may even point to specific simple words and ask if children can read them. Another important piece of information comes from students' attempts to tell the story based on the title and the illustrations. This can show their sense of what stories are all about.

Students reveal many of their cognitive processes when they read to the teacher. Oral reading shows fluency, that is, how quickly and accurately students can decode print. A short fluency test is a good way to screen students to see what they know at the beginning of the year and also serves as an efficient progress-monitoring tool as the year progresses. Most commercial classroom-based assessment systems include a fluency measure, and teachers can easily locate such measures if they are developing their own approach. Rubrics for scoring oral reading are readily available (e.g., Rasinski, 2003, 2004; Zutell & Rasinski, 1991).

When children can read fluently, they demonstrate that they understand letter-sound correspondences and can apply their understanding with relative ease. This is certainly true when students read word lists, but fluency becomes an even more nuanced concept when considering how students read continuous text. Fluent reading of text that is at the appropriate reading level is marked by overall smoothness, attention to punctuation and other markers of thought units, appropriate phrasing, variations in expression aligned to the reader's interpretation of text, and minimal disruption to an ordinarily conversational style. Readers may make errors, but generally, they self correct and move on.

For young readers, fluent reading, even of short texts, is strongly correlated with comprehension, because when children read fluently, they are monitoring what the text says and how it says it (Pinnell et al., 1995). When reading orally, even fluent readers often make miscues, that is, they deviate from the actual written text. When teachers are listening to students read orally as part of an assessment system, they can use a procedure called a running record to track the miscues students make (Clay, 1993). Miscues take many forms and all reveal something about students' cognitive activity as they try to read. Some miscues are phonetically similar to the word in the text but don't make sense within the context of the story; these show that students know letter-sound correspondences but are not monitoring comprehension. Other miscues may bear little resemblance to the original word phonetically but make perfect sense within the text. Reading "house" for "horse" is an example of a meaning-changing miscue, but reading "pony" for "horse" would not change the meaning.

Oral reading fluency and analysis of miscues should not be the only indicator teachers use to measure students' comprehension, however. Asking students to retell what they have read and asking questions to prompt them to think about the reading are two important ways to determine how well students have comprehended. When students retell a story they have understood, they should be able to provide a beginning, middle, and end, the main character, and usually the main plot events. Learning to retell stories begins even before students can actually read, with teachers prompting students to talk about stories that have been read to them. As students engage in retellings, teachers may have to prompt and probe a bit to gather the documentation they need so that students can structure their responses to show how much they have actually comprehended.

Teachers can also ask students questions about what they read, but the questions need to be carefully developed. Questions that tap the literal level of comprehension ("What color was the dog?") can tell whether students comprehended and can remember details, but it is important to use questions that are more engaging and thoughtful. Questions can ask students to engage in many levels of thinking about what they read, including making simple inferences or evaluating the text. Asking students to make personal connections to the text is also important, because this process engages students in reflection and emphasizes the importance of students' knowledge and experiences in making sense of text. For example, asking a student to tell how an event in a story reminds them of something that has happened to them requires the student to delve into background knowledge—an essential comprehension skill that is easier to model than to explain to young readers. Questions of this sort can work, even with very young learners, because they invite them to think deeply about the text. Kindergarten teachers can start to accustom students to think about text in these kinds of ways by asking similar questions about stories they have read aloud.

Students' written products are also an important data source that teachers can use to gain insight into what goes on inside students' minds as they try to externalize their knowledge about various aspects of reading and about their reactions to what they read. There are two commonly used formats for the written products: spelling tests and students' attempts to write continuous text. The tests consist of a series of words that demonstrate different regular and irregular spelling patterns, and students are encouraged to spell the words as well as they can. The written product shows their stage of invented spelling, that is, the way they are at that particular time applying—or misapplying—their knowledge of letter-sound correspondences. Researchers (Clay, 1985, 1993; Richgels, 1995) have shown that students pass through distinct stages in their ability to spell in traditional ways, and that knowing how they are orchestrating their phonics knowledge helps teachers tailor instruction to students' needs. If students are in the process of learning English, their spelling may show the influence of the phonic knowledge in their home and school language. Teachers need to be sensitive to this so that they can help children overcome their confusion.

If the classroom climate is literacy rich and teachers are supportive, even beginning kindergarteners will "write" when asked to do so, and pre-readers will often "read" a story they have written or dictate what the story says so that teachers can transcribe their words into traditional orthography. As students move along the developmental continuum extending from kindergarten to grade 2, they should be encouraged to continue to write both on their own and in response to teacher requests (Dyson, 1993). Teachers can collect representative samples and compare them against the many rubrics that are available to explain what the writing shows about phonics, letter formation, left-to-right orientation of print, purposes for writing, and even story structure. Analyzing writing samples at a given point in time help teachers monitor progress and plan ongoing instruction.

Teachers' observations and anecdotal records can also be an invaluable part of the assessment data that teachers keep about their students' growth. One current textbook (Fields, Groth, & Spangler, 2004, p. 312) for training teachers suggests that "Most teachers talk way too much in school. Instead of trying to keep kids quiet so they can hear you, try keeping yourself quiet so you can hear children. You will be amazed at how much you will learn." Teachers can find or develop checklists that will help them document students' oral language or their demonstrations of specific reading or writing behaviors that are benchmarks along the developmental continuum of literacy growth.

Teachers' anecdotal notes about students' learning are also very important, whether they are taken during instructional interactions or when they periodically step back from involvement with the students to conduct an environmental scan. Teachers might note students who seem reluctant to try to read new words, who like to go off by themselves in the library corner, or who seem to prefer writing to reading. Notes on these and countless other behaviors can help teachers figure out what's going on with students as they try to master literacy and figure out how to help them move forward.

After all their reading and discussion, the teachers and the reading coach devise a plan for an efficient but effective classroom-based assessment system that can be used in kindergarten to grade 2. Table 4.1 summarizes their ideas for screening and progress-monitoring tools. They have integrated the use of the theme tests in their core reading program into their scheme strategies but are convinced that the additional procedures they are proposing will strengthen their ability to monitor progress. They propose setting aside a range of books from each classroom's set of leveled books that can be kept secure for conducting running records, and they have identified words for the spelling test that will give them information on their English-dominant students and those for whom English is a second language.

Their principal likes the proposal and gives approval for the teachers to move forward to the next step of development. This step will be lengthy because it involves finalizing instruments, creating actual recording sheets, developing scoring procedures, trying out the assessment tasks with students, developing training and resource materials, and in all likelihood, refining everything after the pilot year. The development committee has learned firsthand why many schools and districts simply purchase assessment packages or rely primarily on materials accompanying a core reading program. Commercial materials make assessment easy and efficient. Still, for these educators, the work has been worthwhile in terms of what they have learned and what they hope to learn about their students by using this locally grown assessment system.

Table 4.1
Proposed Contents of an Early Reading Assessment System, Kindergarten to Grade 2

Activity/task	Target of assessment	Grades	Data source	Comments
Screening: Given near the beginning of year or as children enter class during the year				
Oral language interview	Vocabulary: extent and specificity; facility with English (for ELLs)	All	Teacher observation	Teacher engages students in conversation about books and reading done at home and listens as students interact w ith others to get an initial sense of language facility. Used at beginning of school year or when new student enters class
Alphabet, environmental print, and sight word check	Students' familiarity with alphabet and common words observed in environment	K–1	Student response	Teacher asks students to view and read from a list of upper and lower case letters; list also contains common examples of environmental print, such as STOP, and common sight words. Used at beginning of school year or when new student enters class
Concepts of print	Knowledge of book parts and book handling skills	K–1	Student response, teacher observation	Teacher engages students in discussion of a book with pictures and one line of print per page; teacher observes students' familiarity with book handling and book parts. Used at beginning of school year or when new student enters class
Fluency check	Decoding speed and accuracy	1–2	Student response	Teacher asks students to read a list of words and checks accuracy, mistakes made in decoding, and self-corrections. Used at beginning of school year or when new student enters class

Progress Monitoring: Used at least three times per year

Running record	Reading rate and fluency; pacing in oral reading; accuracy of decoding and apparent decoding strategies; comprehension as indicated by retelling and answers to questions	1–2	Student response, teacher observation	Running records provide information about decoding, pacing, and rate, all of which correlate with comprehension. Students read orally in an unfamiliar book; teacher notes deviations from text to analyze later for information about decoding strategies; teacher also notes omissions, insertions, and requests for help. After reading, students retell what they read, and teacher notes thoroughness of retelling. If necessary, teacher probes to gain the maximum amount of information. Simple comprehension questions may also be asked. Used quarterly
Reading comprehension	Comprehension; ability to orchestrate emergent and developing reading skills	Upper 1–2	Student response Student writing	Students read orally or silently depending on ability, retell the story, and answer questions. They should find the task challenging enough to require them to use multiple reading strategies. Advanced students may be asked to answer questions in writing. Used quarterly
Spelling assessment	Ability to apply letter-sound knowledge in encoding	Upper K–2	Student writing	Teacher dictates grade-appropriate list of words and encourages students to spell the words as well as they can. Each word is read separately, in a sentence, and then separately again. Teacher analyzes spellings to gain insight into ability to apply letter-sound knowledge. Used quarterly
Writing assessments	Orchestration of prerequisite skills; familiarity with story structure and conventions of writing; syntax; vocabulary		Measures of reading, spelling reflected in writing	A minimum of four samples are collected quarterly and analyzed at that time; entire set is analyzed at end of year to determine growth.

Satisfied with their work so far, the development committee turns to the guidance counselor for information on the third tier of the assessment model—diagnostic tests. There actually are many from which to select. Some are very focused, such as the *Reading Fluency Indicator* (Williams, 2004) or the *Test of Word Reading Efficiency (TOWRE)* (Torgesen, Wagner, & Rashotte, 1999); others are far more comprehensive (see Rathvon, 2004). The guidance counselor appreciates the assessment development committee members' interest in diagnostic testing and says she will work with the early-grades teachers if their screening identifies students who need additional testing. She cautions them that diagnostic testing is only the start of the process of securing intervention for students, however, quoting cautionary words from the *TOWRE* administrator's manual (Torgesen et al., 1999, p. 47: "Too often examiners forget the dictum that 'tests don't diagnose, people do' and base their diagnoses exclusively on test results, a hazardous enterprise at best. . . . The questions concerning the why of the test performance are the very essence of diagnosis, and they can be answered only by an insightful, competent examiner."

Appropriately, Torgesen's comment reminds the committee members that developing tools and procedures is a necessary first step in improving their assessment and teaching, but it is only a beginning. Their next steps include trying out their instruments with their students to answer questions about their sensitivity to student differences, the comprehensiveness of the data they gather, and of course their ease of use. They also know that they will need to develop training and resource materials for their colleagues if the assessment system is going to be used in all the early grades in their school.

The principal is happy with the work that the teachers, reading coach, and school counselor have done and especially applauds the collegial way in which they have worked to create a useful assessment system. She recognizes the professional development value of the work for committee members and looks forward to the learning that will take place when other early-grades teachers are trained to use the system. The principal is aware of the pressure within the district to adopt the test that is issued to the district's Reading First schools, however (see Salinger, 2004). This test is DIBELS. Because of the pressure, the principal asks the development committee to investigate DIBELS further, and to let the reading coach, who has been trained, administer the test to children whom the screening measure identifies as potentially at risk for difficulties. This seems reasonable, because many teachers in district Reading First schools praise the test and see it as valuable.

THE DYNAMIC INDICATORS OF BASIC EARLY LITERACY SKILLS OR DIBELS

DIBELS was developed as an early reading extension of the curriculum-based measurement tools created at the federally funded Institute for the

Development of Educational Achievement (IDEA) at the University of Oregon (see http://reading@uoregon.edu; www.dibels@uoregon.edu; Rathvon, 2004). Now in its sixth edition, it is a set of short, individually administered tests that measure six aspects of fluency: initial sound, letter naming, phoneme segmentation, nonsense word, and oral reading. There are also measures of retelling and word use, both of which also depend on students' fluency. Each measure takes about three to four minutes to administer. The two primary purposes for using DIBELS are to determine whether students have achieved specific benchmarks in skills acquisition and to monitor progress. Teachers use the tests frequently, as often as every two weeks. DIBELS is also widely used as an outcome measure.

DIBELS is a comprehensive system in that it provides a vast array of materials, including reusable test booklets for all measures, consumables for student use, videos, and so forth. The materials can be downloaded from the DIBELS website or purchased commercially (see www.dibels@uoregon.edu or www.sopriswest.com). Teacher training is also available. A software company has also made a handheld computer available for teachers to keep track of their DIBELS data as they administer the tests (see www.wirelessgeneration.com). The University of Oregon DIBELS website also provides data management services so that schools can track their students' scores easily and perform various analytic procedures. The cost is relatively minor, and this service, for an assessment system that may be used every two weeks, is often perceived as good value. Scott Foreman has published an intervention program, *Early Reading Intervention,* tied directly to DIBELS (http://scottforesman.com).

Websites for DIBELS and the Florida Center for Reading Research (see www.dibels@uoregon.edu; www.assessments@fcrr.org) contain links to reports on the psychometric properties of the test and attest to the care that the developers have taken to investigate the test's validity and reliability. Other researchers have also conducted studies. For example, Hintze, Ryan, and Stoner (n.d.) use a validated, commercial test of phonological processing to investigate DIBELS' concurrent validity and diagnostic accuracy. One of their results was that DIBELS designated far more students as at risk for reading failure than the validated, comprehensive diagnostic instrument against which it was compared. Early identification of students who need intervention is positive and a definite goal of the three-tier model of assessment, but clearly schools need to be cautious about dependence on a test that can potentially overidentify potentially struggling readers.

Many reading researchers have also thought deeply about the test, analyzed its use and its properties, and reached decisions that are not always positive about the consequences of depending on DIBELS as the primary measure of young students' reading development (see Lewis & Fabos, 2005; Manning, Kamii, & Kato, 2005). Tierney and Thome (2006) maintain that because it uses only quick fluency tests, DIBELS "does not enhance teachers' knowledge of student literacies in a manner that supports the full range of their literacy development" (p. 52). Goodman (2006) suggests that the short tests used in DIBELS may produce inaccurate measurement of what young readers actually know. He suggests that learners who "are coming to understand that reading is supposed to make sense are likely to be underscored.... [T]he more thoughtful and concerned with the meaning a young reader is the more likely they are to perform more slowly or to lose time as they are distracted by the search for meaning" (p. 15). This view is supported by Lewis and Fabos (2005), who point out that testing students primarily on fluency narrows the definition of early reading and may consequently narrow students' view of "the needs they will have for their literate and social futures at home, at work, and in their communities" (p. 498).

DIBELS has had powerful and positive effects on many teachers, in that they have become more accustomed to thinking about data and using data to monitor their students and to plan instruction. The criticisms of the test, however, point out three possible negative consequences. The first is its potential to narrow teachers' definitions of early reading development. DIBELS tests students' fluency—speed and accuracy—and teachers who teach to this particular test will undoubtedly stress fluency in their instruction. Doing so may produce students who know how to decode quickly and accurately, but who do not necessarily comprehend well, enjoy reading, or see reading as a valuable part of their lives. Teaching to DIBELS will undoubtedly also produce an early literacy curriculum that avoids the use of children's literature, writing, and discussion about what is read. This is the second negative consequence: DIBELS has the potential to narrow the curriculum. These two negative consequences are the same as those that have long been feared because of overuse of standardized, group-administered, paper-and-pencil tests.

The third potential negative consequence is overidentification of struggling readers based on a test with a narrow conceptualization of reading. Learning to read involves the acquisition of knowledge about print, books, and language and the development of many complex cognitive skills. Decoding words quickly and accurately is one part of this developmental process, admittedly a very important part, but only one. The various tests in DIBELS sample this aspect of reading in different ways (letter-sound correspondence, words, nonsense words, etc.), but they do not assess the sense that students are making of what they are reading by asking them to read and discuss continuous text.

REACHING SOME COMPROMISES

At the end of the trial year for the proposed assessment system, the development committee members conclude that even though they have to fine tune some of their measures, their proposed system of screening and progress-monitoring assessments, as summarized in Table 4.1, is aligned with their approach to instruction. It allows them to collect multiple forms of evidence and has encouraged them to look closely at distinct times in students' learning and also at evidence collected over time. They like having the different pieces of evidence to supplement theme tests in their core reading program, especially the samples of students' writing.

The teachers, reading coach, and guidance counselor also report to the principal that DIBELS has provided useful information about the students who might be struggling with beginning reading. The data were detailed, specific, and helpful in determining how to help students *before* they encountered severe difficulties. Thus, they see that DIBELS has potential as one form of evidence. They reject the idea that its small tests of different forms of fluency can replace a more comprehensive approach to collecting data on young learners, but they see its potential value in gaining insight into one aspect of the complex process of learning to read.

WHAT'S AHEAD FOR THE TEACHERS AND THEIR STUDENTS

Refining a teacher-developed, classroom-based assessment system to the point where it will consistently yield reliable and valid information about students' reading development takes considerable dedication and many years of work. Whether the members of the committee discussed in this chapter persevere in their efforts remains to be seen, but their story speaks to the importance of teachers working together to understand their students' reading development and their own instruction. Assessment opportunities built into the fabric of classroom life are an essential part of this understanding and enrich the information that can be obtained from core reading programs or narrowly focused measures like DIBELS. Such assessment usually reflects the instruction that teachers provide, so the question of teaching to the test is moot.

At grade 3, students' reading is assessed, often for the first time, with a standardized, paper-and-pencil test. These tests usually contain multiple-choice items and ask about a full range of reading behaviors, including phonics knowledge and simple reading comprehension (see Rathvon, 2004). The tests may have been commercially developed or created in students' own states to align to the state reading and English language arts standards.

Students whose development up to 3rd grade has been monitored carefully and whose teachers have acted upon multiple forms of evidence from that monitoring should be prepared for the test: learning to read well in a broad sense is better preparation than learning the content of discrete sections of the test through teaching to the text. It is also important, however, that students be prepared for the format and requirements of a standardized testing situation.

Teachers can provide a proactive form of test preparation by helping students understand what Calkins, Montgomery, and Santman (1998) refer to as the specific genre of reading tests. Sitting still, working silently, not asking questions, and bubbling in answers ought not to be natural parts of young learner's school day, but they have become a category of basic skills that students need to master. As Calkins has stated: "if our children's achievement on standardized tests matters to us or to them, then our children deserve to be acclimated to the genre of standardized tests. They deserve some wise instruction in its particular demands" (Calkins, Montgomery, & Santman, 1998, p. 68).

CONCLUSION

Students and teachers both benefit when teachers use ongoing assessment to keep track of students' early reading development, and doing so in thoughtful, instructionally sensitive ways that are embedded within that very development process makes sense. Nevertheless, teachers also owe it to their students to prepare them for the kinds of external measures of reading that they encounter at grade 3, if not earlier. Thoughtful teachers can accomplish both goals when they take on the responsibility of becoming evaluation experts.

REFERENCES

Calkins, L. M., Montgomery, K., & Santman, D. (1998). *A teacher's guide to standardized reading tests: Knowledge is power.* Portsmouth, NH: Heinemann.

Clay, M. M. (1979). *Reading: The patterning of complex behaviours.* Auckland, New Zealand: Heinemann.

Clay, M. M. (1985). *The early detection of reading difficulties* (3rd ed.). Auckland, New Zealand: Heinemann.

Clay, M. M. (1993). *An observation survey of early literacy achievement.* Portsmouth, NH: Heinemann.

Clay, M. M. (2000). *Concepts about print.* Portsmouth, NH: Heinemann.

Dyson, A. H. (1993). *The social worlds of children learning to write in an urban primary school.* New York: Teachers College Press.

Fields, M. V., Groth, L. A., & Spangler, K. L. (2004). *Let's begin reading right.* (5th ed.) Upper Saddle River, NJ: Pearson Merrill Prentice Hall.

Gambrell, L., Palmer, B. M., Codling, R., & Mazzoni, S.A. (1999). Assessing motivation to read. In S. J. Barrentine (Ed.), *Reading assessment: Principles and practices for elementary teachers* (pp. 215–232). Newark, DE: International Reading Association.

Goodman, K. S. (Ed.).(2006). *The truth about DIBELS: What it is, what it does.* Portsmouth, NH: Heinemann.

Harrison, C, &. Salinger, T. (Eds.). (1998). *Assessing reading 1: Theory and practice* (pp. 182–204). London: Routledge.

Hintze, J. M., Ryan, A. L., & Stoner, G. (n.d.). *Concurrent validity and diagnostic accuracy of the Dynamic Indicators of Basic Early Literacy Skills and the Comprehensive Test of Phonological Processing.* Amherst, MA. Authors.

Holdaway, D. (1979). *The foundations of literacy.* Sydney, Australia: Ashton Scholastic.

Johnston, P. (1987). Teachers as evaluation experts. *The Reading Teacher, 40,* 744–748.

Kamii, C. (Ed.). (1990). *Achievement testing in the early grades: The games grown-ups play.* Washington, DC: National Association for the Education of Young Children.

Lewis, C., & Fabos, B. (2005). Instant messaging, literacies, and social identities. *Reading Research Quarterly, 40,* 470–501.

Manning, M., Chumley, S., & Underbakke, C. (2006). *Scientific reading assessment: Targeted intervention and follow-up lessons.* Portsmouth, NH: Heinemann.

Manning, M., Kamii, C., & Kato, T. (2005). Dynamic Indicators of Basic Early Literacy Skills (DIBELS): A tool for evaluating student learning? *Journal of Research in Childhood Education, 20*(2), 81–96.

McKenna, M. C., & Kear, D. J. (1999). Measuring attitude toward reading: A new tool for teachers. In S. J. Barrentine (Ed.). *Reading assessment: Principles and practices for elementary teachers* (pp. 199–214). Newark DE: International Reading Association.

Morrow, L. M. (1988). Retelling stories as a diagnostic tool. In S. M. Glazer, L. W. Searfoss, & L. M. Gentile (Eds.), *Reexamining reading diagnosis: New trends and procedures* (pp. 128–149). Newark, DE: International Reading Association.

National Institute of Child Health and Human Development. (2000). *Report of the National Reading Panel: Teaching children to read: An evidence-based assessment of the scientific research literature on reading and its implications for reading instruction: reports of the subgroups* (NIH Publication No. 00–4769). Washington, DC: U.S. Government Printing Office.

National Research Council. (1998). *Preventing reading difficulties in young children.* Washington, DC: National Academy Press.

Nichols, S. L., Glass, G., & Berliner, D. (2005). High-stakes testing and student achievement: Problems from No Child Left Behind. Originally published in *Education Policy Studies* (March), Educational Policy Studies Laboratory, Educational Policy Research Unit, EPSL0509–105-EPRU. In K. S. Goodman (Ed.), *The truth about DIBELS: What it is, what it does* (pp. 50–59). Portsmouth, NH: Heinemann.

Parker, E. L., Armengol, R., Brooke, L. B., Carper, K. R., Cronin, S. M., Denman, A. C., et al. (1999). Teachers' choices in classroom assessment. In S. J. Barrentine (Ed.), *Reading assessment: Principles and practices for elementary teachers* (pp. 68–72). Newark, DE: International Reading Association.

Pearson, P. D. (2006). Foreword. In K. S. Goodman (Ed.), *The truth about DIBELS: What it is, what it does.* (pp. v–xx). Portsmouth, NH: Heinemann.

Pinnell, G. S., Pikulski, J. J., Wixson, K. K., Campbell, J. R., Gough, P. B., & Beatty, A. S. (1995, January). *Listening to children read aloud: Data from NAEP's Integrated Reading Performance Record (IRPR) at Grade 4.* Washington, DC: National Center for Education Statistics.

Rasinski. T. V. (2003). *The fluent reader: Oral reading strategies for building word recognition, fluency, and comprehension.* New York: Scholastic.

Rasinski,. T. V. (2004). *Assessing reading fluency.* Retrieved November 15, 2006, from www.pre;.org/programs/rel/rel.asp.

Rathvon, N. (2004). *Early reading assessment: A practitioner's handbook.* New York: Guilford Press.

Richgels, D. (1995). Invented spelling ability and printed word learning in kindergarten. *Reading Research Quarterly, 30,* 96–109.

Salinger, T. (2001). Assessing the literacy of young children: The case for multiple forms of evidence. In S. B. Neuman & D. K. Dickinson (Eds.), *Handbook of early reading research* (pp. 390–418). New York: Guilford Press.

Salinger, T. (2004). Assessing the literacy of young children: Policy considerations. In S. B. Neuman & D. K. Dickinson (Eds.), *Handbook of Early Literacy Development* (Vol. 2). New York: Guilford Press.

Shepard, L.A., Flexer, R. J., Hiebert, E. H., Marion, S. F., Mayfield, V., & Weston, J. T. (1996). Effects of introducing classroom performance assessments on student learning. *Educational Measurement: Issues and Practice, 15*(3), 7–18.

Stanovich, K .E. (1984). The interactive-compensatory model of reading: A confluence of developmental, experimental, and educational psychology. *Remedial and Special Education, 5,* 11–19.

Sulzby, E. (1991). Assessment of emergent literacy: Storybook reading. *The Reading Teacher, 44*(7), 498–500.

Teale, W. H., & Sulzby, E. (Eds.). (1986). *Emergent literacy: Writing and reading.* Norwood, NJ: Ablex.

Tierney, R. J., & Thome, C. (2006). Is DIBELS leading us down the wrong path? In K. S. Goodman (Ed.), *The truth about DIBELS: What it is, what it does* (pp. 50–59). Portsmouth, NH: Heinemann.

Torgesen, J. K., Wagner, R. K., & Rashotte, C. A. (1999). *Examiner's Manual: Test of Word Reading Efficiency.* Austin, TX: Pro-Ed.

Valencia, S. W., Hiebert, E. H., & Afflerbach, P. P. (Eds.), (1994). *Authentic reading assessment: Practices and possibilities.* Newark, DE: International Reading Association.

Williams, K. T. (2004). *Reading fluency indicator.* Circle Pines, MN: AGS Publishing.

Zutell, J., & Rasinski, T. V. (1991). Training teachers to attend to their students' oral reading fluency. *Theory into Practice, 30,* 211–217.

Chapter Five

ORAL LANGUAGE

Lynne Hebert Remson

Research and clinical professionals in disciplines as diverse as linguistics, psychology, anthropology, communication disorders, education, and neurology all claim expertise in the knowledge of oral language. Although it is often referred to as a skill, oral language is actually a complex network of coordinated knowledge and movement that allows individuals to communicate with each other by talking and listening. It is the complexity of this process that generates an appeal across so many disciplines.

For the purposes of this discussion, oral language is treated as the modality for symbolic communication that relies on speech production and reception. Communication is defined as the ability to construct meaning between at least two individuals. Symbolic communication refers to the use of language, or a system of shared symbols to represent meanings. Speech is one physical form for producing such symbols. Other forms are written and gestural. These three forms constitute the oral, written, and gestural modalities, reflecting shared linguistic knowledge. Each modality also requires other, more specialized knowledge about that particular form. Oral language, then, is the use of speech to share meanings through an agreed-upon set of symbols—spoken words.

Competence as a communicator depends on the individual's linguistic system (the combined knowledge about a language). It includes word meanings, speech sounds (or another output modality such as writing or gesturing), morphology, syntax, and pragmatics. Phonology refers to the implicit rules for using the speech sounds of a language to construct words. Semantics refers to word meanings. Morphology is the set of rules for modifying root words to alter meanings. Syntax is the grammar of a language, or the rules for ordering words in phrases and sentences. Pragmatics concerns the rules for how language is used socially within a community. These five components comprise the form, content, and use of language (Bloom & Lahey, 1978). By the time children are six years old, their linguistic system is very similar to an adult's, although they continue adding complexity to the system throughout the school years.

Researchers tend to agree that interaction among biology, learning, and culture contributes to the acquisition of a first language (Berko Gleason, 1993; Haynes, Moran, & Pindzola, 1990; Norris, 1998). Debate continues, however, concerning the relative contributions of each process. Similarly, there are different ways of examining the components of language. Some linguists, known as structuralists, prefer to study each of the five components as separate systems that interact. In contrast, functionalists are more interested in how people actually use language, or the functions of language and how they are expressed. Functionalists consider pragmatics to be the overarching component upon which the other four depend. Thus, social interactionists believe that children begin to acquire oral language because they enjoy social interaction with others. Infants exhibit a very early preference for the human voice as against other sounds. This helps babies attend to and learn speech. Parents also use certain techniques, collectively known as motherese, that facilitate language learning by infants. As they gain motor control and cognitive awareness, infants use vocalizations and other behaviors to influence the actions of others. This presymbolic, or prelinguistic, communication develops from random, reflexive behaviors that attentive caregivers interpret as meaningful. With repeated interactions, infants learn to pair looking, vocalizing, reaching, or other gestures to make requests, call attention, and express rejection.

As the infant refines these gestures and vocalizations to intentionally elicit specific responses from others, phonetically consistent forms (PCFs) begin to emerge. These are sounds that the infant uses consistently to represent such things as favorite objects, sounds recognizable only to familiar caregivers and close family members. Through these, the child hopes to achieve a particular result with particular people. Thus, social interaction is crucial for shaping early utterances and refining them into true words. As children mature, they gain the understanding and use of a large number of phoneme sequences (words), which they organize to express more complex meanings. The choice of sounds, words, morphology, and syntax is dependent upon the level of linguistic development of the child and also upon the pragmatic demands of the situation. For example, children must learn that ways of talking with their parents differ from ways of talking with strangers or with friends. Later, choice of words, morphology, and syntax is heavily influenced by the degree of formality of the social situation. Casual conversation with family requires different language choices from those required for presenting a formal speech in a large conference hall.

RELATIONSHIP BETWEEN ORAL AND WRITTEN LANGUAGE

Earlier models of language acquisition represented oral language and written language as separate, sequential processes. It was thought that children first learned to understand and then speak oral language; later, they learned to read and write. Carol Westby (1991) described a continuum of language use with oral language at one end and written language at the other. Oral language was believed to be more casual and immediate; written language was considered more formal and more displaced in time. Many now view oral and written language as merely two different modalities that represent a shared base of linguistic knowledge (Norris & Hoffman, 1993; Westby, 1991). Both modalities rely on similar knowledge of the components of language that comprise surface structure/form (phonology, morphology, and syntax), meaningful content, and social functions. Both modalities can be casual or formal and both can represent information that is dependent upon the immediate context as well as information that is more displaced in both time and space, that is, more decontextualized. That is, we can both talk and write about persons and events that are in the past or future or are located in different geographical places, including hypothetical places. Development in both modalities can be simultaneous because they reflect shared linguistic knowledge in the component areas.

The primary difference between oral and written language, then, lies in the physical form of the symbol. For oral language, it is the spoken word, conveyed through spoken phonemes (speech sounds). Pragmatic nuances are expressed in the oral modality through prosody, loudness levels, gestures, facial expression, and so forth. The form for written language is the written word, composed of graphemes. The pragmatic functions correlates are expressed through written conventions such as punctuation, underlining, and emoticons.

THE COMPONENTS OF LANGUAGE

The remainder of this discussion is devoted to describing each of the five components of language—phonology, morphology, syntax, semantics, and pragmatics. These are organized as the three aspects of language—form, content, and use—as described by Bloom and Lahey (1978).

Form

Language form includes three areas. In oral language, these are phonology, morphology, and syntax. Phonology is the sound system used to express words in oral language. In English and other alphabetic languages, orthography (the writing system) is the equivalent to phonology for written language. That is, words, phrases, and sentences can be spoken using phonemes or written using graphemes (letters). In alphabetic languages, the morphology and syntax are shared. Each of these areas will be is discussed separately, although in language acquisition and actual use, there is a great deal of interaction among them and the other components of language.

Phonology. Phonology refers to the knowledge that speakers have about the sounds of a language, how they can be combined, and what combinations are allowed and disallowed. The smallest identifiable linguistic unit is the phoneme, or individual speech sound. A phoneme is defined as the smallest unit that can change meaning. For example, the phoneme /k/ distinguishes *cake* from *Kate*. So, /k/ and /t/ are separate phonemes because they cannot be used interchangeably without affecting meaning. The /k/ in the initial position is actually slightly different from the /k/ in the final position, however. The initial consonant is slightly aspirated (produced with a slight /h/ after the /k/). In English, this difference does not affect meaning. Aspirating the final /k/ in the word *cake* by saying /k^hek^h/ instead of /k^hek/ does not change the meaning. In other words, /k^h/ and /k/ are allophones—sounds in the same phoneme family.

INFANTS

Within the first weeks of life, infants learn to recognize sounds that are in their native languages as opposed to those that are nonspeech sounds or sounds that might be in another language. The configuration of the vocal tract, however, is very different from the adult configuration. This influences early vocalizations. Infants have smaller mouths and smaller lips. The larynx and palate are shorter and the tongue is relatively large and forward in the mouth. In addition, infants do not yet have teeth. All of these features influence the character of the sounds produced by an infant. As infants grow physically and the dimensions of the vocal tract change, they are able to produce a greater variety of sounds with better control. The period from birth to 12 months is characterized by prelinguistic development of sounds. This means that the infant is learning how to use the vocal tract to produce sounds and modify pitch and loudness rather than using sounds for symbolic communication.

Prerepresentational phonological development characterizes the period from 12 to 18 months. The infant begins to produce a variety of vowel sounds and combine them with consonant-like sounds that will eventually become consonants. Sounds and syllables produced with high frequency during babbling often emerge in the infant's first words. The first consonants to emerge are typically the ones that are easiest to see—/m/, /b/, and /d/. These are almost always present in the first words of children. The infant produces reduplicated consonant-vowel (CV) strings such as "dadadadada" or "muhmuhmuh." Attentive caregivers attach meaning to these random sounds and syllables, rewarding the infant with attention and reciprocal babbling. Very soon, these reduplicated syllables give way to variegated babbling, in which the infant uses different consonants and vowels in the strings. Infants also begin imitating the prosody, or melody, of the speech they hear, playing with pitch and loudness levels.

At 18 months, children have several words that they use consistently to communicate with caregivers based on these early syllables. When children have about 50 such words, they begin to organize speech sounds as single phonemes rather than as syllables. This stage is known as representational phonology. Children are characterized by their ability to perceive nearly all adult phonemes. However, at this stage, they are still unable to produce many of the speech sounds. By the time children are three, they can produce all the vowel sounds and many of the consonants in the language. At first they produce these sounds in single words, and then they learn to smoothly transition between words in increasingly longer utterances. They learn the distinctive features (the place and manner of articulation) that identify each phoneme as a separate sound. This means that changing the sounds in a word changes the meaning: toy and boy are not the same. Children learn that /k/ and /w/ can go together at the beginning of a word, as in quit, but that /z/ and /r/ cannot. They also know that two words can be reduced, for example, got and to can be reduced to gotta, but that the words got and two, as in He got two toys from the shelf, cannot be reduced.

The average person can understand most of what a three-year-old child says. Toddlers and preschool children, however, continue to have difficulty with many consonant clusters such as initial blends (e.g., /sl/ in sleep) and final clusters (e.g., /ndz/ in ends), and they mispronounce complex words or those with several syllables or those that are motorically complex (e.g., elephant or piano). The ways of simplifying sounds in words so that young children can say words they would otherwise be unable to pronounce are collectively known as phonological processes (systematic modifications of the distinctive features of sounds in words). Examples include weak syllable deletion (e.g., saying te'phone for telephone); final consonant deletion (e.g., saying daw for dog); and cluster reduction (e.g., saying s'im for swim). Such errors are very common in toddlers, but they begin to disappear by the time the child is around three years old.

Between the ages of four and seven, children complete the phonetic inventory. That is, by the time children are six or seven years old, they have acquired all the consonant and vowel sounds of the language, although they may still have some difficulty with words that are five or six syllables in length. The typical five-year-old is almost completely intelligible to the average listener. As children complete the phonetic inventory and master more advanced phonology, phonological processes gradually fade. Between the ages of 7 and 12, children acquire more advanced phonology, such as the sounds for th and r. They also learn how to combine sounds in multisyllable words, such as *outrageous, ridiculous,* and *Bohemian,* that require many fine adjustments. By the age of 12, the phonological system is similar to that of an adult.

Some researchers have begun to look at the connection between early phonological development and learning how to spell in English. Jan Norris and Paul Hoffman (1989) found that children undergo a developmental process of learning to spell that is similar to the process of acquiring speech sounds. In fact, spelling errors in young children often resemble their earlier speech errors. For example, children who say the word tooth accurately nonetheless may write it initially as tuf, substituting f for th as they once substituted /f/ when learning to talk. The progression of early scribbling from random movements to coordinated patterns resembling real words can be likened to the vocal play, babbling, and jargon speech demonstrated by infants as they gain control of the articulators, moving from random and vegetative sounds to speech-like strings of variegated (differentiated) syllables.

Morphology. The second component of form is morphology. A morpheme is the smallest unit of meaning. Some morphemes are single words, such as hat, elephant, walk, and enormous. These are known as free morphemes because they are meaningful even when standing alone. Other words have two or more morphemes. Words such as hotdog and sailboat are compound words because they combine two free morphemes. These words can be modified, however, by bound morphemes. Bound morphemes are meaning units that must be attached to other meaning units. For example, the word hat can be modified by adding the bound morpheme –s to denote plural. The word that is formed, hats, has two morphemes. There are two types of bound morphemes—inflectional (or grammatical) and derivational.

Inflectional morphemes occur only at the ends of words and are used to modulate or change state or make the meaning of the free morpheme more precise. Inflectional morphemes mark verb tense, subject-verb agreement, possession, plural, and so forth. Once an inflectional morpheme has been added to the end of a word, no other morphemes can be attached. Inflectional morphemes are usually acquired by the age of five.

Roger Brown (1973) identified 14 inflectional morphemes that most children acquire in a predictable order and at predictable ages. Known as Brown's grammatical morphemes, these meaning units inflect, or mark, nouns and verbs, thereby changing their meanings. Children first learn to mark progressive verbs with –ing to indicate that an action is ongoing. Soon afterward, they mark regular noun plurals by adding –s. Also among the earliest of Brown's grammatical morphemes to emerge are the prepositions in and on, although these are actually free morphemes. These first four markers begin to appear around 18–30 months. Sometime between the ages of two and three years, the possessive marker –s emerges, as in Mommy'*s* book. Children between the ages of approximately three and a half and four and a half begin to mark past tense verbs with –ed. Irregular past tense verbs, such as ate and fell, emerge shortly after, although the child may double mark these verbs at first, producing such words as ated and felled. During this same time period, children master acquire the definite article, the, and the indefinite articles a and an. The –s marker appears at the ends of third person singular verbs in the present tense to mark agreement, as in the sentence The boy play*s* in the sandbox. In addition, utterances now include the contractible copula, as in the sentence He'*s* big. As the child nears the age of five, the last inflectional morphemes are mastered. These include the contractible auxiliary (e.g., He'*s* playing), the uncontractible copula (e.g., *Is* it ready?), the uncontractible auxiliary (*Is* he running?), and the irregular third person singular verbs (He *has* a new toy).

In contrast, derivational morphemes change whole classes of words to other classes. Development of derivational morphology occurs over a long period of time and is not usually complete until adulthood. In English, derivational morphemes can either be suffixes, found at the ends of words, or prefixes, found at the beginnings of words.

Derivational morphemes are used to change the grammatical categories of words. For example, the derivational morpheme –er is used to transform the verb bake into the noun baker. The morpheme –ly changes the adjective quick into the adverb quickly. We can change adjectives such as happy into nouns such as happiness by using the derivational morpheme –ness. Other common suffixes include –ism, –tion, –able, –ment, and –al. Derivational morphemes can also be prefixes, such as un–, in–, pre– and a–.

Derivational morphemes can be added to free morphemes or to other derivational morphemes. For example, the verb transform consists of the root word form and the prefix trans–, a derivational morpheme. It can become the noun "transformation" by adding the derivational morpheme –ation. By adding –al to –ation, the adjective "transformational" is created. Inflectional morphemes such as –s can be added to derivational morphemes, as in as in the word "developments." The free morpheme, develop, is first modified by the derivational morpheme, –ment, changing the word from a verb to a noun, and then by the inflectional morpheme –s, denoting pluralization. Once an inflectional morpheme has been added to the end of a word, no other morphemes can be attached, however.

Syntax. Morphology is closely related to syntax, the third component of form, because of the relationship to grammatical categories and to verb tense formation. Syntax refers to the order of words in sentences and the relationships among the words and phrases. The order of words in a sentence contributes directly to the meaning of the sentence. Word order expresses certain relationships among and between words that the child must come to understand. An example of one kind of relationship is animacy. An entity person, character, or object that can act and move freely has animacy. Thus words that entail animacy can be used in certain ways; words that do not entail animacy cannot. The boy kicked the door is a grammatical sentence in English, but The door kicked the boy is not. Doors cannot, by definition, perform an action; therefore, the word door cannot be used as the subject of the verb kicked, because that particular verb requires an animate subject capable of kicking.

Differences in word order signal other types of meaning differences. Interrogatives, or questions, are formed by inverting the order of the subject and the verb. The sentence Catherine Murphy is here is a declarative sentence, making a statement of fact. Changing the order of the words to Is Catherine here? makes the statement become a question rather than an observed fact. Changing the order of words so that the subject receives the force of the action expressed by the verb creates the passive voice. In the previous example, The boy kicked the door, the subject actively exerts a force against the object of the verb door. But if door is in the subject position, the sentence is in the passive voice: The door was kicked by the boy. To accomplish this transformation, we must also change the verb morphology—by adding the auxiliary (helping) verb, was. Question formation often requires auxiliary verbs as well, especially forms of the verb do. For example, to transform the statement, Allyson eats crackers, into question form, we must begin the question with the word do(es), as in the question, Does Allyson eat crackers?

Roger Brown (1973) noted that, in children who are first acquiring English, the development of inflectional morphemes is directly related to the average number of words the child is able to combine in an utterance. He found that this average, or the mean length of utterance (MLU), is related to syntactic complexity. As MLU increases, the child uses more complex syntax. MLU is roughly equivalent to chronological age in years up to the age of five. That is, children who are one year old have an MLU of one word; children who are two years old have an MLU of two words, and so on.

Brown (1973) examined the language development of three children, whom he called Adam, Eve, and Sarah. Based on the ways that these children learned to talk, he identified stages of syntax development from 18 months until about the age of five. These stages, known as Brown's stages of development, describe the sequence of syntax development, from the single-word level, to simple phrases consisting of two or three words, to complete sentences with a subject noun phrase and a verb phrase, through lengthier sentences that have two main clauses (sentences composed of a subject and verb that can stand alone) or a main clause and a dependent clause (a subject-verb combination that cannot stand alone as a complete sentence, such as, who is sitting). Remarkably, subsequent research has supported Brown's general findings despite the extremely limited number of children in the original study.

Brown (1973) described the increases in complex syntax by examining the sequence of development for using grammatical morphemes, expressing negation (using, for example, no, not, and don't), asking yes/no questions, asking wh– questions (questions starting with what, where, when, and why), elaborating noun phrases, elaborating verb phrases, and forming complex sentences. As children acquire inflectional morphemes (such as –ing, plural –s, past tense –ed, etc.), they are able to express more ideas in each utterance. Increases in inflectional morphology and MLU correspond to more complex syntax.

In order to discuss the way children develop complex syntax, it is first necessary to clarify the terms that Brown and other linguists use. A noun phrase consists of a single word that names a person, place, object, event, or concept, or a pronoun standing in place of the noun, such as I, you, it, her, one, and all. The noun phrase also includes all the words that modify the noun or pronoun, such as my book or the big one. Noun phrases can be elaborated by adding modifiers in front of the noun. Such modifiers can be the articles a, an, or the; the demonstratives this, that, these, and those; possessive pronouns such as my or his; possessive nouns such as Mommy's or children's; quantifiers such as all or some; or adjectives such as big, silly, or interesting. In the sentence The little boy laughed, the subject noun phrase is the little boy. Noun phrases can also occur in the object position as part of the verb phrase, as in the sentence The little boy threw the ball. In this sentence, the noun phrase, the ball, is the object of the verb, threw. Thus, there are subject noun phrases and object noun phrases.

A verb phrase consists of the main verb in a sentence plus any auxiliary (helping) verbs as well as any phrases or clauses that come after the verb and complete it. A phrase is simply a group of words, and a clause is a group of words that has a subject and a verb. Some clauses can stand alone as a grammatical sentence. These are called main clauses or independent clauses. Examples include I go, The book fell off the table, and The dog ran all the way home. Complex sentences have two clauses. Dependent clauses cannot stand alone and must be attached to an independent clause. In the sentence, I talked to the woman who was sitting on the bench, the clause "who was sitting on the bench" has a subject and a verb (who; was sitting) but it cannot stand alone as a grammatical sentence. It is, therefore, a dependent clause. "Sitting" is the main verb for that clause and "was" is the auxiliary verb. The complete verb phrase in this dependent clause, however, is "was sitting on the bench." This is because the verb phrase also includes any noun phrases that complete the verb.

Such sentences, called complex sentences, are generally mastered by the time a child is only five years old!

In Brown's stage I, children are learning their first words and the semantic roles expressed by these words, such as agent (performer of an action) and action (movement). These roles will be explained in more detail in the section devoted to semantics and the meaning of language. Children do not yet use any of the grammatical (inflectional) morphemes, previously discussed, in a consistent way, and they express negation at first with the single word no. Later, they learn to use no or not with a noun or verb, as in no cookie (I don't want a cookie) or not go (I don't want to go). They ask yes/no questions as statements with rising intonation: drink? or Baby go? Children ask what this? or what that? often spoken as a single "giant word" as in (whasat?) Some children begin to use elaborated noun phrases when there is no verb. For example, they might say big dog, but not big dog bark.

Occasionally, they might elaborate the verb phrase by using particles, as in sit down or put on.

Brown's stage II is characterized by mastery of the first grammatical morphemes, particularly the –ing verb ending, –s for noun plurals, and the preposition in. In this stage, children learn modulation of meaning. That is, they learn how to modify words and word order to change meanings. MLU increases to 2.0 with occasional utterances being three or four morphemes in length. Simple what and where questions emerge. For example, children might say, What doing? or Where Daddy? They are beginning to elaborate noun phrases when they appear in the object position. At this stage, children can elaborate only noun phrases that follow the verb and, importantly, only if they omit the subject; they cannot elaborate noun phrases when they are the subjects of sentences. Thus, children at this stage might say, Get big cookie, but cannot yet say, I get big cookie or Bad dog go home. Another important characteristic of stage II is the appearance of use of the semiauxiliary (helping) verbs gonna, gotta, wanna, and hafta. Sentences such as I hafta go and wanna run are now possible.

The semiauxiliary verbs gonna, gotta, wanna, and hafta function as auxiliary (helping) verbs at this stage rather than as main verbs with infinitival clauses (e.g., I'm going to eat dinner now; I have to sit down) as they do in the speech of adults. Sentences such as these are now possible: I wanna go, you gotta, hafta play.

Utterances of children in Brown's stage III are beginning to sound more like adult sentences. The MLU is now around three morphemes and children master the preposition on and the possessive –s. They express negation in sentence form with utterances such as I not go or Baby not sleeping. Later in this stage, they are able to use auxiliary verbs to form negation, such as I *did*n't jump, and copula verbs as in I'*m* not happy. Early in this stage, they still ask yes/no questions by using rising intonation, but as they transition to stage IV they begin to invert the auxiliary verb with the subject to form adult-like questions, such as, *Is* he running? or *Can* I go? They now ask wh– questions by combining who, why, and how with a statement, as in Why baby sick? or Who in there? or How doggie bark? Children can now manage to elaborate the subject noun phrase with demonstratives such as this or that, and occasional articles (a and the) or other modifiers, and at the same time also include the verb in the sentence. In fact, they almost always use verbs in nearly all their utterances at this stage, and use such auxiliary verbs as can, will, be, and do. The past tense –ed may appear, but children also apply it to irregular verbs such as sleep, fall, eat, and go. Sentences that are now possible include That doggie sleeped or Kitty can eat. Finally, in stage III, children begin to use more complex utterances, with a full sentence taking the place of the object of the verb. For example, they can now say, I see bunny hopping. Simple infinitive phrases, such as I want to play, emerge as children transition to stage IV. In these sentences, the subject of the main verb is also the subject of the infinitive (verb forms such as to go, to eat, to play, etc.).

During Brown's stage IV, at around ages three and a half to four and a half, children almost always use noun or pronoun subjects as well as verbs in their utterances. Noun phases now include possessives (e.g., Mommy's big book) along with other modifiers, such as articles, demonstratives, and adjectives. Examples include a little bird or that chocolate cookie. Noun phrases can be joined with a variety of different verb forms that include the occasional use of the past tense –ed, the past tense modals (e.g., could, would, should, must, and might), and forms of the verb be plus the present progressive –ing (e.g., is seeing, am giving, are going). Possible sentences now include That little bird fly, I didn't taked that one, Mommy's big book gone, He's running away, and She should say sorry.

The hallmark of stage IV is embedding—sentences that contain certain kinds of phrases or that combine two clauses into one clause. Embedding at this stage usually occurs as prepositional phrases that consist of a preposition, such as, in, on, under, or to, and its object noun or pronoun. Examples of prepositional phrases are in the box, to me, and under my bed. Children also use the word "and" to conjoin two simple sentences, as in I sit here and Daddy sit there.

In Brown's stage V, children acquire five more grammatical morphemes: regular and irregular past tense verbs; the regular third person singular, present tense agreement marker –s; definite and indefinite articles; and the copula, or linking, verb (forms of the verb be such as He'*s* happy or I *am* here). Yes/no questions now include past tense modals and be verbs (e.g., *Could* I be a pirate?). The most important milestone in stage V is the ability to use relative clauses to produce complex sentences with both independent and dependent clauses, as in the sentence Give me the one *that's big*. Infinitives are also more complex now, with subjects that differ from the subject of the main verb. Children can generate sentences with infinitives that have different subjects from the main verb. An example is the sentence I want Mommy to fix it. Children also use if clauses, as in If you go, I'll go too.

Brown (1973) identified two additional stages, known as stage V+ and stage V++. The MLU of children in stage V+ is between 4.5 and 5.0 words. During this stage, children master the final four grammatical morphemes: the contractible auxiliary, the uncontractible copula, the uncontractible auxiliary, and irregular third person singular verbs. These morphemes allow the child to achieve more complex verb phrases, such as, He's eating all the cookies; Is that candy for me? Are we gonna walk to the park? and She has my best favorite doll. Children can also use past tense forms of the verb be (was and were). These increases in verb development overlap those in stage 5++. In this final stage, children are nearly approaching the age of five and the MLU is between five and six words. They now use when and so as conjunctions (words that connect other words, phrases, or clauses). Examples include such sentences as When I start counting, you hide and He took my cookie so I told. Although children continue to make errors with verb tenses and with marking agreement between subjects and verbs, most sentences are well formed and adult-like by this stage.

Thus, by the age of five or six, most children have progressed from random, reflexive, vegetative noises to intentional verbal communication. They produce this through verbal symbols (words) requiring coordination of motor patterns to reflect a complex phonological system. They organize words with highly organized, complex syntax conveyed through the coordination of motor patterns expressing an equally complex phonological system. However, although it is true that most of a child's first language is acquired by the age of five, children continue to develop and refine language form throughout adolescence and beyond, although the rate of development slows considerably.

Sentences in which the order of events is inverted pose problems for preschool children to understand. An example is the sentence Before you get your cup, pick up your toys. Young children must figure out that the first action mentioned is not the first action to be performed. They also continue to refine their understandings of embedded ideas. Embedding gives us ways to include an unlimited number of ideas in one sentence. For example, we can keep adding prepositional phrases to the sentence There's a hole on the bottom of the sea, to create new sentences such as There's a wart on the frog on the bump on the log in the hole on the bottom of the sea.

During the school years, the major focus of language learning shifts from oral to written language. With this shift, children are introduced to even more complex syntax not typically encountered in conversation. In oral conversations, syntax is usually simple and linear. That is, words are ordered in a straightforward manner to enhance listener comprehension in real time. Language is highly contextualized, as children and caregivers talk about persons and objects present at the time of conversation and about immediate events. However, Carol Westby (1991) maintains that, through storybooks and storytelling, children encounter language that is more distant in time and space than the highly contextualized language of everyday, routine activities at home. Adverbial phrases (words that tell when, where, how, how much, how many, how often, or why, or express affirmation or negation) such as once upon a time, all of a sudden, at last, and after a while are common in storybooks but are less frequent in storybooks than they are in everyday conversations. Adverbial phrases are groups of words that function as adverbs. They modify verbs, adjectives, and other adverbs to tell when, where, how, how much, how many, how often, or why. They also express affirmation and negation (e.g., I will *absolutely* do it; I *never* saw it.) In sentences such as Even though her mother told her not to, Little Red Riding took a shortcut through the woods, adverbial phrases are moved to appear at the beginning of the sentence, a condition known as adverbial fronting. This type of syntax is rarely used in conversational speech, although young children begin to use such constructions in their oral retellings or when "reading" books from memory to family, playmates, or dolls. Much less is known, however, about how children continue to develop and refine complex sentences during the school years.

Cheryl Scott (1995) has studied the ways children continue to develop and refine complex sentences during the school years. She noted that much less is known about how advanced syntax emerges in typically developing school-aged children and adolescents for several reasons. First, language development tends to slow in rate during the school years, with gradual growth measured over periods of years rather than in months as with preschool children. Another problem involves modality and genre. Scott (1995) has demonstrated that older children use more complex syntax when writing than they do while speaking, and that these differences are highly influenced by the nature of the discourse. That is, the social context of the language and the purposes for which it is used as well as the topics being discussed all interact to influence the choice of word and the syntax used by the child. As we have already seen, written language tends to use different conventions that may be harder to apply in conversational language. Conversation is fleeting and spoken words last only a moment before the sound signal fades altogether. In contrast, written language remains on the printed page and can be referred to over and over again, as many times as the child likes. Once spoken, a word cannot be retrieved. However, written words can be examined, erased, reordered, or modified because the conversational partner, the reader, does not have immediate access to them. Thus it is difficult to measure increases in oral language complexity as children enter adolescence.

MEANING

Content

The component of language that deals with meaning is semantics. This component includes the lexicon, or mental dictionary, of the language as well as other knowledge we have about words, such as what part of speech a word is, how it can be used in a sentence, what other words have similar meanings, and so forth. According to Erika Hoff (2001), the average adult knows the meanings of over 100,000 words.

Children begin to learn word meanings sometime between the age of six months and one year. They understand the meanings of some words long before they begin to produce them. The process of learning word meanings is called reference. Children must associate the verbal symbol (the spoken word) with its real world referent (the object or person it represents). The first few words are spoken between 10 and 15 months of age and are context dependent. That is, first words are tied to a particular object or person in a single context. When the child says mama, it means only this person who is the child's own mother.

First words are usually associated with a frequent social routine or word game, such as waving and saying bye-bye. In fact, because first words seem to be conditioned responses that the infant has learned in very specific circumstances, some linguists believe that these utterances are not really words at all. This is because the child has not really used the word as a symbol to identify a specific referent. Rather, he is just making sounds the way a parrot can be trained to make sounds similar to words. Gradually, these context-bound words become attached to referents and become true words that are symbolic. It takes many repeated opportunities to hear a word and associate it with the referent before the child learns to use the word. This process is relatively slow at first.

By the time children are about 18 months old, they can use approximately 50 true words. First words usually fall into a limited number of categories such as naming words, action words, modifiers, personal-social words, and function words. Specific nominals are words that name a particular person, animal, or object such as Mamma or Fido. General nominals refer to general instances of people, animals, or objects, such as book or water. Action words describe actions and may or may not actually be action verbs. An example is the word "up" when the child uses it to ask to be picked up. Modifiers are often function words, adjectives or adverbs that describe or tell about some quality. These can include words like more or again (to request recurrence), big, and allgone. The fifth category contains personal-social words such as yes, no, and please. The final category is function words. These are words needed for grammatical functions and they do not correspond with concrete referents. Examples are words like is, for, to, and where. Children have very few of these words in their early vocabularies.

In English, children learn more nominals (nouns) as part of their first 50 spoken words than any other grammatical category (verbs, adjectives, adverbs, prepositions, pronouns, and conjunctions). One reason is that caregivers usually stress nouns in their speech to young children. It is also easier to map words to concrete referents such as persons and objects than to map words such as verbs or adjectives. Verbs also denote relationships. In other words, although a noun simply names a person or object, verbs and other parts of speech entail relationships among objects or actions that the child must understand. For example, adults know that "Don't say me that" is ungrammatical because the verb say cannot take the indirect object "me." This is an example of relationships that are part of understanding the meaning of the verb say versus the verb tell. The verb tell is needed in this example. Evidence that children actually do not fully understand the first words that they use comes from the way that children overuse or underuse first words. For example, the word dog may first mean only the family dog. The child does not apply this word to any other dog. Later, the word dog may be overgeneralized and applied to any animal with four legs, including cats and cows. With experience, the child learns the conventional meaning of dog, a particular kind of four-legged animal, with fur and a tail, that barks and behaves in particular ways and is found in particular places.

After children can produce about 50 words, they experience a rapid growth in new words known as the word spurt. The rate of learning new words now increases dramatically from about 10 per month to about a new word every day or two. Toddlers seem to approach the learning of new words in one of two different ways. Some children seem to learn more names for objects than anything else. This learning style is known as referential. Other children tend to learn more personal-social words, a style known as expressive. Other factors that seem to influence word learning include birth order, gender, temperament, and the amount and type of speech used by the mother.

As children refine their understandings of word meanings, they begin to understand various semantic roles, mentioned previously in the section describing Brown's stage 1 in syntax development. Nouns, or naming words, can be agents that perform actions or objects that receive actions. They can also possess, as in baby toy to mean the baby's toy. Words can identify locations, as in cookie table to mean the cookie is on the table. Other words express actions, such as go and eat. Still others express quantities, such as lots, or recurrence, such as more or again.

Between 18 and 24 months, toddlers begin to combine single words into two-word combinations. These combinations are based on semantic, or meaning, relationships rather than syntactic relationships. An utterance such as Daddy up may mean Daddy, pick me up; Daddy is upstairs; Daddy, go upstairs; or Is Daddy upstairs? In this way, the child can use a handful of words, and ways of combining them can give the child a way to express many different meanings. The interpretation, therefore, is dependent upon the adult's knowledge of the context in which the child is speaking.

Early combinations typically consist of content words known as lexical words. These words are nouns, verbs, adjectives, and adverbs that carry the meanings the child is trying to convey. These words can be contrasted with functional category words that consist of words needed to express syntactic or grammatical relationships. Functional category words include auxiliary verbs, pronouns, articles, prepositions, and conjunctions. These are often missing in the speech of very young children.

For this reason, early speech has been called telegraphic, with a reliance on lexical words.

Children continue to add new words to their mental lexicon at a very fast pace throughout the preschool years. According to Rhea Paul (2001), the average five-year-old child has over 5,000 words in his or her vocabulary. This is more than doubled by the time the child is 18 years old and includes a greater variety of types of words in all grammatical categories. Some of the growth is accounted for by greater and more varied experiences as the child matures, especially by reading. Knowledge of derivational morphology that allows the child to take a known word and change the grammatical class (e.g., bake/baker) is another important contributor to semantic development.

During the preschool and early school years, children explore meanings through word play and school lessons that involve concepts such as synonyms (words with similar meanings) and antonyms (words with opposite meanings), and rhyming words. During the school years, children organize their knowledge of words in ways that facilitate the ability to remember and use words as needed. For example, they recognize hierarchies of word families. An example is the relationships among the basic category word, cat, and its subordinate categories, such as wild and domestic. They understand that subordinate categories of domestic cats are Siamese, Persian, and tabby, as compared with wild cats such as lions, tigers, and leopards. Children understand superordinate categories, such as feline, mammal, and vertebrate. They also organize words according to semantic fields, or areas of related terms, such as those associated with math, music, banking, or sports.

Children acquire an appreciation of figurative language, especially idioms, slowly throughout childhood and adolescence. Expressions such as hit the roof and raining cats and dogs cannot be interpreted literally. Children also begin to understand and use such language as similes, in which the comparisons are explicit (as white as snow), and metaphors, which only imply comparisons (Her hair is straw). Figurative language is especially important for comprehending the literate language of textbooks and literature.

Use of Language

Language is a social tool, acquired within a community of speakers. Children learn not only the native language of the parents but also the nuances of the parents' particular dialect. Children learn not only what words are in the language and how those words are ordered in sentences, but they also learn when to talk and when to be quiet, and how tone of voice changes meaning. They learn that there are different ways of talking to different people in different contexts and that some words are taboo. They learn which words to use with which people, which words to avoid using, and what happens when they use these words. This component of language is pragmatics.

As with all other components, pragmatics begins to develop very early in infancy, before verbal communication. Early evidence of pragmatic development is apparent in what is known as the prelinguistic, intentional communication of infants just before and as they transition into the use of verbal speech and language. It occurs when the children intentionally use gestures paired with vocalizing or eye contact to communicate with caregivers. Early intentions that children can express this way include requesting objects, requesting actions, and requesting social attention, and rejecting or refusing. Soon afterward, the children begin to use words along with gestures and eye contact to express these early intentions. The gestures eventually fade as children establish a spoken vocabulary and begin to develop syntax.

John Searle (1969) proposed that using words accomplishes specific functions that he referred to as speech acts. Examples of speech acts are requesting information, naming, acknowledging, commenting, and protesting. John Dore (1974) identified nine "primitive speech acts" accomplished in the single-word utterances of infants and toddlers: labeling, repeating, answering, requesting action, requesting an answer, calling, greeting, protesting, and practicing. With more complex language, greater cognitive ability, and the ability to shift perspectives from one's self to that of another, older children exhibit a wider range of pragmatic intentions, which include, among others, deception and joking.

The study of pragmatics also includes the organization of language into discourse, the use of language beyond the level of a single sentence. Three types of discourse characterize oral language: conversational, narrative, and expository discourse. Conversational discourse is the earliest to develop, with infants and toddlers engaging in rudimentary conversations as they learn to talk. Early conversations occur during familiar interaction routines with the mother or other primary caregiver, who provides support by altering her language to maintain the conversation. By the time children are two years old, they can respond to invitations to conversation, initiate conversations, take turns, shift topics, and respond to invitations to conversation.

As children approach school age, they soon learn that there are polite ways of talking and that people do not always say exactly what they are thinking. They begin to understand and make indirect requests. Preschoolers learn registers, or different ways of talking with different people in different situations. They also learn acceptable ways of maintaining and closing conversations, issuing directives, and making requests, and they learn how to shift perspectives. The ability to appreciate the perspective of another is crucial in discourse, because it allows the speaker to decide what knowledge is already shared and what information is new and must be explicitly stated. It is also necessary for understanding and correctly using pronouns such as I and you or these and those.

During the preschool years, children learn other important aspects of conversation. Grice (1975) argued that conversation involves a tacit agreement among participants to cooperate with each other to construct meaning. He called this the cooperative principle. Grice proposed that conversational participants expect each other to provide new information without repeating what is already known, to be honest, to speak directly, to use precise vocabulary and syntax, and to avoid being ambiguous. Communication breaks down when participants violate this agreement unless they agree to certain exceptions. Examples of such agreements are using sarcasm, or telling jokes, or creating suspense.

As children enter the school years, they begin to understand and make indirect requests. Prior to this time, they have not understood that, when someone says, Is your mother home? this is actually a request to call the mother to the telephone or to the door. Another area of growth for school-aged children is the ability to make conversational repairs. Preschool children simply repeat what they have already said when listeners do not understand them. When the listener lets a preschool child know he has not been understood, the child simply repeats the utterance. Because this strategy does not give the listener any more information, it usually results in frustration for both the child and the listener. By the time a child is six, he can sometimes add a little more information. It is not until children are around nine years old that they can rephrase or elaborate when conversation breaks down, and make effective repairs, partly because they are more adept at taking on the listener's perspective.

Narrative discourse is also important during the school years, with brief personal and fictional narratives emerging during the preschool years. Westby (1991) considers narratives to be the bridge between the highly contextualized language of the preschool years and the more abstract, literate language of the school years. According to Westby (1991), narratives are characterized by a speaker who assumes responsibility for most of the discourse, by fluency and prosody that are not typical of conversation, and by distancing from the present context and often from personal perspectives. These characteristics are similar to those of early books designed to help children learn to read, as well as the more advanced literature encountered in higher grades.

Norris and Hoffman (1993) identified a developmental progression as children learn to construct increasingly more complex narratives. First efforts are characterized by list-like sequences of statements about a topic known as a descriptive list. Next, children begin to order events in a chronology. Such narratives constitute an ordered sequence. Children need more complex syntax to express causal relationships among events when their narratives are organized at the level of a reactive sequence. By the end of the preschool years, children are often able to attribute intentionality to characters as they engage in events. This level is an abbreviated structure. A complete structure occurs when the narrative expresses an overarching moral or theme. The required components of a story grammar—initiating event or problem, response, consequences, and resolution—are present at this level. Older school-aged children are able to develop complex episodes with multiple plots, with lessons learned from one episode carrying over into other episodes. Finally, in adolescence and adulthood, interactive structures are possible, with independent story episodes that may be related from multiple perspectives.

The third type of discourse is expository, or language that describes or explains. Preschool children engage in expository discourse when they explain how to play a game, make a sandwich, or use a toy. Studies of classroom discourse show that the ability to understand and to produce expository discourse is critical to school success. Teachers use expository discourse to explain mathematics, science, or social studies lessons. And they expect students to be able to define, list, enumerate, and describe, as well as explain, compare and contrast, and argue. These kinds of structures are organized differently from both conversational and narrative discourse. Thus far, most of the research has focused on identifying the nature of the organization of expository discourse, but little is known about the process of how children acquire the ability to use these ways of organizing and communicating information.

REFERENCES

Berko Gleason, J. (1993). Language development: An overview and a preview. In J. Berko Gleason (Ed.), *The development of language* (3rd ed.). New York: Macmillan.

Bloom, L., & Lahey, M. (1978). *Language development and language disorders.* New York: Wiley.

Brown, R. (1973). *A first language: The early stages.* Cambridge, MA: Harvard University Press.

Dore, J. (1974). A pragmatic description of early language development. *Journal of psycholinguistic research, 4,* 343–350.

Grice, Paul. (1975). Logic and conversation. In P. Cole and J. Morgan (Eds.), *Syntax and semantics: Speech acts* (Vol. 3). New York: Academic Press.

Haynes, W., Moran, M., & Pindzola, R. (1990). *Communication disorders in the classroom.* Dubuque, IA: Kendall/Hunt.

Hoff, E. (2001). *Language development* (2nd ed.). Belmont, CA: Wadsworth/Thomson Learning.

Norris, J. (1998). Early sentence transformations and the development of complex syntactic structures. In W. Haynes and B. Shulman (Eds.), *Communication development.* Baltimore: Williams & Wilkins.

Norris, J., & Hoffman, P. (1989). On the nature of phonological development: evidence from normal children's spelling errors. *Journal of Speech and Hearing Research, 32,* 787–794.

Norris, J., & Hoffman, P. (1993). *Whole language intervention for school-age children.* San Diego, CA: Singular Publishing Group.

Paul, R. (2001). *Language disorders from infancy through adolescence* (2nd ed.). St. Louis, MO: Mosby.

Scott, C. (1995). *Syntax for school-age children: a discourse perspective.* In M. Fey, J. Windsor, S. Warren (Eds.). *Language intervention preschool through the elementary years.* Baltimore: Paul H. Brooks Publishing.

Searle, J. (1969). *Speech acts.* Cambridge, MA: Cambridge University Press.

Westby, C. (1991). Learning to talk; Talking to learn: Oral-literate language differences. In C. Simon (Ed.), *Communication skills and classroom success: Assessment and therapy for language and learning disabled students.* Eau Claire, WI: Thinking Publications.

Chapter Six

THE IMPORTANCE OF PHONOLOGICAL AWARENESS AND DECODING FOR EARLY LITERACY INSTRUCTION

Benita A. Blachman

In just 30 years, educators have made enormous strides in understanding how young children learn to read and what teachers and parents should do to promote early literacy acquisition (Dickinson & Newman, 2006). There is a consensus among researchers and practitioners that reading is a language-based skill. As a consequence of the emphasis on language, educators have come to expect that oral language experiences will be valued in classrooms, that reading to children will be commonplace, that basic concepts about print (such as how to hold a book) and the functions of reading and writing will be developed, and that children will have daily opportunities both to talk and to write about their experiences (Anderson, Hiebert, Scott, & Wilkinson, 1985). It is important to remember, however, that children come to school with differing levels of language—especially vocabulary knowledge and world knowledge. Hirsch (2003) emphasizes the strong relationship between vocabulary knowledge and oral and written language, pointing out that a "high-performing first grader knows about twice as many words as a low-performing one and, as these students go through the grades, the differential gets magnified" (p. 16). One way of building both vocabulary and world knowledge is "through the stories that teachers read aloud and through the discussions that follow" (Walsh, 2003, p. 25).

Another area in which children differ when they enter school is in their knowledge about the connections between spoken and written language (Adams, 1990). Although as literate adults, it is obvious that we have an alphabetic writing system in which letters more or less represent speech sounds, we cannot assume that young children have this important insight into the relationship between print and speech. Understanding how print and speech are connected provides the foundation for learning to read words accurately and fluently—a critically important skill that is strongly related to good reading comprehension (Snow, Burns, & Griffin, 1998). The ability to read words accurately and fluently frees up conscious attention that children would otherwise have to devote to sounding out words—allowing children to focus instead on the meaning of what they are reading.

Recently, two prestigious panels (Snow et al., 1998; and the National Reading Panel [NRP] report, National Institute of Child Health and Human Development, 2000a) have provided research-based guidance regarding early literacy practices that have been proven to reduce the number of children who have trouble learning to read. These practices include a strong focus on learning how print and speech are connected. The NRP report reviews the importance of instruction in phoneme awareness (an awareness that spoken words can be segmented into individual sounds or phonemes—the sounds that are represented by the letters of the alphabet). Other important practices reviewed by the NRP include instruction in phonics (helping children use their knowledge of letter-sound correspondences to read and spell words), as well as the importance of developing fluency, vocabulary, and comprehension. This chapter will focus on phoneme awareness and learning to decode (sound out words) by providing children with systematic phonics instruction. I will provide examples of research-based practices that have been used in the classroom and have been found to facilitate the acquisition of reading and spelling in young children.

WHAT IS PHONOLOGICAL AWARENESS AND WHY IS IT IMPORTANT?

Phonological awareness is the awareness that speech can be segmented into words, syllables, and even smaller units called phonemes. Phonemes are the smallest units of sound in a given language and the segments of speech that are represented by the letters in an alphabetic writing system. It is important for children to understand that spoken language can be segmented—especially into phonemes. If children don't understand that the spoken word *sun*, for example, has three phonemes (or segments of sound), it will be very hard for them to understand why the word must be written with three letters. Awareness that speech can be segmented into the phonemic units represented by the letters of the alphabet does not develop naturally as a consequence of learning to speak. It is only when children start to learn to read and write that this awareness becomes important. Educators now know that failure to develop this awareness can be a major stumbling block for many young children.

Researchers have used many different tasks to assess a child's phoneme awareness. For example, children have been asked to demonstrate their awareness of phonemes by tapping out the sounds in spoken words, categorizing spoken words on the basis of common sounds (for example, knowing that the spoken words *hen* and *hot* go together because they both start with /h/), and deleting sounds (say *sat* without the /s/). Regardless of the task used to measure this crucial skill, the children who perform well are the children who are more likely to be successful readers in the early grades; and the children who perform less well on these tasks are the children who are more likely to have difficulty learning to read. Twenty years ago, Williams (1987) offered an explanation for the connection between phoneme awareness and reading when she wrote that "Sometimes children have trouble learning to decode because they are completely unaware of the fact that spoken language is segmented—into sentences, into syllables, and into phonemes" (pp. 25–26).

Why is it so difficult for children to develop the understanding that *spoken* words can be segmented? When we see the *written* spelling of the word, the segments (represented by letters) are obvious. On the other hand, the segments in the spoken word are not obvious, because when we pronounce a word, the sounds merge or overlap (think about the overlapping shingles on a roof)—the consonants are actually folded into the vowels. This phenomenon is called coarticulation. Liberman and Shankweiler (1991) explained it this way:

> Though the word "bag," for example, has three phonological units, and correspondingly, three letters in print, it has only one pulse of sound: The three elements of the underlying phonological structure—the three phonemes—have been thoroughly overlapped and merged into that one sound—"bag." (p. 6)

Given what educators now know about speech production—and coarticulation in particular—it is easy to understand why a young child might have difficulty detecting the separate segments in spoken words (Moats, 2000, p. 230). Large-scale research studies in the United States and elsewhere (see Blachman, 2000, for a review) have shown repeatedly that when teachers include phoneme awareness activities (showing children how to segment spoken words) in early literacy programs, along with activities to illustrate how the phonemes are represented by the letters of the alphabet, many of the reading difficulties experienced by young children can be prevented.

According to research reviewed in the National Reading Panel report (National Institute of Child Health and Human Development , 2000b), effective phoneme awareness instruction has many important characteristics. Two specific phoneme awareness activities, phoneme segmentation (breaking spoken words into their individual sounds or phonemes) and phoneme blending (blending the segmented phonemes and saying the word naturally), have been shown to have the most direct transfer to reading. Thus, it is important that any phoneme awareness program include these two activities. Research has also shown that phoneme awareness instruction is most effective and has a greater influence on reading and spelling when children are taught explicitly how the segmented phonemes are represented by letters in print. Finally, research has shown that phoneme awareness programs do not require extensive amounts of time in kindergarten classrooms. Programs that took less than 20 hours had the most impact on reading. Although the NRP makes a strong point of saying that this last point should be interpreted with caution (different children might require different amounts of instructional time), the finding is consistent with what I and my colleagues found in our research.

In our work with kindergarten children, our first study (Ball & Blachman, 1991) included 28, 15- to 20-minute lessons spread over 7 weeks for a total of 7 to 9 hours of instruction. Children who participated in the 28 phoneme awareness lessons had higher reading and spelling skills at the end of kindergarten than children who did not participate in these lessons. In our second study (Blachman, Ball, Black, & Tangel, 1994), we expanded the intervention for children who began with fewer early literacy skills (on average they knew only two letter sounds in January of their kindergarten year). The expanded program included 41, 15- to 20-minute lessons spread over 11 weeks and taking 10 to 13 hours. Again, we found that children who participated in our phoneme awareness instruction in kindergarten were better readers and spellers at the end of kindergarten and they maintained this advantage at the end of 1st grade. Others who have followed children for a longer period of time have found that the advantage of this instruction lasts well beyond the time that children participate in the activities (National Institute of Child Health and Human Development, 2000b).

To illustrate activities that include both phoneme segmenting and phoneme blending, and also illustrate how to combine phoneme awareness with letter-sound instruction, I will describe the three-part program that we used in our research. Although no one program has been found to be superior to all other models of phoneme awareness instruction, the research is clear that all children need to learn about the segmental structure of speech and how to connect these segments to printed letters. Children who develop this understanding are more likely to be better readers and spellers than children who lack this important insight about the structure of spoken words.

Research-Based Strategies to Build Phonological Awareness and Letter-Sound Knowledge

In our intervention studies, we used a simple three-step lesson plan. At the beginning of each lesson, children participated in a phoneme segmentation and blending activity called *say-it-and-move-it.* This activity is followed by a second activity to reinforce phoneme awareness, and finally there is an activity each day to teach letter names and sounds. Although these activities have been designed with small groups in mind (four or five children), they have also been adapted for larger groups and used with individuals.

The children begin each lesson with a say-it-and-move-it activity designed to teach children to segment spoken words into phonemes and then to blend the phonemes and say the word naturally. Each child in the group is given an 8 1/2-by-11-inch sheet of laminated paper. On the top half of this sheet is a picture (e.g., boat or clown) or geometric shape that serves as a holding place for the disks (tiles, buttons, or blocks) that will be used to represent the sounds in spoken words. A thick black line divides the paper into two sections. Below the line is a black arrow going from left to right. The children are taught to move the appropriate number of disks down to this arrow to represent the individual sounds pronounced by the teacher. For example, the teacher might say "I'm going to say a sound: /a/. Now I'm going to say-it-and-move-it." The teacher models for the children, moving the disk out of the square in the top half of the page to the black arrow in the bottom half of the page as she stretches out the sound, /aaaaaaaaaaa/. When the disk is on the black line, the teacher says "/a/, one sound" and then sweeps the disk back to the top of the page to get ready for the next sound or word. After modeling for the children, the teacher has the children "say-it-and-move-it," using the same sound that she used for demonstration. When the children are successful at moving one disk to represent one sound, the teacher can move on and model how to move two disks for a sound that is repeated twice, such as /a/ /a/. Again, the children repeat the sounds and move one disk to represent each sound. Next, two-phoneme words (such as *at*) are introduced, and finally three-phoneme words (such as *sun*). After modeling by the teacher, the child repeats the word slowly, stretching out the sounds, and moves a disk to represent each sound. Once the children have demonstrated how many sounds they hear in a spoken word (such as *sat*) by moving one disk to represent each sound, the children blend the sounds and say the word naturally.

During the first few weeks of instruction, it is helpful to use continuous sound letters in the initial position. These are sounds that the children can stretch out or hold with a minimum of distortion, such as /s/ in *sun,* /f/ in *fan,* and /l/ in *lip.* After children are comfortable segmenting three-phoneme items beginning with continuous sound letters, stop consonants (a stop consonant, being a "speech sound that is articulated with a stop of the air stream" [Moats, 2000, p. 235], such as /t/ and /b/), can be used in the initial position.

Once children are successful segmenting one-, two-, and three-phoneme items using blank tiles or disks, the teacher can begin to add letters to the disks, being careful to select only those letters whose names and sounds have been mastered by the children. For example, we often start by adding the letter *a* to one of the tiles, once we know that the child can automatically give the name and sound of that letter. We usually select letters from among the first eight letters that we teach *(a, m, t, i,* s, *r, f, b*), although children do not need to know all of these letters before one of them can be added to a letter tile. (There is no agreed-upon sequence for teaching letter names and sounds. We start with these letters because they can generate a significant number of simple words with the consonant-vowel-consonant pattern, such as *mat, sat, fit.* Other letters may have been learned first by the children if a teacher has been using a specific sequence in a classroom reading program. The important point is that the first letters that are put on the tiles should be letters that the children know automatically.)

The children who are ready for the letter tiles can use a combination of letter tiles and blank tiles when segmenting a word, while other children in the group can continue to use all blank tiles if that is what they need to be successful. Eventually, children who have mastered more letter names and sounds can be given enough letter tiles to produce a consonant-vowel-consonant real word (e.g., *lip*) during the segmentation activities. The children use the same procedure that was described above, saying the word slowly (stretching out the word and segmenting the sounds, as in *llliiiippp*) and moving one letter tile as each sound is pronounced. When the three letter tiles have been moved to the black arrow on the bottom half of the sheet, the children blend the sounds and read the word *lip.* This is an important stage for the children to reach, because now they have made the connection that spoken words can be segmented and that each segmented sound can be represented by specific written letters (graphemes). This is the point at which phoneme awareness and the alphabetic principle (the knowledge that letters stand for spoken sounds) meet. The insight that written letters stand for spoken language sounds—whether the children develop this insight informally through language play and being read to or through explicit instruction—increases the likelihood that children will become successful readers and spellers.

After the say-it-and-move-it activity, children are given an opportunity each day to practice phoneme awareness with a related activity or game. For example, a teacher might introduce sound categorization, a game adapted from Bradley and Bryant (1983) in England. Using pictures of words that rhyme or that share initial, final, or medial sounds, the teacher displays three pictures with shared sounds, such as *hat, hen, hug,* and one picture that does not belong because it does not start like the others (such as *bus*). The children select the picture that does not belong and explain their choice. In another activity, adapted from what Elkonin (1973), a Russian psychologist, called "sound analysis," the children get booklets containing one picture on each page of an object representing simple words (*fan, sit, lip*). Underneath each picture is a series of connected boxes corresponding to the number of phonemes in the word. As in the say-it-and-move-it activity, children using the Elkonin cards are taught to say the word slowly and simultaneously move a disk into a box to represent each phoneme in the word. In yet another phoneme awareness task, children learn to hold up a finger for each sound they hear in a word spoken by the teacher. To reinforce blending words, as opposed to segmenting them, the children also have the opportunity to practice correcting mistakes made by a puppet with a movable mouth who tells the children stories. At several points in the story, the puppet mispronounces a word by segmenting it into its constituent phonemes (saying the word very slowly and stretching out the sounds). The bashful puppet turns away from the children until the children fix the mispronounced word by pronouncing it or blending it correctly.

A final activity in each lesson involves direct, explicit instruction in *letter names and letter sounds.* As noted earlier, the results of previous phoneme awareness intervention studies demonstrate that phoneme awareness instruction has a greater influence on early reading and spelling when connections are made between the sound segments of the word and the letters representing those segments (Bradley & Bryant, 1983). As indicated in the discussion of the say-it-and-move-it activity, teachers in our research projects start teaching children eight letters (*a, m, t, i,* s, *r, f, b*). Children learn key words and phrases to help them remember the sound of each letter. Illustrated alphabet cards are used to reinforce initial sounds. For example, the *r* card has a picture of a *red rooster* in *red* running shoes and the *f* card is illustrated with *five funny faces.* Children also play games such as "Post Office" to reinforce letter names and sounds. In this game, children select a picture, identify the letter that represents the first sound of the pictured item, and mail the picture card in the appropriate letter pouch. On another day, a bingo game might be selected, with pictures that illustrate a subset of letter names and sounds (for example, one set of cards might reinforce the letters *a, m, b,* and *t*). Once children have mastered several letter names and their corresponding sounds, these letters can be put on the manipulatives (e.g., disks, buttons, tiles, or blocks) and used in the say-it-and-move-it activity, as described earlier.

Phonological Awareness—Some Final Thoughts

The research on phonological awareness has lead to some important conclusions. Teachers need to understand and be able to provide for the differences in phonological awareness that they will encounter in their classrooms. Some kindergarten children will not yet know how to rhyme—an early indicator of phonological awareness—while others will already know how to segment spoken words into their constituent sounds. Some children appear to make discoveries about the connections between speech and print effortlessly by being read to, by opportunities to write, and by playing oral language games with parents, preschool teachers, or other caregivers. Other children are not as fortunate. Even with exposure to preschool literacy experiences, differences or deficiencies in phonological ability might make it difficult for them to discover the connections between print and speech. Other children lack the necessary preschool literacy experiences that facilitate making these connections. The latter two groups especially need teachers who understand why they may be lagging behind in early reading. Their teachers may need to provide explicit instruction to help them understand that spoken language can be segmented into the sounds that are represented by the letters of the alphabet. Thus, even though not every kindergarten child will need as explicit a program in phoneme awareness as the one just described, every teacher of young beginning readers, especially in kindergarten and 1st grade, needs to know how to provide such a program for those children who need it. Next, it is important to help young children use the insights they have gained from instruction in phoneme awareness and the alphabetic principle (understanding how letters represent the sounds of speech) to learn to decode words and to spell.

WHAT IS DECODING AND WHY IS IT IMPORTANT?

Research has shown that decoding (figuring out the pronunciation of a word by using one's knowledge of the systematic relationships between sounds and letters) (Snow et al., 1998, p. 52) is made much easier when a child has phoneme awareness. In a now classic article, Stanovich (1986) described children who fail to learn to decode words in 1st grade and the downward spiral that can result. These are the children who are more likely to dislike reading, practice less, and fail to develop the fluency that comes with practice. Without fluency, children must use valuable resources to continue to focus attention on decoding words and are left with less attention available to devote to the meaning of what they are reading. In addition, these children gain less from their reading—in terms of new vocabulary and general knowledge—than the children who are initially successful in learning to decode in 1st grade. Juel (1994) confirmed these observations when she followed 54 children from grade 1 to grade 4 and found that the 4th-grade poor readers were the ones who entered 1st grade with the most limited phonological awareness. This contributed to their difficulty in learning the correspondences between spoken sounds and letters and to their slowness in learning to decode. At the end of grade 4, Juel reported that the decoding of the poor readers was not yet equivalent to that of the average readers at the beginning of grade 2. Consistent with Stanovich's hypothesis, the poor readers in the Juel study liked reading less, did less of it, and, consequently, lost the valuable opportunities for vocabulary growth and exposure to new ideas that come from reading widely. Although no one is suggesting that all is lost if children fail to learn to read in 1st grade, the point is that it gets harder and takes longer to remediate difficulties the older children get (Torgesen, 2005). Thus, our goal should be to get all children off to a good start by teaching children to decode words accurately and fluently.

Research-Based Strategies to Build Accurate and Fluent Decoding—The Foundation for Good Comprehension

As with phoneme awareness, there is no one model that is superior to all others for providing explicit and systematic instruction to insure that all children learn to decode words accurately and fluently. The research is clear, however, that this is an important goal for all children. In the studies I have conducted with my colleagues, we have provided teachers with a framework for organizing beginning reading instruction that has proven successful with children in regular classrooms, as well as children with special needs in programs taught by reading and resource teachers. In one of our classroom studies (Blachman, Tangel, Ball, Black, & McGraw, 1999), classroom teachers and their teaching assistants followed a five-step plan to facilitate accurate and fluent word recognition and to provide opportunities for students to read stories out loud with corrective feedback from teachers. Children who participated in this project were better readers at the end of 1st grade than children who did not participate in this structured program, and they maintained their advantage when assessed one year later. More recently, we (Blachman et al., 2004) reported the results of a remedial study in which 2nd- and 3rd-grade children who had been identified as struggling readers (scoring below the 25th percentile on individually administered reading tests) participated in eight months of one-to-one tutoring that replaced the special remedial program the school was providing. We used an expanded version (50 minutes instead of 30 minutes) of the five-step plan as will be described below. At the end of the intervention and again one year later, the participating children demonstrated superior reading, fluency, and spelling skills when compared to the children who had participated only in the remedial programs available in the school.

Explicit and Systematic Decoding Instruction in the Regular Classroom

The model that we have used in our research is based on five relatively simple steps. Each small-group lesson takes between 30 and 40 minutes, although all times are only suggested guidelines. Each part of the lesson can be adapted easily by the teacher to meet the needs of a particular group (spending less time on one step and more time on another). As noted earlier, in our remediation study, resource and reading teachers expanded the length of the lesson to a 50-minute tutorial.

Step 1. Each lesson begins with a brief and quick-paced (1 to 2 minutes) review of sound-symbol associations in which the child gives the name of the letter, the sound it makes, and a word that starts with that sound (such as *a* says /a/ as in *apple*). A pack of index cards can be used as a sound pack, with each card containing one grapheme (a grapheme is a letter, such as *t* or *a,* or a letter cluster, such as *ai,* representing a single speech sound or phoneme). To keep this activity brief and quick-paced, not all sounds are included each day. In order to highlight the vowels (such as *a*) and later the vowel combinations (such as *ai*), the vowels are written in red and the consonants in black. In the early stages of letter-sound instruction, when the children are just learning vowels, we have found that it is especially important to have a consistent key word for each of the short vowels and make sure that the children can name the letter, give the sound, and identify the key word. These are the key words we have used:

- *a* says /a/ as in *apple*
- *i* says /i/ as in *itch*
- *o* says /o/ as in *octopus*
- *u* says /u/ as in *up*
- *e* says /e/ as in *Ed*

Step 2. After the letter-sound review, teachers instruct the children in phoneme analysis and blending. In this step, children learn new decoding skills. That is, they learn how to build words and sound them out *accurately* using the letter sounds that they already know from Step 1. The primary activity at this step requires the use of a pocket chart that we refer to as a "sound board" (an 8 1/2-by-11-inch piece of card stock with three pockets—the top pocket holds cards with the consonant letters or consonant digraphs, such as *sh, ch, th,* that the children learned in Step 1, the middle pocket holds the vowels also learned in Step 1, and the third or bottom pocket is used to put these letters together to make new words). When used in a regular classroom, this step might take only six to eight minutes, depending on the ability of the children. The group might build six to ten words—using fewer words when working with the younger children (beginning 1st graders).

To get started on this phoneme analysis and blending technique (adapted from Slingerland, 1971), the teacher pronounces a word, such as *fat,* emphasizing the medial (vowel) sound. The children repeat the word, listen for the vowel sound, and select the appropriate vowel grapheme card (vowels are color-coded red) from the middle pocket and place it in the lower pocket. The teacher then repeats the word and asks the children to select the letter card that represents the first sound in the word and place it in the appropriate position (i.e., in front of the vowel) in the bottom pocket. The teacher might then say, "Now we have /fa/. Our word is *fat*. What is the last sound we hear in *fat*?" The children then select the *t* and place it at the end of the word. The whole word is then read naturally (as we would say the word in normal speech), either by an individual child or by the group.

Once the children are successful in constructing words, phoneme manipulation is introduced. For this task, the teacher works through a series of preselected words and might ask the children to change *fat* to *fan* and, when new vowels are mastered, change *fan to fin*. A later lesson might require changing *fin to shin* and, eventually, as new syllable types are introduced on the sound board, changing *shin to shine*.

As with all of our activities, teachers have developed a variety of ways to improvise and adapt instruction. For example, the same activity can be conducted with a set of magnetized letters on a cookie sheet or with Scrabble tiles. Scrabble tiles are especially useful with older children, giving the activity a more sophisticated look, and can be used when students are building longer phonetically regular words (words that can be sounded out, such as *backpack* or *pancake*). Blank Scrabble tiles can be purchased and a black marker can be used to create special tiles, for example, for consonants digraphs (e.g., *sh, ch*) and vowel teams (e.g., *ai, ee*), putting the two letters that make a single sound on one tile, just as we would when we create letter cards for the sound board described above.

Step 3. Whereas the goal of Step 2 is *accuracy*, the goal of Step 3 is *fluency*. Once children can construct and accurately read on the sound board a pool of phonetically regular words, these words (and different words with the same phonetic pattern) are put on flash cards and the children practice reading them quickly. Often the children need to read the words more than once—the first time for accuracy and the second time to build automaticity. Teachers have found that the use of a stopwatch or hourglass encourages children to move quickly. Both the stopwatch and hourglass can be used by pairs of children when the teacher is working with groups. Each child tries to beat his or her own time on his or her own set of words. In that way the children in the pairs are not competing with each other. Children like to graph their progress on this activity.

Step 3 also includes the opportunity to practice high frequency words that have to be memorized, such as *said*. Words can be selected from a variety of sources. Basal reading programs, the core program used in most elementary schools, often have a predetermined list of high-frequency words that the children are required to learn at each grade level, and these can be incorporated into this step. There are also published lists (see, for example, the lists of instant words in *The Reading Teacher's Book of Lists* by Fry & Kress, 2006) that include the most frequently used words in written English. These lists are a valuable resource for classroom teachers, reading teachers, and resource teachers. The teachers in our research projects write the high-frequency words in a different color font (or print them on a different colored index card) than the phonetically regular words, to remind the children that these are words that need to be memorized. For approximately two to three minutes daily, children can practice reading phonetically regular words and irregular high-frequency words.

Step 4. The fourth step in the lesson includes using a variety of books for oral reading. We encourage teachers, especially during the early stages of instruction, to select books that will give children the opportunity to practice the decodable patters they have learned and to reinforce the importance of accurate and fluent reading as a foundation for comprehension. For this purpose, we include a variety of decodable texts in our early lessons, selecting books from several series, such as Primary Phonics (Educator's Publishing Service, 1995), the Steck-Vaughn Phonics Readers (Steck-Vaughn, 1991), and Dr. Maggie's Phonics Readers (Creative Teaching Press, Inc., 1999).

Teachers are also encouraged to include stories that are not phonetically controlled by whatever basal series (core reading series) is being used in their school district, as well as having children read from trade books, including both narrative (e.g., the Arthur series by Marc Brown; the Amelia Bedelia series by Peggy Parish) and expository texts (e.g., the Curious Creatures series, Curriculum Associates, 1997). In the early stages of instruction, teachers (and/or parents) may need to provide extensive support when books that are not phonetically controlled are being introduced. This might mean that the teacher will be doing most of the reading, alternating reading with the child, or just supplying unknown words. Gradually, as the children become more proficient, they will be reading these books independently. Trade books should be selected based on the appropriateness of the reading level and on the child's interests.

As noted in the *Report of the National Reading Panel* (National Institute of Child Health and Human Development, 2000a, p. 11): "Fluent readers are able to read orally with speed, accuracy, and proper expression. Fluency is one of several critical factors necessary for reading comprehension." The NRP further explains that "If text is read in a laborious and inefficient manner, it will be difficult for the child to remember what has been read and to relate the ideas expressed in the text to his or her background knowledge" (National Institute of Child Health and Human Development, 2000a, p. 11). In order to develop this important component of reading, children should have frequent opportunities to read and reread texts with corrective feedback from an adult. As early as possible, teachers should begin to help children self-monitor by having the children ask themselves, for example, if what they just read makes sense. Focusing children's attention on the meaning of the text should be part of their earliest reading experiences—whether the teacher, parent, or child is doing the reading (Snow et al., 1998).

Step 5. The last step of each lesson includes a short writing to dictation activity. Teachers dictate preselected words used in earlier steps of the lesson (such as words practiced on the sound board or encountered in phonetically controlled text) *or* new words with the same phonetic pattern. The number of words dictated will depend on the age of the children. In our research projects, we have asked teachers to dictate four to six phonetically regular words and one sentence (that may include one or more high-frequency words) when working with small groups of first graders—this usually takes about five to seven minutes. For reading and resource teachers working with somewhat older children (2nd and 3rd graders) who are struggling readers, we have encouraged them to dictate six to eight words and two sentences. Reading and resource teachers often have more than 30 minutes in which to conduct their lesson and, therefore, can spend somewhat more time on each step.

Regardless of the number of words dictated, children are directed to print vowel headings at the top of each dictation page (e.g., *a* and *i,* or, later in the year, *ai, oa, ea*). These headings represent the particular vowel sounds that the teacher targeted for that day's lesson. The teacher says the word she wants the children to write, such as *lid,* and the children repeat the word slowly, stretching it out and listening for the vowel sound. If the dictation paper has the headings *a* and *i,* for example, the child might stretch out the word *lid* and then write it under the appropriate heading. After the words for the day are dictated, the children are asked to read the words back to the teacher. Only phonetically regular words—words that can be decoded—are dictated in this step of the lesson. The goal is to help children see the connection between reading and writing by learning that they can write the words they can decode. This procedure for learning to spell is quite different from the usual classroom activity of having children memorize lists of unrelated words for the Friday spelling test.

The dictation activity gives teachers an opportunity to evaluate student progress on the target sounds for the day's lesson. The dictation notebooks also become a record of student growth over the year. Students, teachers, and parents can review the progress as students move from writing and reading simple closed-syllable words (*ham*) to more complex syllable types (*lake, float, perch*) and multisyllable words (such as *reptile, bugle, and tarnish*) made up of the syllable patters they have learned.

Many of the early activities in the five-step plan focus on developing accurate and fluent word identification. Accurate and fluent word identification can be developed in part by learning the six basic syllable patterns used in the English language. All six of the syllable patterns can be introduced using the five-step plan just described. These patterns include the following:

- closed syllables, such as *fat* and *flat*
- final "e" syllables, such as *cake* and *shine*

- open syllables, such as *me* and *cry*
- vowel team syllables, such as *pain*, *teach*, and *crawl*
- vowel + *r* syllables, such as *burn* and *start*
- consonant + *le* syllables, as in *bottle* and *table*.

The syllable patterns are reinforced when children read decodable books and also when children have the opportunity to read a wide variety of trade books and books representing various genres. The goal in teaching these patterns is for children to begin to read appropriate grade level texts fluently and with good comprehension as early as possible.

Vocabulary development and comprehension, although not the focus of this chapter, should never be neglected. Teachers are encouraged to make sure that children know the meaning of all the words that they are asked to read *or* spell, and a variety of strategies, such as retellings and making predictions, can be used to support comprehension. It is especially important to help children learn to self-monitor their reading and detect from an early age when something does not make sense. As word recognition increases, more time in each lesson can be devoted to reading new stories and rereading old ones. If time becomes a problem, teachers may alternate the use of the sound board and dictation. This allows more time to be spent on oral reading of text with corrective feedback from the teacher.

CONCLUSION

In this chapter, I have focused on the importance of phonological awareness and decoding for early reading instruction. As the NRP (National Institute of Child Health and Human Development, 2000a, 2000b) points out, however, although both are critical for early reading success, neither constitutes a total reading program. There is also no one-size-fits-all reading program and, regardless of the core program that teachers are using to teach reading, teachers need to differentiate instruction for children in their classrooms. Unless all children learn about the systematic relationships between speech sounds and spellings, teachers will be doing a disservice to young readers. Making sure all children have this foundation can help to level the playing field for children who come to school with different levels of early literacy skills and experiences. The ultimate goal is for more young children to learn to read fluently and with good comprehension and, just as important, to learn to enjoy reading.

REFERENCES

Adams, M. J. (1990). *Beginning to read: Thinking and learning about print.* Cambridge, MA: MIT Press.

Anderson, R. C., Hiebert, E. H., Scott, J. A., & Wilkinson, I.A.G. (1985). *Becoming a nation of readers: The report of the commission on reading.* Washington, DC: National Academy of Education, Commission on Education and Public Policy.

Ball, E. W., & Blachman, B. A. (1991). Does phoneme awareness training in kindergarten make a difference in early word recognition and developmental spelling? *Reading Research Quarterly, 26,* 49–66.

Blachman, B. A. (2000). Phonological awareness. In M. L. Kamil, P. B. Mosenthal, P. D. Pearson, & R. Barr (Eds.), *Handbook of reading research* (Vol. 3) (pp. 483–502). Mahwah, NJ: Lawrence Erlbaum Associates.

Blachman, B. A., Ball, E., Black, R., & Tangel, D. (1994). Kindergarten teachers develop phoneme awareness in low-income, inner-city classrooms: Does it make a difference? *Reading and Writing: An Interdisciplinary Journal, 6,* 1–17.

Blachman, B. A., Schatschneider, C., Fletcher, J. M., Francis, D. J., Clonan, S. M., Shaywitz, B. A., et al. (2004). Effects of intensive reading remediation for second and third graders and a 1-year follow-up. *Journal of Educational Psychology, 96*(3), 444–461.

Blachman, B. A., Tangel, D. M., Ball, E. W., Black, R., & McGraw, C. K. (1999). Developing phonological awareness and word recognition skills: A two-year intervention with low-income, inner-city children. *Reading and Writing: An Interdisciplinary Journal, 11,* 239–273.

Bradley, L., & Bryant, P. (1983). Categorizing sounds and learning to read: A causal connection. *Nature, 30,* 419–421.

Dickinson, D. K., & Neuman, S. B. (Eds.). (2006). *Handbook of early literacy* (Vol. 2). New York: Guilford Press.

Elkonin, D. B. (1973). U.S.S.R. In J. Downing (Ed.), *Comparative reading* (pp. 551–580). New York: Macmillan.

Fry, E. B., & Kress, J. E. (2006). *The reading teacher's book of lists* (5th ed.). San Francisco: Jossey-Bass.

Hirsch, E. D. (2003, Spring). Reading comprehension requires knowledge—Of words and the world. *American Educator,* 10–29.

Juel, C. (1994). *Learning to read and write in one elementary school.* New York: Springer-Verlag.

Liberman, I. Y., & Shankweiler, D. (1991). Phonology and beginning reading: A tutorial. In L. Rieben & C. A. Perfetti (Eds.), *Learning to read: Basic research and its implications* (pp. 3–17). Mahwah, NJ: Lawrence Erlbaum Associates.

Moats, L. C. (2000). *Speech to print: Language essentials for teachers.* Baltimore: Brookes.

National Institute of Child Health and Human Development. (2000a). *Report of the National Reading Panel: Teaching children to read: An evidence-based assessment of the scientific research literature on reading and its implications for reading instruction* (NIH Publication No. 00–4769). Washington, DC: U.S. Government Printing Office.

National Institute of Child Health and Human Development. (2000b). *Report of the National Reading Panel: Teaching children to read: An evidence-based assessment of the scientific research literature on reading and its implications for reading instruction: Reports of the subgroups* (NIH Publication No. 00–4754). Washington, DC: U.S. Government Printing Office.

Slingerland, B. (1971). *A multi-sensory approach to language for specific language disability children: A guide for primary teachers.* Cambridge, MA: Educators Publishing Service.

Snow, C. E., Burns, M. S., & Griffin, P. (Eds.). (1998). *Preventing reading difficulties in young children.* Washington, DC: National Academy Press.

Stanovich, K. E. (1986). Matthew effects in reading: Some consequences of individual differences in the acquisition of literacy. *Reading Research Quarterly, 21,* 360–407.

Torgesen, J. K. (2005). Recent discoveries from research on remedial interventions for children with dyslexia. In M. Snowling and C. Hulme (Eds.), *The science of reading: A handbook* (pp. 521–537). Oxford, UK: Blackwell.

Walsh, K. (2003, Spring). Basal readers: The lost opportunity to build the knowledge that propels comprehension. *American Educator,* 24–27.

Williams, J. P. (1987). Educational treatments for dyslexia at the elementary and secondary levels. In W. Ellis (Ed.), *Intimacy with language: A forgotten basic in teacher education* (pp. 24–32). Baltimore: Orton Dyslexia Society.

Chapter Seven

FOSTERING EARLY LITERACY DEVELOPMENT

Diane H. Tracey and Lesley Mandel Morrow

Our knowledge of how best to facilitate children's literacy development in schools and at home has grown tremendously. The earliest educational recommendations date back to ancient Greece and the period of Plato (ca. 428–347 B.C.) and Aristotle (384–322 B.C.), who suggested that the mind was like a muscle that needed to be exercised through practice for learning to take place. People believed that learning occurred as a result of associations made in the mind, such as the associations made between items that are similar and those that are opposite, and that these associations needed to be practiced to enhance learning. These concepts, known as the theories of mental discipline and associationism, dominated educational thought throughout ancient times, the Middle Ages, and the European Renaissance. For about 2,000 years, educators emphasized practice as the main route to all educational learning (Gutek, 1972).

In the 1700s, however, a new way of thinking about learning emerged that proved to be extremely influential, particularly in the education of young children. Known as unfoldment theory, this idea suggested that learning unfolds naturally in young children's minds as a result of their curiosity. Educators such as Rousseau (1712–1778), Pestalozzi (1746–1827), and Froebel (1782–1852) seized this idea and began to design programs for young children that emphasized the creation of environments that would stimulate children's natural desire to learn. The contributions of popular educators of the early twentieth century, such as Maria Montessori and John Dewey, extended unfoldment theory and applied it to literacy education. Many current early childhood education programs still reflect this important educational belief.

Beginning in the 1950s, educators began to design alternative educational initiatives that would be more proactive than those based on unfoldment theory. The new orientation, called reading readiness, identified subskills thought to be most highly related to early reading achievement, and then directly taught those subskills in a sequential manner. Skills frequently addressed in reading readiness programs included the following: auditory discrimination of familiar sounds, similar sounds, rhyming words, and sounds of letters; visual discrimination, including color recognition, shape, and letter identification; left-to-right eye progression; visual motor skills, such as cutting on a line with scissors and coloring within the lines; and large motor abilities, such as skipping, hopping, and walking a straight line. While the practice of many of these skills can still be seen in today's classrooms, new research has extended our understanding of the ways in which young children's literacy abilities develop, and, subsequently, has impacted our classroom practices.

In the mid-1960s, ideas regarding the best way to facilitate young children's literacy development changed once again. This change was prompted by the research findings of Durkin (1966), who discovered that children's progress in literacy learning was positively correlated with a variety of previously unrecognized conditions. These included the frequency with which parents read aloud to children at home, the frequency with which parents themselves read, the frequency of conversations about books held in children's homes, the number of books in children's homes, and children's at-home access to writing materials. These conditions, when present, were considered indicators of a rich at-home literacy environment.

CURRENT THOUGHTS REGARDING EARLY LITERACY DEVELOPMENT

Marie Clay (1966) extended Durkin's findings and created emergent literacy theory. In addition to recognizing the importance of a rich at-home literacy environment, emergent literacy theory emphasizes that children's literacy development begins at birth and is an ongoing, lifelong pursuit. Emergent literacy theory suggests that the processes of listening, speaking, reading, and writing are all related and develop concurrently. This theory argues that gains in any one of these literacy processes has a positive effect on the other processes and, similarly, that a deficit in any one area will adversely affect the others.

The central concepts from emergent literacy theory have now been applied to early childhood education classrooms. When these concepts are combined with those from unfoldment theory and with direct instruction, originally associated with reading readiness, a "balanced literacy" program is created. A balanced literacy program is a popular approach to literacy programs for young children.

Balanced literacy programs are ideal for fostering early literacy development in schools. The first way in which programs are balanced is that they address the physical, emotional, social, and cognitive dimensions of all children. For example, a balanced literacy program is sensitive to the fact that young children are not able to be physically still for long periods of time and, as a result, a balanced literacy program includes many active learning experiences during the school day. A balanced literacy program also addresses the emotional needs of young learners by prioritizing the importance of a warm, positive, and nurturing affective climate in the classroom. A balanced literacy program recognizes the importance of social interactions in learning, and works hard to create positive learning communities in schools. Finally, a balanced literacy program creates cognitive experiences for children that are developmentally appropriate.

A balanced literacy program also heavily emphasizes the physical environment of the classroom. The classroom should be designed to support whole-group, small-group, and individual learning experiences. Reflecting ideas about a rich literacy environment, the physical environment of an early childhood classroom should include the following: appropriately sized clustered desks or worktables, and a literacy center including: a rug, rocking chair, pillows, bean bag chairs, stuffed animals, storytelling items, manipulatives, a writing table, and books organized by difficulty and genre and stored in baskets on bookshelves. The classroom would also have an abundance of labels in the room (e.g., "desk," "clock," and "door"), to help children associate printed words and objects, a dramatic play area enhanced by items for reading and writing (e.g., a menu, pad, and pencil within a play restaurant), and learning centers for other academic subjects, such as a science center, a math center, and a social studies center In short, the classroom should be filled with print and opportunities for listening, speaking, reading, and writing.

The curriculum of a balanced, early literacy program addresses the following areas: oral language/vocabulary, phonemic awareness, word identification strategies (including phonics instruction), comprehension, and fluency instruction. Other vital areas addressed are children's texts, motivation, writing, technology, and parent involvement. Each of theses areas is further described below.

Oral Language and Vocabulary Development

Oral language is believed by many to be the foundation for children's reading and writing achievement. Children whose oral language develops easily and at an early age tend to be children who learn to read with ease and success; conversely, when children's oral language is delayed or follows a deviant pattern, children tend to be at risk for reading and writing difficulty (Snow, Burns, & Griffin, 1998). A child who has had a normal oral language history but is experiencing excessive difficulty with early reading tasks may have a reading disability.

There are valuable strategies that teachers and parents can use to facilitate children's oral language and vocabulary development. For example, "scaffolding" is used when adults reduce the difficulty of a conversation so that children can better understand what is being said. "Extensions" are adults' restatements of children's words in grammatically correct sentences. "Topic continuations" are seen when adults provide extra verbal information about a topic to children so that their background knowledge is increased as a result of a conversation. "Open-ended questions" are those that have require more than a one word (Yes of No) response to appropriately answer. "High-level questions" are those that require children to use critical thinking skills to answer (e.g., "Why is using bricks to build a house better than using straw?"). Adults can use all of these strategies during daily conversations and storybook reading to help build children's oral language.

Phonemic Awareness

Another important aspect of early literacy development is phonemic awareness. Phonemic awareness refers to the ability to hear sounds within words. A phoneme is the smallest unit of sound in the English language. For example, the word "boat" has three phonemes since the letters "oa" create a single sound. Children's ability to hear sounds within words is closely related to their ability to match sounds and letters, a skill essential for both reading and writing. Proficiency in phonemic awareness is linked to success in early reading and writing while deficits in this area are linked to reading and writing difficulties. Many researchers believe that a deficit in phonemic awareness processing is the most common cause of reading disability (Stanovich, 2000). The possibility of a phonemic awareness deficit should be investigated in all children displaying early reading and writing problems.

It appears that phonemic awareness skill develops naturally and quite easily in most children. Furthermore, weaknesses in this area appear to be responsive to remedial interventions. Some of the best activities to strengthen children's phonemic awareness are the following: sound matching activities, sound isolation activities, blending activities, sound addition or substitution activities, and segmentation activities (Yopp, 1992). In sound matching activities, children identify words that begin with particular sounds. In sound isolation activities, children listen to a word and are asked to decide if a target sound is at the beginning, middle, or end of the word. In blending activities, children put sounds together to make new words. For example, if a child hears three sounds, c/a/p, she or he would have to blend them together to create the word "cap." In sound addition or substitution activities, the child changes one word to another word by changing single sounds. In segmentation activities, children isolate sounds within a word. Additional ideas for strengthening students' phonemic awareness skills can be found in Yopp and Yopp (2000).

Word Identification Skills

Another essential area for fostering early literacy development is known as word identification skills. Word identification skills are the skills that children use to identify words during the reading process. Word identification skills include the ability to memorize high-frequency sight words, the ability to break words down into their individual sounds (decoding), the ability to break words down according to word families (phonograms), and the ability to break words down using word parts such as prefixes, roots, and suffixes (structural analysis).

High-frequency words are those that occur most often in the English language. Because of their great frequency, there is a high payoff for young children in learning how to read and write these words. For example, according to Fry and Kress (2006), the 25 most common words in the English language make up about one-third of all printed material, and the first 300 words make up about 65 percent of all written material. *The Reading Teacher's Book of Lists* (Fry & Kress, 2006) lists the most common words in the English language in groups of 25. When children master these words, they are able to automatically read them when they come across them in connected text. Reinforcement activities for teaching sight words include making matching pairs of cards for each word and having children play games.

Children also need to decode to be successful with early reading and writing. Decoding instruction teaches children to break down words based on sound-symbol relationships. Decoding instruction begins when children learn the letters of the alphabet and the sounds associated with each letter. It is easy for children to confuse the name of a letter with the sound that a letter makes. Individual letter sounds are often practiced by having children find items in the classroom that begin with a certain sound, cut out pictures from magazines that begin with that sound, and bring in objects from home that begin with that particular sound.

Within classrooms, teachers often create areas, called centers, designed to provide students with opportunities for independent, hands-on learning. One center literacy activity that children often enjoy is sorting objects according to their sounds. Objects that start with a particular letter (e.g., egg, elephant, elf) can be sorted into an "e" container; objects that begin with a different letter (frog, flower, fly) can be sorted into an "f" container. As children get more skilled in sorting objects and sounds, an increasing number of containers can be used, and the activity can be modified for difficulty. One modification is for children to sort objects according to the location of a sound, such as objects that begin with "e," objects that end in "e," and objects that have "e" as their middle sound.

Because English contains complicated sound-symbol relationships (e.g., "ou" can be pronounced several different ways depending on the word), many educators believe that using knowledge of word families to identify words is an easier and quicker route than traditional decoding (Gaskins, 1998). In this approach, after children learn their consonant letter names and corresponding sounds, their instruction moves directly to learning word families. Simple word families are taught first, such as all the words associated with the "at" family (e.g., bat, cat, fat, hat, mat, pat, rat, sat, tat, vat, brat, drat, flat, scat, slat, spat, that). Once students have mastered the "at" family of words, the next family is introduced, for example, the "ap" family. "Bingo" will also work for word family practice. *The Reading Teacher's Book of Lists* (Fry & Kress, 2006) provides a comprehensive presentation of the major and minor word families (also known as phonograms) and the words associated with each family. As children get older, their knowledge of word families can also be used as the key to break down multisyllable words. This approach is known as decoding by analogy and has been found to be effective for both normal and disabled readers (Gaskins, 1998).

Finally, young readers' and writers' word identification skills are strengthened by instruction in the area of structural analysis. Structural analysis teaches students to separate words into their roots, prefixes, and suffixes. According to White, Sowell, and Yanagihara (1989), 9 frequently occurring prefixes account for 75 percent of all prefixed words (un, re, in, dis, en, non, in (into), over, and mis). Similarly, 10 suffixes account for 85 percent of all suffixed words (s/es, ed, ing, ly, er, ion, able, al, y, and ness).

Comprehension

Comprehension is the goal of all reading. It is the ability to understand what one is reading. It is also conceptualized as the reader's ability to construct a message during the reading process. There are many ways that teachers and parents can help improve children's reading comprehension. These ideas are applicable whether a child is reading to an adult or an adult is reading to a child. The ideas can be thought of as conversations that take place before, during, and after the reading experience.

Before reading, children are assisted in talking about the topic of the text. For example, if a story or book is about a fisherman, a conversation about fishing and people who like to fish would be initiated. The professional term for this activity is "activating and building children's schemata." The term schema refers to a child's knowledge base—everything he or she knows about a specific topic; the plural of schema is schemata. When adults build children's schemata, they add new knowledge to children's already existing knowledge base. An important part of the pre-reading conversation is to introduce key vocabulary that is part of the reading text. Other ways to stimulate pre-reading conversations include predicting what the text will be about based on pictures and/or titles and headings.

Once the reading session begins, conversations during reading will help ensure that children fully understand the text that is being read. This occurs when adults stop and ask questions at particularly important and or interesting points in the reading. The most beneficial questions are those that require much language to answer. Examples of beneficial questions are those that ask children to make predictions, provide explanations, and support opinions.

Comprehension is also enhanced by activities completed at the end of a reading lesson. Follow-up activities can be of a broad variety. Popular choices for young children include artistic responses to the text, such as drawing their favorite part or character of the story. Using storytelling props to retell stories has also been shown to increase young children's comprehension of text (Morrow, 2002). Helping children comprehend what they read is an essential part of promoting early literacy development. Activities can be used before, during, and after reading to accomplish this goal.

Fluency

Recently, the importance of building children's reading fluency has gained recognition as an important component of early literacy instruction (National Institute of Child Health and Human Development, 2000). Reading fluency is the ability to read easily, smoothly, and with proper expression. When children do not have adequate fluency, their reading is slow and labored, with an absence of appropriate expression. Listeners often experience disfluent reading as frustrating and painful. Disfluency can often result from a book that is too difficult for students. If a student is making more than 10 errors per 100 words during oral reading, the book is frustrating for the child, and an easier text should be provided. Sometimes children need fluency instruction even when books are appropriate for their reading abilities. Activities that have been shown to increase readers' fluency include the following: paired reading, repeated reading, choral reading, readers' theater, and taped reading. In paired reading, students are put into groups of two and take turns reading to each other. In repeated reading, a student reads a short portion of a text aloud, then the teacher provides feedback, and then the student rereads the text. In choral reading, all students read the text aloud in unison. In readers' theater, students practice reading scripts and then perform their script reading for other, often younger, students. Readers' theater is an enjoyable and meaningful form of repeated reading for young students. In taped reading, students listen to an audio-recorded version of a book or text and then tape-record themselves reading. All of these activities can help to improve students' fluent oral reading.

Text

Another area that is increasingly recognized as important to early reading success is the text from which children read (Menon & Hiebert, 2005). The difficulty level of a text is evaluated by the number of high-frequency words, the number of easily decodable words, the frequency or repetition of words, the predictability of the text, the clarity of picture-text relationships, and the total number of words. Using these indicators, researchers are currently trying to determine optimal ways of writing beginning texts to facilitate early reading development.

At the present, many publishers code texts for young readers according to readability levels or grade levels that they believe reflect a text's difficulty. Teachers maintain a collection of books at varying levels of readability in their classrooms. These books are often sorted by difficulty and coded by using different colored stickers on their bindings and sorting them into baskets by their code. Such a system allows children to easily find and replace books at their ability level.

A general rule of thumb is that for independent reading, children should be able to read 97 percent of the words in a text without errors. Children should be able to read about 95 percent of the words without errors when a text is used for instructional purposes with help from the teacher. Children should not be given a text in which they cannot read at least 90 percent of the words; such books may be too difficult for them and may lead to frustration and lower motivation. An exception to these guidelines may be made if a child is highly motivated to read about a particular area due to a high level of interest and/or extensive background knowledge on the topic. In cases such as these, providing students with challenging texts may work very well. In general, however, providing children with the right level of text for independent reading and instruction is one of the keys to successful early reading.

Teachers of early literacy often keep a large collection of texts other than beginning-level books in their classroom libraries. These books may be on a wide variety of topics and represent a wide variety of reading levels. Teachers include books that they can read aloud to students to build their vocabulary and background knowledge. Children frequently want to look at these books themselves after their teachers have read them to the class. Teachers also provide books on thematic topics, favorite authors, and poetry. Picture books, word books, and alphabet books are also essential additions to young children's classrooms.

Motivation

Children's motivation to read is another condition that affects early reading success. Four variables have repeatedly been shown to be positively associated with children's motivation to read: choice, challenge, social collaboration, and success (Morrow, 2001). Children are most motivated to read when they have choices about what they will read, when they will read, and how they will respond to reading material. While teachers cannot always give children choices in these areas, they can sometimes give children choices. The use of a literacy center, an area of the classroom with many activities for independent reading and writing, is highly conducive to promoting student choice. When children work in a literacy center, they can usually decide which books they will read and in which order. They can also often choose between literacy activities, such as retelling a story with props, flannel board pieces, or puppets, drawing a favorite part of a story, or playing with literacy-oriented games. Giving children literacy choices helps them identify their reading interests and empowers them as learners.

Challenge is also positively related to reading success. Challenge refers to the difficulty level of any given task. A child's motivation is increased when reading tasks are at the correct level of difficulty. If tasks are too easy, children will be bored Similarly, if tasks are too difficult, students will be frustrated, which also lowers their reading motivation. Since students in any given classroom are at many different levels of reading development, teachers work hard to differentiate activities for learners. With careful planning, the use of a literacy center is highly compatible with differentiating reading tasks for students of different reading abilities.

Social collaboration also contributes to students' motivation to read. Social collaboration refers to activities in which students work together. Most children intrinsically enjoy being together, and research has shown that giving them opportunities to be together will lead to improved learning outcomes (Morrow, 2002) Again, the literacy center is ideal for providing opportunities for social collaboration. Students can read in pairs, retell stories together, and play games that lead to literacy growth.

Success is the fourth condition associated with reading motivation. Success refers to the positive sense of accomplishment that children have at the completion of a task. When children believe that they have completed a task well, they have a feeling of success. Exemplary teachers work hard to design learning experiences in which all children experience success.

Writing

Children's writing ability is closely related to their reading ability. Children use writing to express their ideas and to explore the relationships between sounds and letters. Writing can be incorporated into exemplary early literacy programs in at least three ways—traditional, teacher-directed activities; activities in a writing center; and the use of writing materials placed at other centers in the classroom.

Teacher-directed writing activities can take place in whole-class and small-group settings. Teachers often model writing and engage the class in shared writing activities during the whole-class morning meeting. A teacher can say and write a message while children watch, or transcribe sentences that children orally generate. Teachers also provide whole-class writing instruction to students to help them learn to print the alphabet, write sentences and paragraphs, and use punctuation. Writing instruction can also take place in small groups. Small-group writing instruction is ideal for meeting the differentiated needs of students in a classroom.

The establishment of a writing center is an enjoyable and important way to build young children's writing skills. Writing centers are places in the classroom that are equipped with an assortment of writing implements, such as pencils, colored pencils, markers, crayons, and pens, and different sizes and colors of paper or paper that is cut in special ways including shapes, animals, fruits, and flowers. Block, sponge, and stamp letters that can be used for printing enhance a writing center, as do a computer and a typewriter. Pictures can be used to promote writing ideas, and an index box of high-frequency words helps children learn to spell correctly when writing. A mailbox for each child in the class encourages children to write to each other. Designing activities that facilitate social collaboration at the writing center stimulates children's desire to engage in writing.

Adding writing materials to centers other than the writing center also builds children's writing skills. At the early childhood level, it is especially important to add writing materials to the dramatic play and block areas since young children learn through play. A dramatic play area can include a restaurant with menus and pads and pencils for taking customers' orders. Grocery items, coupons, materials to write a shopping list, play money, and a cash register will lead to playing store. Another idea is to include stuffed animals, a stethoscope, and a prescription pad for a pretend veterinarian's office. Children using writing centers may use pencils, crayons, and index cards to create street and traffic signs. In all of these cases, valuable learning about writing takes place as children interact in play.

Technology

Young children also "play" with technology. Like dramatic play with literacy props, play with technology can also lead to significant literacy learning (Tracey & Young, in press). Opportunities to use technology with young children are found at Internet sites, through software programs, and through the inclusion of electronic books in the classroom. Well-equipped early childhood classrooms have one or more Internet-connected computers for children's use, usually found at the classroom computer center. Peripherals such as a printer, scanner, digital camera, and headsets enhance a teacher's ability to optimally integrate the use of technology in the classroom. Software for very young children (ages two and up) is available to teach children to use a computer mouse, and thereafter enable them to embark on a multimedia journey guaranteed to thrill learners of every age and ability level.

Technology offers teachers another tool through which they can differentiate their literacy instruction. Many software programs are specifically designed to identify students' correct level of educational need, offering increasingly difficult activities for students who succeed at tasks, while providing additional practice for students who are not achieving mastery of a skill. Technology also offers students many learning scaffolds. For example, when reading electronic books, students can click on a word that they don't know and have the computer pronounce the word for them or provide a definition. In fact, if children choose, many electronic books can be read completely aloud to them as the text is highlighted on the computer screen. In one study, kindergartners' independent reading of electronic books was found to be as effective as having parents read traditional storybooks to them (de Jong & Bus, 2004). The use of electronic books in early childhood classrooms may prove to be an extremely valuable tool for literacy development, especially for those whose parents are not able to read to them in English.

Understanding and Promoting Home-School Connections

In addition to the many components of effective literacy programs described above, exemplary programs include strong parent involvement. Parent involvement improves children's academic performance at all school ages, particularly in the area of literacy (Rasinski & Stevenson, 2005). Traditional parent involvement programs provide information to parents about how to interact with their children in ways that have been proven to be educationally effective. These programs are known as transmission programs, because the school transmits information to parents. In contrast, two-way communication programs are more egalitarian in design and seek to create equal partnerships between parents and teachers. These programs seek to elicit information from parents about their children and use that information to help the teacher individualize instruction for his or her students.

A variety of programs have been created to strengthen home-school connections in the language arts. For example, in the "Parents as Partners Program," parents are taught how to improve the quality of at-home storybook reading through a videotape program. In "Three for the Road," teachers send home backpacks with a variety of literacy items related to storybooks, and parents use the books and props to retell stories and extend comprehension. In the "Parents Writing to Children" program, parents came to school and, over a period of 10 weeks, created diaries, memory books, and photo journals with their children. In "Capturing Family Stories," students collected oral retellings, audio- and videotaped recordings, and written family stories from parents in response to prompts such as, "Tell your child about the neighborhood where you lived when you were a child," or "Tell your child about a favorite relative you had when you were young."

Other ideas include encouraging parents to sign up as classroom helpers and/or guest readers. Parents can also be encouraged to come to school to share special skills with children, skills such as knitting, crocheting, or cooking. Young children also like to learn about parents' jobs, especially when parents can bring along some tools of the trade such as plumbing, dental, or gardening equipment. Another event that is very motivating for children and parents is a "pajama party," in which parents, teachers, and children come to school in the evening to share books and popcorn on sleeping bags and blankets. All of these ideas stimulate meaningful parent-child conversations that ultimately contribute to children's literacy development.

IMPLEMENTING EXEMPLARY EARLY LITERACY PROGRAMS

To illustrate the ways in which the literacy components described above are integrated into an exemplary early literacy program, a case study of a kindergarten teacher is highlighted below.

Background Information

Kim Miller is a fifth-year, 1st-grade teacher who recently finished her master's degree in education with a specialization in reading. She works in a northeastern, inner-city, low-income school district in which approximately 65 percent of the children qualify for free and reduced-cost lunches. This case study aims to capture Ms. Miller's classroom in March, after her students have had time to master the classroom routines. At this point in the year she has 20 students in her classroom—14 African American students, four Hispanic students, and two European American students. She has a part-time aide to assist her three mornings a week, and two parent volunteers, each of whom comes to class approximately once a week.

Planning/Standards

Ms. Miller is a strong believer in the importance of planning in effective instruction. Accordingly, she completes educational plans at four levels: yearly, monthly/thematically, weekly, and daily. Her yearly plans are based on the standards established by the state in which she works. She uses these standards to make sure her instructional plans cover all of the essential skills that kindergartners need to learn. Ms. Miller also plans at the monthly level. Each month she uses a different theme, to integrate the skills that children need to master with meaningful and interesting content. Ms. Miller's monthly thematic units are the following: *people in our community, transportation, zoo animals, our bodies, under the ocean, dinosaurs, all about families, cultures of the world, gardening for everyone, and summer fun.* Ms. Miller uses read-aloud books and center activities based on each thematic topic to make learning fun and interesting throughout the year. Focusing on thematic content also helps her students increase their general knowledge of the world and their vocabularies. Ms. Miller stores the materials, books, and lesson plans for each unit in large, separate, see-through plastic boxes, and adds to each unit every year.

Once Ms. Miller knows the skills and thematic topics that she will be teaching during the year, she creates weekly lesson plans for her supervisor. These plans ensure that she is optimally using her instructional time in each academic subject area as well as her "specials"—art, music, physical education, library, and the computer lab. Finally, Ms. Miller creates daily lesson plans based on the needs of the whole child. For example, knowing that young children learn best when active and social, she structures many learning experiences accordingly. She also limits the length of time that her students need to sit still and listen. Ms. Miller's daily lesson plans provide time for whole-group, small-group, and individual activities, and she carefully sequences active and quiet times throughout the day. Ms. Miller typically prepares her yearly and monthly/thematic plans prior to the start of the school year. She completes her weekly plans prior to the start of each week and her daily plans each night before school.

Physical Environment

Ms. Miller is also a strong proponent of the importance of the physical environment in learning. Since this case study was done in March, the class was studying the *all about families* theme. In addition to the standard classroom items described earlier in this chapter, Ms. Miller added thematically related items to all of her centers. The literacy center had a basket of books about families, two posters about families, and two boxes of story retelling props, one for the book *All about Frances* and the other for the book *Frog and Toad.* In the writing center, children were working on making posters about themselves and their families. Ms. Miller was using her classroom aide and parent volunteers to assist the students with this project. Several completed posters were hung as examples. Ms. Miller had added a dollhouse with family member dolls and a playhouse with props to the dramatic play area. The science center had a family of gerbils that the children cared for and studied. The social studies center had picture books showing families from around the world, and also magazines using which the children had to cut out and paste pictures of people they believed were family members. The math center had several sets of teacher-made index cards. There was a pairing game in which picture cards showing different families had to be matched, and a sequencing activity in which picture cards showing different family members had to be sorted by height. Each sets of index cards was a different color to help the children keep them organized.

Assessment

Ms. Miller believes that exemplary literacy instruction is assessment driven. She is aware that all children come to school possessing a wide range of skill levels, and feels that it is her job to assess students' skill level, facilitate their learning, and track their progress. She also believes that the best way to evaluate children's abilities is through the use of multiple assessment tools and methods. Ms. Miller uses quarterly tests to assess items such as phonemic awareness, letter identification, and knowledge of letter-sound correspondences. She also completes a running record on each child, each month, to track word identification, vocabulary, and comprehension skills. During daily instruction, she takes informal, anecdotal notes on small, blank stickers that are dated and then added to students' files.

To keep track of assessments, Ms. Miller keeps an expandable file folder/portfolio for each of her students. The folders have 10 compartments each—one for each month of the year. Ms. Miller files formal tests, running records, anecdotal notes, sample work assignments, and report cards, and uses these folders for parent-teacher conferences and to complete report cards. At the end of the school year, she passes the portfolios to the 1st-grade teachers, who use them to learn about their incoming students.

The Language Arts Block

Each day, as required by her school district, Ms. Miller devotes a 90-minute block of time to language arts. The 90-minute block is divided into three segments: a 20-minute, whole-class mini-lesson, a one-hour center/small-group reading time, and a final 10-minute, whole-class closing time.

The 20-minute, whole-class mini-lesson is designed to reinforce the sense of the entire class comprising a single learning community. In the mini-lesson, Ms. Miller presents a lesson from the kindergarten basal series. The lesson may be related to oral language/vocabulary, phonemic awareness, word identification, comprehension, fluency, and so forth. The lesson is usually designed to present a new concept and reinforce already learned concepts. It typically involves teacher-directed instruction, modeling, and shared reading experiences. Ms. Miller usually follows the teachers' guide when presenting these lessons, and she observes how students respond to the material. She encourages students' participation and questions during the lesson.

At the conclusion of the mini-lesson, Ms. Miller transitions the students to center time by reviewing the activities that the children need to complete at each of the centers. By this time of the school year, Ms. Miller's students are very familiar with her center management system. They know that Ms. Miller's popsicle-stick chart shows the three centers that they must visit that day (not all children will go to the same centers each day), and that they must put their completed work in the center basket when they are done. They know that they are to "read" a book at their desk if they finish their center work before the bell rings. They also know that going to centers is a privilege, and that if they are poorly behaved at a center they will need to return to their seat for the rest of center time that day. Whenever possible, Ms. Miller uses a classroom aide or parent volunteer to help supervise center time. Although the students love this hour of the day, they are still very young and do not always have the independence and self-regulation necessary to stay on task. Ms. Miller helps them develop these strengths by sending the students with the least amount of self-regulation to activities using as blocks, Lego items, computers, and the dramatic play areas. Because these activities are so intrinsically engaging, even the least mature students are often able to succeed in staying on task. As these children's self-regulation matures, Ms. Miller gradually moves them to more academically challenging tasks.

As students begin their center work, Ms. Miller calls a small group of students for a reading lesson. The students have been grouped based on their developing skills. Grouping students for a portion of the literacy block enables Ms. Miller to provide instruction and reading materials that are ideally suited for the children's needs. The small-group setting also facilitates greater student engagement and helps Ms. Miller more easily keep track of students' progress. The small-group lesson takes approximately 20 minutes. During this time, Ms. Miller introduces or reviews a skill that is developmentally appropriate for the students and helps the students use the skill during the reading of connected text. Usually an extension activity from the small group is assigned for homework, such as rereading a story at home. After 20 minutes of instruction, a second small reading group is called. On most days, Ms. Miller calls two to three reading groups and completes a running record on one child at the end of each group. It is important to note that Ms. Miller does not start to use small reading groups until October of each academic year. She gives the students the full month of September to learn the center management system in her presence before she expects them to be able to independently use the centers. Ms. Miller also uses the extra time in September to collect information that will better help her form her reading groups. Although students can and should be moved from group to group throughout the school year depending on their rate of progress, it is always important to initially group the students as accurately as possible.

At the conclusion of center time, Ms. Miller reconvenes the class in a whole group. She asks the students to report on their activities—both successes and challenges. Ms. Miller uses the closure time to reinforce lessons learned that day—academic, social, and emotional. She strives to have students leave the language arts block with a sense of accomplishment and success as well as with ideas for how the time can be used even more productively the next day.

Daily Schedule

Below is Ms. Miller's daily plan for a school day in March:

8:45–9:00. Starting the day. Children arrive at school and put their belongings in their cubbies. They move their name cards into the "here" slot on the attendance board and begin to draw and write in their personal journals. Children who have jobs that week, such as watering the plans and feeding the gerbils, complete their jobs.

9:00–9:20. Language Arts Block: Mini-Lesson. Ms. Miller calls the students to the rug for a morning meeting and a brief language arts lesson. The students review the calendar and a message the teacher has written to the students on a large pad. This message is called the "morning message." Today's lesson focuses on compound words (multisyllable words made up of smaller words, such as "doghouse" and "backyard").

9:20–10:20. Language Arts Block: Center-Time/Small-Group Reading Lessons. Ms. Miller reviews the tasks to be completed at each center and draws students' attention to the chart illustrating the centers that children are to visit that day. She reminds the students to place their completed center work in the basket at each center and that if they finish their work early they are to take a book to their desk. She rings a bell, indicating that the students are to go to their first center, and calls her first guided reading group. After 20 minutes, she rings the bell again, indicating that students are to proceed to their next center, and calls a second reading group. After 20 more minutes, this routine is repeated once more.

10:20–10:30. Language Arts Block: Closing. Ms. Miller discusses the language arts block with the students, with the goal of helping the students become more aware of the ways in which they worked independently in the classroom. She chooses several students who did exceptionally well that morning and praises their accomplishments in front of the whole class. She asks for recommendations as to ways the language arts block could be improved for the next day.

10:30–10:45. Morning Snack. Children eat their morning snack while listening to quiet music. Ms. Miller praises those children who have brought nutrition-rich snacks to school.

10:45–11:30. Math. A 15-minute teacher-directed math lesson is followed by a 25-minute activity-based math experience. The last five minutes of the period are used to review the presented concept.

11:30–12:00. Lunch.

12:00–12:30. Recess.

12:30–12:45. Read Aloud. Ms. Miller reads a story connected to the *all about families* theme.

12:45–1:30. Special (Art, Music, Library, etc.).

1:30–2:15. Science or Social Studies. A 15-minute teacher-directed science lesson is followed by a 25-minute activity-based science experience. The last five minutes of the period are used to review the presented concept.

2:15–2:30. Closing the day. Students gather their items and prepare for home. Ms. Miller reminds the students of their homework and highlights the next day's activities.

CONCLUSION

Early literacy development encompasses children's listening, speaking, reading, and writing skills. Research has shown that these abilities develop concurrently and in an integrated manner. When one area is strengthened, it usually has a positive effect on other areas. When one area is impaired, problems in the other literacy skills are likely.

This chapter has presented a wide perspective of the areas that need to be addressed to foster children's early literacy development. These include the concepts of emergent and balanced literacy, addressing the needs of the whole child, creating literacy rich environments, oral language, vocabulary, phonemic awareness, word identification, comprehension, fluency, text, writing, motivation, technology, and parent involvement. Ideas for implementing an exemplary literacy program in the classroom have been presented. This chapter has included a broad range of information on fostering early literacy; further reading (including the sources in the references) will provide a deeper understanding of associated topics and issues.

REFERENCES

Clay, M. M. (1966). *Emergent reading behavior.* Unpublished doctoral dissertation, University of Auckland, New Zealand.

de Jong, M. T., & Bus, A. G. (2004). The efficacy of electronic books in fostering kindergarten children's emergent story understanding. *Reading Research Quarterly, 39*(4), 378–393.

Durkin, D. (1966). *Children who read early.* New York: Teachers College Press.

Fry, E. B., & Kress, J. E. (2006). *The Reading teacher's book of lists* (5th ed). San Francisco: Jossey-Bass.

Gaskins, I. W. (1998). A beginning literacy program for at-risk and delayed readers. In J. L. Metsala & L. C. Ehri (Eds.), *Word recognition in beginning literacy* (pp. 209–232). Mahwah, NJ: Lawrence Erlbaum Associates.

Gutek, G. L. (1972). *A history of the western educational experience.* Prospect Heights, IL: Waveland Press.

Menon, S., & Hiebert, E. H. (2005). A comparison of first graders' reading with little books or literature-based basal anthologies. *Reading Research Quarterly, 40*(1), 12–38.

Morrow, L. M. (2001). *Literacy development in the early years: Helping children read and write* (4th ed.). Boston: Allyn & Bacon.

Morrow, L. M. (2002). *The literacy center: Contexts for reading and writing* (2nd ed.). Portland, ME: Stenhouse.

National Institute of Child Health and Human Development. (2000). *Report of the National Reading Panel: Teaching children to read: An evidence-based assessment of the scientific research literature on reading and its implications for reading instruction* (NIH Publication No. 00–4769). Washington, DC: U.S. Government Printing Office.

Rasinski, T., & Stevenson, B. (2005). The effects of Fast Start Reading, a fluency-based home involvement reading program, on the reading achievement of beginning readers. *Reading Psychology, 26,* 109–125.

Snow, C. E., Burns, M. S., & Griffin, P. (Eds.). (1998). *Preventing reading difficulties in young children.* Washington, DC: National Academy Press.

Stanovich, K. E. (Ed.). (2000). *Progress in understanding reading: Scientific foundations and new frontiers.* New York: Guilford Press.

Tracey, D. H., & Young, J. W. (in press). Technology and early literacy: The impact of an integrated learning system on high-risk kindergartners' achievement. *Reading Psychology: An International Quarterly.*

White, T., Sowell, J., & Yanagihara, A. (1989). Teaching elementary students to use word part clues. *The Reading Teacher, 42,* 302–308.

Yopp, H. K. (1992). Developing phonemic awareness in young children. *The Reading Teacher, 45*(9), 696–703.

Yopp, H. K., & Yopp, R. H. (2000). Supporting phonemic awareness development in the classroom. *The Reading Teacher, 54*(2), 130–143.

Chapter Eight

READING ALOUD WITH YOUNG CHILDREN

Lee Galda and Lauren Aimonette Liang

Reading aloud from well-written books is one of the best gifts that an adult can give to a child. This common wisdom has been part of the thinking of parents, teachers, and policy makers for many years. The publication of *Becoming a Nation of Readers* (Anderson, Hiebert, Scott, & Wilkinson, 1985), more than 30 years ago, supported this thinking with the claim that "the single most important activity for building the knowledge required for eventual success in reading is reading aloud to children" (p. 23), and that "there is no substitute for a teacher who reads children good stories. It whets the appetite of children for reading and provides a model of skillful oral reading. It is a practice that should continue throughout the grades" (p. 51). Since then, we have learned a great deal about how reading aloud might affect children's literacy development.

Reading aloud often, although certainly not always, begins at home. It also occurs in preschool and early elementary grade classrooms. Although these contexts differ, they all demonstrate the role of reading aloud in children's development of literacy. For example, there are many reports of positive connections between being read to and development as readers and writers (e.g. Baghban, 1984). In the mid-1960s, Durkin (1966) found that children who learned to read before school entrance were read to and had someone to answer their questions. Twenty years later, Wells (1986) followed over a hundred children from just after their first birthday until school entrance, finding a clear connection between the early experience of listening to stories and later achievement, and emphasizing the importance of the conversations that surrounded reading aloud. Heath (1982) looked closely at how parents read to children in different ethnic and socioeconomic groups and how different reading/discussion styles matched the demands of school. Varied cultural practices influence children's literary experiences at home and have different effects on their success at school. What happens at school also has a major impact on the development of literacy. Cochran-Smith (1984) described in detail how teachers' actions construct the ways in which children listen and respond to books read aloud.

At the same time, other studies were beginning to indicate that the type of text that was being read aloud was also important (e.g., Pellegrini, Brody, & Sigel, 1985). From these and other early studies, it was clear that any exploration of reading aloud to children must also include consideration of the text, the way in which it is read, the talk that surrounds the read aloud, and the context in which it occurs.

Literacy researchers now have a more detailed knowledge of how reading aloud to children influences their knowledge of and attitudes toward reading. We have begun to understand the effects of different *ways* of reading aloud, and of the *contexts* in which reading occurs. We know that the *kinds of books* that are read are important. We also realize the importance of *the talk* that surrounds reading aloud in the development of literacy and literate behavior. Although reading aloud is only one of many experiences that are important for literate development, most scholars consider it an important part of a child's early experience (see van Kleeck, Stahl, & Bauer, 2003). Perhaps most important, most scholars now acknowledge the complexity of what might seem a simple act—reading to a child.

For better or for worse, today's schools require that students quickly develop the ability to read and understand text. While our ideas about text are expanding to include the many new types of text that technological advances have provided for us, such as Web sites, computer games, film, and e-mail, school is still about books. Reading aloud allows children access to the world of books. For children not yet reading fluently on their own, reading aloud enables them to share the riches that books have to offer, to have a broad range of experiences, and to develop resources upon which to draw as they continue to learn about their worlds. As children develop cognitively, they link new information with what they already know. If they have listened to a number of books, they have in their repertoire many more experiences from which to draw than they would have without books. For example, children who have never left the city they live in can understand what it is like to live in the country by listening to books, and their rural counterparts can understand city life by the same means. By listening to books, children can explore the world they live in through the many excellent nonfiction and fiction titles available to them. As they listen, they come to understand how the world works. They can visit the zoo, ride on a train, watch a skyscraper being built, sleep by a campfire, make a new friend. A piece of nonfiction might explain a natural phenomenon, explore a familiar social routine, or describe a place such as a farm or a post office. A story might explore feelings or introduce new experiences. A poem presents new ways of thinking about the world. Experience with different kinds of books opens new horizons for children.

Reading aloud to children also helps children learn what to do with books, both physically and cognitively. Immersion in the world of books helps children develop basic understandings about books and reading in much the same way that they learn about language—through interactions with other readers. Children learn about books by seeing what others do with books, by being read to and talking about what they are doing. Children who are read to learn how to be physically comfortable with books—how to hold them, how to turn the pages. They will often "read" to toys, pets, and other children long before they can actually decode the words on the page, demonstrating their skill and pleasure. Children who are read to also learn to view reading as a positive experience. Reading aloud is a special time between caregiver and child, or between teacher and children, a time when they share the experience of a book. As they listen to and discuss books with other readers, children learn the ways in which we think and talk about books (van Kleeck, Alexander, Virgil, & Templeton, 1996). In these discussions, children learn to think beyond the book, to make inferences and judgments about what they read, to think about books in terms of what they know and what they are learning. They try out their own ideas and listen to the ideas of others, expanding their understandings of the book they have heard, just as they are expanding their understandings of the world. They also learn about how written language works.

When young children are read to at home or at school, they develop important knowledge about how print works. They learn, for instance, that books are read (in English) from front to back, top to bottom, left to right—the principle of directionality that is important in early reading development (Clay, 1979). They learn to distinguish words on a page by following along in books as others read to them, and asking questions about how print functions. A three-year-old who asks, "What that white space for, Mommy?" is becoming aware of the concept of word and the function of white spaces, something essential to learning how to read. The children who ask about white spaces will soon be asking the oral reader to point out specific words—Where it say elephant?—as they solidify their understanding that print carries meaning. Some research suggests that being able to point to individual words as they are being read, something that many adult readers encourage children to do, enhances children's ability to recognize words, an important skill for learning to read. Children also begin to notice punctuation marks, indentations, all of the conventions of print, as they follow along with the oral reader. These understandings about the conventions of print are a foundation for learning to read.

Children who are read to develop a sense of the kind of language and literary structures found in stories, poems, and nonfiction. The two-year-old who hands her mother a storybook while saying, "Read me," yet says, "Sing me," when she chooses a poetry book has a clear understanding of the differences in the language of story and poem. Children who are read to before they can read themselves develop ideas about how literature works, ideas that they can draw on as they learn to read and encounter new texts. Hearing storybooks read aloud, for example, helps children develop their understanding of narrative language and story structure, as well as the differences between oral and written language (Smith, 1978). Children who are read to also develop an understanding of abstract or decontextualized language, the kind of language that is necessary for success in school (Dickinson, DeTemple, Hirschler, & Smith, 1992; Olson, 1977; Snow & Ninio, 1986). Books are created from language that refers to things and ideas that exist in our minds, rather than referring to actual things that we can see, taste, touch, hear, or smell. This language experience is quite different from the contextualized oral language that surrounds children. Thus the language of books introduces children to the use of abstract language.

More experience with varied books also develops a better sense of how texts can be organized, and this, in turn, makes it easier to predict and understand new texts. Listening to stories helps children understand that plots are usually sequential, occurring over time. Listening to poetry helps children understand that poems, unless narrative, are different from stories, play with sound by using rhythm, rhyme, alliteration, and onomatopoeia, and are brief capsules of new and interesting feelings. Listening to nonfiction helps children learn that informational texts usually provide details that lead up to a larger idea. When these books are picture books, they also help children learn that information can come from both words and pictures, and that the two are related. All of this often tacit knowledge helps children understand new texts as they encounter them, either by listening or by reading themselves.

Children who are read to also develop their vocabulary and their knowledge of the possibilities of language structure, or syntax, even as they are developing their concept of the word (Morrow & Gambrell, 2000). Written language, especially the carefully crafted language found in the best books for children, is infinitely more varied than oral language, and offers a variety of language models for children to try on as their own. The child who marches around home or classroom declaring, "I trust that is not a rat!" is using Beatrix Potter's (1906) words in his own way. While vocabulary is certainly developed through other experiences, children who are read to a lot have larger vocabularies than do those who have less extensive experiences with books. Repeated storybook readings increase vocabulary for young children (Morrow & Brittain, 2003), especially when reading is accompanied by talking about the words found in books. Talk about books that includes talk about words and activities that require the use of new words result in increases in vocabulary development in preschool children (Senechal, LeFevre, Thomas, & Daley, 1998). Encountering new and interesting words in books, learning to notice and savor them, and having opportunities to use them in meaningful ways, gives children the resources and the tools to become facile language users.

One of the greatest powers of reading aloud may be its ability to motivate children to engage in the world of print. We know that young children who were read aloud to at home often come to school with a strong desire to learn to read. Children who are read to learn at an early age that books can provide information and pleasure. These children seek out exciting stories, interesting information, and compelling poems. Reading aloud can help motivate children to engage in the important task of learning to read, and to participate in literary discussions and activities that promote higher-order thinking and deeper comprehension of text. In the many studies examining the relationships between reading aloud and literacy development, successful early reading (reading before starting school) occurs most often in children who are read aloud to (Clark, 1984).

Beyond the home environment, reading aloud in school leads to greater motivation to read and subsequent, successful literacy development. Listening to books read aloud led to increased levels of motivation for and interest in reading in at-risk students, more appropriate book selections, greater engagement during reading, and higher reading competency in fluency and comprehension (Wood & Salvetti, 2001). Several similar research studies in the 1990s found that students in classrooms where daily read alouds took place scored better on various measures of decoding ability, vocabulary, and comprehension than students in classrooms without read alouds (e.g., Bus, van Ijzendoorn, & Pellegrini, 1995; Senechal, Thomas, & Monker, 1995). While being read aloud to is not the only experience that contributes to children's literacy development, for most children it does make a difference (Teale, 2003).

It has become increasingly clear, however, that it is not simply the reading of books to children that is important for literacy development, but rather the combination of reading aloud and talking about books with children. Reading aloud to children, either individuals or groups, is a social experience. When a text is read aloud, it can then be commented on, before, during, or after the reading, as reader and listener(s) share the experience of the book. This provides opportunities for talking about books that often lead to increased linguistic development, comprehension of the text, higher-order thinking about the content, and an ability in children to think about themselves and others as readers. The positive experience of sharing in a book with someone becomes a motivating factor for children to explore other books together.

There has been considerable research on the sorts of interactions and discussions children and adults have when engaging in a read aloud, as shared discussion around a text is often a natural part of reading aloud. Discussions and related activities, such as role playing, retelling, and predicting, before, during, and after story reading has been found to enable children to better integrate the information in the story. Sharing personal reactions, relating concepts to other texts and experiences, and extending information are all important parts of discussion around story read alouds. Talk that goes beyond the information given in a book, in which reader and listener make predictions, analyze information, talk about meanings of words, and make connections between the book and the listener's experiences with the world and with other books, has a positive influence on their literacy development (DeTemple & Snow, 2003). Conversations that are marked by a high level of interaction between parent or teacher and children and that promote analytic talk (about words, ideas, connections, for example) result in increased positive outcomes for children's literacy skills (Reese, Cox, Harte, & McAnally, 2003).

The interactive nature of the read aloud and discussion helps to engage students in the text and often motivates them to more actively construct meaning (Klesius & Griffith, 1996). The connections to life and other books that children made in the classroom that Cochran-Smith (1984) focused on, and that children who are frequently read to make spontaneously, are evidence of this active construction. For example, a five-year-old who was adjusting to life in a new city drew upon her literary experience when she saw an old, vine-covered building and asked, "Mommy, are we in Paris?" She had, of course, been listening to Bemelmans' (1962) *Madeline.*

The conversation that surrounds reading aloud, then, is a crucial element in the effectiveness of reading aloud, both at home and at school. These conversations, or good discussions, certainly vary widely, developing in complexity as children develop in their cognitive ability. Generally they are marked by adult support, or scaffolding, as parents and teachers provide the structures that enable children to successfully connect with the book and participate in the discussion. Over the years, research has documented the many different ways that parents and teachers do this, varying according to the particular book and the individual child (van Kleeck, Stahl, & Bauer, 2003). In classrooms in which book talk is an essential part of the literacy program, this talk is marked by an engaged exploration of the world of the book, an intense interest in and concentration on the issues and ideas that the book raises, and multiple connections between the world of the book and the worlds of the child (Roser & Martinez, 1995).

Good conversations about books in school are marked by extensive preparation for discussions on the part of the teacher. Knowing the focal book well and preparing questions or activities that will encourage children to spend time thinking about the book set the foundation for fruitful talk. Engaging in true conversations, as opposed to asking questions to test children's knowledge, is also essential. Conversations are opportunities to discover what others think, and thus require thoughtful responses. Intense listening as children are talking is essential, as this enables teachers to build on ideas, support developing thoughts, and clear up misconceptions. Teacher modeling of ways of thinking and talking about books offers children effective strategies. Many successful teachers, for example, help children make connections between what is in the book and their own lives, helping them learn that the ideas in books have relevance in the real world and can be understood in relation to what children know and do (Galda, Rayburn, & Stanzi, 2000). They encourage children to build on their own and others' speculation and comments, to combine their insights and ideas, and to return to the book to assess the ideas that they develop.

Even very young children demonstrate a rather sophisticated understanding of the opportunities that hearing a book read aloud can provide. In a series of studies of young children's comments about picture books during read-aloud sessions in school, Sipe (in press) documented how kindergarten and 1st-grade children responded analytically, that is, made narrative meaning, analyzed the book as a cultural artifact, analyzed the language of the text and the illustrations, and analyzed the relationship between fiction and reality. They also linked books to other books, compared the book to their own lives, and entered into the world of the book. The responses of these children also indicated their growing understanding of how texts work, and their engagement during read alouds.

While many students respond positively when discussing a shared read aloud, sometimes young listeners will offer negative comments about the story, complaining about certain elements (Sipe & McGuire, 2006). It is important that parents and educators remember that these seemingly negative comments are evidence that the child is engaged with the story and attempting to make meaning of it. These early critiques are not a negative reaction to reading but rather the early development of critical literacy, and evidence that the child is likely beginning to engage in higher-order thinking about the text; they are signs of a motivated listener.

Active participation by children before, during, and after a read aloud is key. When adults engage children in talk and activities about the words and structures of books, children learn vocabulary, grammar, and a sense of the possibilities of language. When engaged in a consideration of illustrations and text, children learn how picture books work and develop their visual literacy skills. And when drawing upon prior knowledge and experience or linking and applying new ideas to prior knowledge and experience, children are learning very basic, crucial comprehension strategies. These kinds of active participation are, of course, predicated on a safe and supportive atmosphere that is established by the adult reader. New ideas and understandings flourish best in contexts in which children feel comfortable. They also flourish best when the books that are being read are outstanding examples of the many wonderful books that are published for young children each year.

Just as how adults talk with children about the books they read together makes a difference in what occurs during a read aloud, so does the book itself. We know that different genres, or types, of books provide different opportunities for children at various points in their development. Generally, nonfiction books offer children specialized vocabulary and concepts, and often generate more child participation in discussion of these books with parents or caregivers. On the other hand, storybooks offer children the opportunity to learn about story structure and to make inferences about characters' motivation, for example. The familiarity of the book being read also seems to change the dynamic of the interaction between parent and child, with children taking on a more active role the more familiar the book is, even as discussion tapers off with familiarity. Finally, the complexity of a book's language also influences the interaction that surrounds book reading, as it relates to a child's cognitive development (van Kleeck, 2003).

It is important that we choose books that will engage children, provide wonderful language models, and expand their literary understanding. Reading from outstanding examples of all types of literature—realistic fiction, historical fiction, fantasy, science fiction, folklore, poetry, biography, and nonfiction—helps shape children's literary taste. Most of the books that young children experience during read alouds are picture books, that special genre that combines verbal and visual art. Picture books may be realistic or fantasy, contemporary or historical, fiction, nonfiction, or poetry, but all are marked by a combination of words (if present) and illustrations that, together, create a template for meaning making. Just as it is important for the language to be rich, it is also important that the illustrations be examples of excellent art that effectively serve the development of meaning. Further, for some children, the illustrations they see in picture books are the primary source of their exposure to art. Fortunately, there are thousands of outstanding picture books available.

Careful selection considers children's interests and experiences, both to connect with and expand upon them. Language that will tickle the ear and delight the tongue is also important. Children won't expand their own language if they encounter only words they already know. Ideas—often called themes or concepts—need to be interesting to children but also to provide new ways of thinking about the world. Complexity of ideas, language, and illustration will vary, depending on the audience. For example, reading Emily Arnold McCully's (1984) wordless picture book, *Picnic,* with a three-year-old generates a different experience than reading Barbara Lehman's (2004) *The Red Book* with a seven-year-old. *Snow* is about familiar routines and family relationships. *The Red Book* invites readers into the world of the imagination, asking them to participate in the character's fantastic journey into the world of a book, to entertain possibilities for their own lives. Both are wonderful wordless books, offering rich opportunities for discussion and meaning making.

There are so many good books to choose among that it is virtually impossible to recommend specific titles for generic children. A simple checklist of considerations of quality, looking at prize-winning book lists such as the American Library Association's Caldecott Award, and the use of "touchstone" picture books for comparison with other books help parents and teachers make wise selections. First, all picture books should have rich language, with interesting words used in interesting ways, artistically excellent illustrations, and an appealing design. With picture storybooks, the text and illustrations together should establish the mood, setting, characters, and theme of the story just as they also reveal the plot. Nonfiction picture books need to have accurate text and illustrations, both of which impart information, and to be organized in a way that helps children grasp the concept being explored. Picture books that contain poetry should have lyrical language and illustrations that match the feeling established by the text. Beyond this, the "artfulness" of the book as a whole should be apparent. Asking the question, "What makes this book special?" and being able to answer it in terms of language and art probably indicate a book of good enough quality to read aloud to children.

Picture storybooks such as Virginia Hamilton's (2003) *Bruh Rabbit and the Tar Baby Girl,* stunningly illustrated by James Ransome, exemplify the qualities that make a book special. First, the story is both engaging and entertaining, and captivates young listeners with its humor, language, and beautiful art. Hamilton's use of the Gullah dialect is sparing, adding just enough flavor to the telling of the tale that children understand words they have probably not heard before, words such as nary, dayclean, and scarey-crow. The language is cadenced, inviting children to chime in. Ransome's watercolor pen-and-ink illustrations add detail to the story, inviting readers to look closely, and extend the humor of the tale. Before the story even begins, we learn about the happy-go-lucky nature of Bruh Rabbit. Other picture storybooks that could be considered touchstones include Jacqueline Woodson's (2004) *Coming on Home Soon,* illustrated by E. B. Lewis; Peter Sis's (2002) *Madlenka's Dog;* Peggy Rathman's (1995) *Officer Buckle and Gloria;* Amy Schwartz's (2003) *What James Likes Best;* Kevin Henkes's (2004) *Kitten's First Full Moon;* and many others.

Lisa Westberg Peters's (2003) *Our Family Tree: An Evolution Story,* is the perfect marriage of informative text and beautiful illustrations that match and extend the information presented in the words. Lauren Stringer, the illustrator, spent more than a year doing the research that would allow her to accurately depict the processes that Peters explained in her lucid prose. The result is a book about a complex process that is presented simply, yet accurately, for a young audience. Other books that could be considered touchstones of nonfiction include Steve Jenkins's (2004) *Actual Size;* Rachel Isadora's (2000) *ABC Pop!;* Sandra Markle's (2000) *Outside and Inside Dinosaurs;* and Maria Kalman's (2002) *Fireboat: The Heroic Adventures of the John J. Harvey.*

Poetry picture books offer a special experience for children when they are the brilliant combination of words and art that typify books such as Kristine O'Connell George's (2001) *Toasting Marshmallows,* illustrated by Kate Kiesler, and *Fold Me a Poem* (2005), illustrated by Lauren Stringer. In both of these books the language fairly leaps off of the page while the illustrations add depth and texture. Other poets such as Douglas Florian and Jane Yolen offer children important experiences with the language tools of the poet and the artistic tools of the illustrators.

Reading well-written books to children offers them the opportunity to learn many things. Good books read aloud introduce children to new, interesting words and sentence patterns, and allow them access to different styles of written language. Reading aloud helps children understand that print carries meaning, develops a sense of story, poetry, and exposition, enriches children's general knowledge, and motivates children to read more for pleasure and information. Reading aloud from picture books helps children understand the relationship between word and illustration, and, when selected wisely, introduces them to wonderful art. Reading aloud also models the sound of fluent reading. Reading books that offer rich and varied language and illustrations in the presentation of intriguing ideas, creates multiple opportunities for the kinds of conversations that will promote the many positive outcomes that are possible in the context of effective read- alouds.

REFERENCES

Anderson, R., Hiebert, E., Scott, J., & Wilkinson, I.A.G. (1985). *Becoming a nation of readers: The report of the commission on reading.* Washington, DC: National Institute of Education.

Baghban, M.J.M. (1984). *Our daughter learns to read and write: A case study from birth to three.* Newark, DE: International Reading Association.

Bemelmans, L. (1962). *Madeline.* New York: Viking.

Bus, A. G., van Ijzendoorn, M. H., & Pellegrini, A. D. (1995). Joint book reading makes for success in learning to read: A meta-analysis on intergenerational transmission of literacy. *Review of Educational Research, 65,* 1–21.

Clark, M. M. (1984). Literacy at home and at school: Insights from a study of young fluent readers. In J. Goelman, A. A. Oberg, & F. Smith (Eds.), *Awakening to literacy* (pp. 122–130). London: Heinemann.

Clay, M. (1979). *Reading: The patterning of complex behavior.* Auckland, New Zealand: Heinemann.

Cochran-Smith, M. (1984). *The making of a reader.* Norwood, NJ: Ablex.

DeTemple, J., & Snow, C. E. (2003). Learning words from books. In A. van Kleeck, S. A. Stahl, & E. B. Bauer (Eds.), *On reading books to children: Parents and teachers* (pp. 16–36). Mahwah, NJ: Lawrence Erlbaum Associates.

Dickinson, D. K., DeTemple, J. M., Hirschler, J., & Smith, M. W. (1992). Book reading with preschoolers: Co-construction of text at home and at school. *Early childhood Research Quarterly, 7,* 323–346.

Durkin, D. (1966). *Children who read early.* New York: Teachers College Press.

Durkin, D. (1974–1975). A six year study of children who learned to read in school at the age of four. *Reading Research Quarterly, 10,* 9–61.

Galda, L., Rayburn, S., and Stanzi, L. C. (2000). *Looking through the faraway end: Creating a literature-based reading curriculum with second graders.* Newark, DE: International Reading Association.

George, C. O. (2001). *Toasting marshmallows.* New York: Clarion.

George, C. O. (2005). *Fold me a poem.* San Diego: Harcourt.

Hamilton, V. (2003). *Bruh Rabbit and the tar baby girl.* New York: Blue Sky Press.

Heath, S. B. (1982). What no bedtime story means: Narrative skills at home and school. *Language in Society, 11,* 47–76.

Henkes, K. (2004). *Kitten's first full moon.* New York: Greenwillow.

Isadora, R. (2000). *ABC pop!* New York: Viking.

Jenkins, S. (2004). *Actual size.* Boston: Houghton Mifflin.

Kalman, M. (2002), *Fireboat: The heroic adventures of the John J. Harvey.* New York: Putnam.

Klesius, J. P., & Griffith, P. L. (1996). Interactive storybook reading for at-risk learners. *The Reading Teacher, 49*(7), 552–560.

Lehman, B. (2004). *The red book.* Boston: Houghton Mifflin.

Markle, S. (2000). *Outside and inside dinosaurs.* New York: Atheneum.

McCully, E. A. (1984). *Picnic.* New York: HarperCollins.

Morrow, L. M., & Brittain, R. (2003). The nature of storybook reading in the elementary school: Current practices. In A. van Kleeck, S. A. Stahl, & E. B. Bauer (Eds.), *On reading books to children: Parents and teachers* (pp. 140–158). Mahwah, NJ: Lawrence Erlbaum Associates.

Morrow, L. M., & Gambrell, L. (2000). Literature-based reading instruction. In M. L. Kamil, P. B. Mosenthal, P. D. Pearson, & R. Barr (Eds.), *Handbook of Reading research* (Vol. 3, pp. 563–586). Mahwah, NJ: Lawrence Erlbaum Associates.

Olson, D. R. (1977). From utterance to text: The bias of language in speaking and writing. *Harvard Educational Review, 47,* 257–281.

Pellegrini, A. D., Brody, G. H., & Sigel, I. E. (1985). Parents' book reading habits with their children. *Journal of Educational Psychology, 77,* 332–340.

Peters, L. W. (2003). *Our family tree: An evolution story.* San Diego: Harcourt.

Potter, B. (1906). *The tale of Jeremy Fisher.* London: Warne.

Rathman, P. (1995). *Officer Buckle and Gloria.* New York: Putnam.

Reese, E., Cox, A., Harte, D., & McAnally, H. (2003). Diversity in adults' styles of reading books to children. In A. van Kleeck, S. A. Stahl, & E. B. Bauer (Eds.), *On reading books to children: Parents and teachers* (pp. 37–57). Mahwah, NJ: Lawrence Erlbaum Associates.

Roser, N. & Martinez, M. (1995). *Book talk and beyond: children and teachers respond to literature.* Newark, DE: International Reading Association.

Schwartz, A. (2003). *What James likes best.* New York: Atheneum.

Senechal, M., LeFevre, J. A., Thomas, E., & Daley, K. (1998). Differential effects of home literacy experiences on the development of oral and written language. *Reading Research Quarterly, 32,* 96–116.

Senechal, M., Thomas, E., & Monker, J. (1995). Individual differences in 4-year-old children's acquisition of vocabulary during storybook reading. *Journal of Educational Psychology, 87,* 218–229.

Sipe, L. R. (in press). *Constructing literary understanding with young children: A grounded theory.* New York: Teachers College Press.

Sipe, L. R., & McGuire, C. E. (2006). Young children's resistance to stories. *The Reading Teacher, 60*(1), 6–13.

Sis, P. (2002). *Madlenka's dog.* New York: Farrar Straus Giroux.

Smith, F. (1978). *Understanding reading* (2nd ed.). New York: Holt Rinehart Winston.

Snow, C. E., & Ninio, A. (1986). The contracts of literacy: Chat children learn from learning to read books. In W. Teale & E. Sulzby (Eds.), *Emergent literacy: Writing and reading* (pp. 116–137). Norwood, NJ: Ablex.

Teale, W. (2003). Reading aloud to young children. In A. van Kleeck, S. A. Stahl, & E. B. Bauer (Eds.), *On reading books to children: Parents and teachers* (pp. 114–139). Mahwah, NJ: Lawrence Erlbaum Associates.

van Kleeck, A. (2003). Research on book sharing: Another critical look. In A. van Kleeck, S. A. Stahl, & E. B. Bauer (Eds.), *On reading books to children: Parents and teachers* (pp. 271–320). Mahwah, NJ: Lawrence Erlbaum Associates.

van Kleeck, A., Alexander, E., Virgil, A., & Templeton, D. E. (1996). Verbally modeling thinking for infants: Middle-class mothers presentation of information structures during book sharing. *Journal of Research in Childhood Education, 10,* 101–113.

van Kleeck, A., Stahl, S. A., & Bauer, E. B. (2003). *On reading books to children: Parents and teachers.* Mahwah, NJ: Lawrence Erlbaum Associates.

Wells, G. (1986). *The meaning makers.* Portsmouth, NH: Heinemann.

Wood, M., & Salvetti, E. P. (2001). Read-alouds for students at risk. *The Reading Teacher, 55*(1), 76–83.

Woodson, J. (2004). *Coming on home soon.* New York: Putnam.

Chapter Nine

CHOOSING AND USING INFORMATIONAL TEXT FOR INSTRUCTION IN THE PRIMARY GRADES

Barbara A. Marinak and Linda B. Gambrell

There is now broad agreement among reading educators and researchers about the importance of exposing young children to more informational books. The Committee on the Prevention of Reading Difficulties in Young Children (Snow, Burns, & Griffin, 1998) concluded that young children must have opportunities to read a rich array of both fictional and informational text. In addition, the International Reading Association (IRA) has taken the position that young readers should be exposed to a variety of genres, including picture storybooks, fiction and nonfiction material, magazines, and poetry (International Reading Association, 1999).

For many decades, classroom reading collections contained primarily fiction. Current definitions of literacy, however, focus on individual competence with a wide variety of print materials (Harris & Hodges, 1995). In addition, the demands seen in virtually all state academic literacy standards require competence in reading and comprehending both narrative (story) and informational (expository) text. A one-dimensional, fiction-only collection in a classroom lacks the rigor and depth required for developing high levels of literacy. As Menon and Hiebert (2005) noted, a range of well-designed curricular materials is necessary for teachers to plan highly effective instruction.

DEFINITIONS OF INFORMATIONAL TEXT

Various definitions of informational text are now used in the field of literacy. According to Harris and Hodges (1995), informational text can be defined as a nonfiction work of facts and concepts about a subject or subjects. This definition would include both textbooks and nonfiction literature. Some researchers have used more complex definitions. Duke and Bennett-Armistead (2003), for example, define informational text as having the primary purpose of conveying information about the natural and social worlds. According to this definition, informational text does not include biographies or how-to books.

Kletzien and Dreher (2004) define informational text more broadly to include three distinct types: narrative-informational, expository-informational, and mixed. Narrative-informational text conveys factual information using a story format. Expository-informational text also conveys factual information (including biographical information) but does not use a story structure. Mixed text is defined as a hybrid of styles and structures. An example often cited of this type of informational text is the *Magic School Bus inside the Human Body* (Cole, 1990). These mixed texts typically convey information, contain some story elements, and use cartoon-like formatting.

In this chapter, we use a broad definition of informational text. We include text that is primarily designed to convey information, including narrative-informational, expository-informational, and mixed text. Such text comes in many forms, including books, magazines, reference books, encyclopedias, newspapers, posters, pamphlets, and electronic sources such as Web sites.

WHY CHOOSE INFORMATIONAL TEXT?

Research suggests that in primary grade classrooms, the reading collections as well as the reading materials used for instruction are skewed toward fiction, and informational text is underrepresented (Duke, 2000). Both the amount of informational text available to young readers and the number of minutes spent reading informational material are far less than needed in a balanced, comprehensive reading program (Yopp & Yopp, 2000). These studies, based on book counts and surveys of teachers, have found that both instructional reading materials and classroom libraries contain mostly fiction. Current instructional demands and recent research reveal a number of compelling reasons to include more informational text in primary reading programs.

High-Quality Informational Text Is Now Readily Available

There was a time when many of the informational texts for young readers were poorly conceived and poorly written. As many classroom teachers are finding, however, there has been a recent explosion of high-quality informational books for young children. The number of informational children's books being published for the early grades has increased by 200 percent over the last 10 years (Cooperative Children's Book Center, 2006).

Some Children Prefer Informational Text

In a recent study by Mohr (2006), nonfiction books were the overwhelming choice of 1st-grade students. One hundred and ninety 1st graders from 10 different schools were invited to visit a book display. The display included a range of genres, ethnicities, and male/female protagonists. The children had unlimited time to browse and select a book that was theirs to keep. Approximately 85 percent of the children chose nonfiction over fiction.

A study conducted by Pappas (1993) revealed that children as young as kindergarten age showed a preference for informational text. Pappas analyzed children's pretend readings of two stories and two informational books to gain insights into their use of strategies in dealing with these two genres. Young children were just as successful in reenacting the informational books as they were the stories, and they preferred the informational text. Pappas challenged the "narrative as primary" notion, stating that an exclusive emphasis on reading "story" in the early grades limits children's experiences with other text forms and may result in creating a barrier to full access to literacy.

Informational Text Can Help Minimize the 4th-Grade Slump

The 4th-grade slump refers to the overall decline in reading scores that occurs as children enter 4th grade, where they are expected to read and learn from informational text and content area textbooks (Chall, Jacobs, & Baldwin, 1990). Greater exposure to and comfort with informational text may help minimize the effects of the 4th-grade slump. Evidence that reading informational text bolsters reading achievement can be found in data from the National Assessment of Educational Progress (NAEP). Trends on the NAEP from 1990 to the present indicate that 4th graders' reading achievement increases as the diversity of their reading experiences increases. In other words, 4th graders who reported reading a wide variety of text (narrative, information, etc.) had higher reading achievement than students who reported reading only one type of text. Exposing young children to informational text positions them to handle the literacy demands of their later schooling (Duke & Bennett-Armistead, 2003).

Informational Text Supports the Development of Strategic Readers

The primary grade years (K–2) were once thought of as the time when children "learned to read," while "reading to learn" took place in the upper elementary grades and beyond (Chall, 1983). Research in emergent and adolescent literacy suggests that learning to read and reading to learn occur at all grade levels. A study by Kamil and Lane (1997) found that primary students were able to read text well above their grade placement. The students learned strategies for dealing with complicated informational text that should have been beyond their capabilities.

Hall, Sabey, and McClellan (2005) found that text structure instruction in the primary grades is effective for promoting informational text comprehension and that young children benefit from well-structured texts. A number of researchers have shown that text structure awareness is crucial for facilitating text comprehension and recall (Richgels, McGee, Lomax, & Sheard, 1987). These studies found that readers who understand the organizational structures of text typically find greater success in identifying important information and relationships between ideas.

In an attempt to better understand why primary classroom reading collections are not more balanced, researchers discovered several important perceptions. Donovan (2001) found that teachers' preferences for fiction grew out of a lack of comfort and familiarity with informational text. When choosing children's literature, teachers tended to assume that informational text was too difficult and too boring for young readers. In addition, classroom teachers were not sure how to support children's comprehension using informational text and, more specifically, lacked methods to productively teach specific structures.

In the following section, we describe the elements that are common to informational text. We know that young children become aware of and comfortable with narrative story structure (characters, setting, problem, events, solution) at an early age. It is just as important that they become aware of and comfortable with the predictable elements that occur across informational text. In the following section, elements of informational text are described and examples of instructional activities are provided.

Informational Text Elements

As young readers interact with printed materials to construct meaning, comprehension is significantly affected by the characteristics of each selection. For example, knowing the text type—fiction, nonfiction, book, magazine, picture book, a novel with short chapters—helps the reader anticipate what the text might contain. Awareness of the actual elements of the text enhances predictability and can foster comprehension (Williams, 2005).

Fictional text contains a story structure that has been taught in classrooms for many decades. Primary and elementary teachers routinely organize their instruction with regard to fictional text around the basic elements of characters, setting, problem, events, and solution. Informational text also contains predictable elements, but with less informational text being used in primary classrooms, instruction using these elements has not occurred as frequently.

There are five text elements that commonly occur across most informational text. These include the author's purpose, major ideas, supporting details, aids, and vocabulary.

These five elements provide an instructional framework for supporting young children in becoming aware of common features of informational text:

1. Author's Purpose: To provide information about the topic.
2. Major Idea(s): The key points the author wants the reader to understand.
3. Supporting Details: The information that supports and clarifies the major ideas.
4. Aids: The variety of pictorial, graphic, typographic, and structural representations used to convey information.
5. Vocabulary: Technical words that are needed for a full understanding of the text.

The practical suggestions provided in the following section use these five common elements of informational text during three instructional contexts that commonly occur across the early literacy curriculum: read alouds, discussion, and writing.

READALOUDS, DISCUSSION, AND WRITING

Theories of child development suggest that it is the social environment that provides learners with the opportunity to observe higher levels of cognitive processing (Vygotsky, 1978). Read alouds, discussion, and writing activities provide opportunities for primary students (kindergarten through grade 3) to witness how others (e.g., teachers and peers) work together to collaborate and construct meaning using informational text. It is especially in the primary grades that teachers model awareness of informational text features during read alouds and think alouds and that students are engaged in learning the language of informational text (major ideas, supporting details, etc.).

Using Informational Text Elements during Teacher Read Alouds

Using teacher read alouds is an effective way to introduce young readers to high-interest informational text, and to begin teaching the predictable elements found in most informational books. A teacher read aloud is the oral sharing of a book for the purpose of modeling strategic reading behaviors and generating instructional conversation. According to McGee & Richgels (2003), teacher read alouds can be used to promote deeper understanding and interpretation of text; allow children to take an active role in understanding text; and prompt children to begin using mental activities that will become automatic as they begin reading independently.

Using Informational Elements during Interactive Read Alouds

An interactive read aloud requires a great deal of conversation between children and their teacher. This give and take conversation around a shared text engages children in predicting, inferring, and thinking and reasoning

Engaging children in an interactive read aloud of an informational text is not only an effective way to increase the amount of informational text that children experience, but it is also an effective way to introduce children to the common elements of this type of text.

In the classroom vignette shown in Table 9.1, a primary grade teacher uses an interactive read aloud to help children become familiar with the elements of informational text (author's purpose, major ideas, supporting details, aids, and vocabulary). The text used for the interactive read aloud is *Outside and inside Sharks* by Sandra Markle (1996).

Table 9.1
Interactive Read Aloud: *Outside and Inside Sharks* by Sandra Markle

Informational elements	Teacher dialogue	Focus
Author's purpose	"Boys and girls, today our read aloud is an informational book called *Outside and Inside Sharks* by Sandra Markle. What was Sandra Markle's purpose for writing this book?"	Sandra Markle wrote *Outside and Inside Sharks* to teach readers about a shark's anatomy and behavior.
Major ideas	"The title of this book gives a hint about the two major ideas in this book. Remember, the book is called *Outside and Inside Sharks.* What do you think the two major ideas are?"	The major ideas in this book are the features found on the outside of a shark and the features found on the inside of a shark.
Major ideas	"Do you think our major ideas are correct? Which major idea are we reading about first?"	The first major idea in the text describes the outside of a shark (fins, gills, etc.).
Supporting details	"What two supporting details did we learn about the outside of the shark? What did you learn about the gill and tail of the shark so far?"	The two supporting details related to the outside of the shark are gills and tail.
Aids	"What did we find on these three pages to help us? What important information did we learn about sharks from the photograph?"	The aids in the text are color photographs and a photo-diagram (a labeled photograph) of sharks.
Vocabulary	"What do you notice about important vocabulary words such as oxygen and operculum on page 5? What does the author do in the sentences that contain italicized vocabulary words to help you learn new words?"	The vocabulary is italicized to help the reader recognize new or challenging words. The definitions of the italicized vocabulary words are found in the same sentence.

Using Informational Element Sorts

In the next example, a primary grade teacher uses an interactive read aloud as the basis for a vocabulary activity that is designed to help children become familiar with the elements of informational text. This activity will also help students learn some of the specific vocabulary from the book. The text used for the interactive read aloud is *Fighting Fires* by Seymour Simon (2002) and the vocabulary activity is an informational element sort.

The Informational element sort is an activity where children engage in sorting words by categories (Zuttell, 1999). In this activity, the teacher guides the students in grouping or sorting words into the categories of author's purpose, major ideas, supporting details, and vocabulary. Once the text has been shared, the teacher engages children in thinking about the words and sorting them into the informational element categories. Word sort activities enhance vocabulary development and comprehension by actively involving students in the categorization process (Gillett & Kita, 1979).

An informational element sort encourages children to reflect on the content of the text as they sort words into categories that reflect the elements of informational text. For example, after reading aloud *Fighting Fires* by Seymour Simon, the teacher presents the elements of informational text as the sort categories. In our example, shown in Table 9.2, 12 words are selected from the text by the teacher. The students sort the words into each of the element categories used in this activity. (Note that in this example only four categories are used because the aids in this text are photographs that are not accompanied by captions. Without captions there are no aids words to sort.) In the example, an informational element sort shows the teacher-selected vocabulary as well as an example of the completed sort, including some annotations.

Depending upon the words selected, interesting discussions might take place as children discuss the best category for each word. For example, in our sort, the words "bucket" and "buckets" appear. In this story, a "bucket" is a piece of equipment on a pumper truck and "buckets" are said to have been used to fight fires before fire trucks were available. Including interesting word choices provides for an excellent vocabulary discussion about multiple-meaning words and singular and plural word forms.

USING INFORMATIONAL TEXT ELEMENTS DURING DISCUSSION

Rich discussions occur when the thoughts, ideas, feelings, and responses of all participants contribute to a better understanding of the text. Discussion is a balanced oral exchange, where roles of leadership and understanding may frequently shift. In a discussion, the teacher does not lead the students to interpretation; rather. interpretation is mutually constructed by the group. Students

Table 9.2
Element Sort: *Fighting Fires* by Seymour Simon

Teacher-selected words

water	hoses	bucket	off-road
buckets	foam	rescue	collapsed
fireboats	pumper	special	tiller

Completed sort with annotations

Informational elements	Sort words	Examples of teacher's and/or students' reasons for including a word in a category.
Author's purpose	Special	Seymour Simon describes the special types of vehicles that are used to fight fires.
Major ideas	Pumper, off-road, fireboats, tiller	The major ideas in this book are the 11 types of vehicles used to fight fires.
Supporting details	Water, hoses, foam, bucket*	The supporting details are examples of the substances and/or equipment found on fire-fighting vehicles.
Vocabulary	Buckets,* rescue, collapsed	These are a few important vocabulary words that describe fire fighting.

*In this case, bucket(s) is an interesting word. It is both a supporting detail and a vocabulary word.

who are invited to talk about what they have read are more likely to engage in reading, resulting in deeper comprehension (Gambrell & Almasi, 1996).

Using Informational Elements to Guide Discussion

The five elements of informational text can serve as an organizer for teacher-guided discussions of informational text. Table 9.3 presents questions that are appropriate for informational text.

In the next example, the teacher has read aloud (or the children have silently read) *The President's Cabinet and How It Grew,* by Nancy Winslow Parker (1978). Table 9.4 shows teacher-constructed questions based on informational elements and possible responses that children might give. The teacher-posed questions use language that is specific to the information text elements (major ideas, supporting details, etc.) that children need to know and understand. Using questions of this type helps children become more comfortable with the predictable elements of informational text.

USING INFORMATIONAL TEXT MAPS DURING DISCUSSION

An informational text map is a type of graphic that can be used *following* reading to organize information using the five elements of informational text.

Table 9.3
Guiding Discussion Using Informational Elements

Informational elements	Generic discussion questions
Author's purpose	Why did the author write this book/selection? What information did the author want to convey?
Major ideas	What are the major ideas of the book/selection? How are the major ideas presented?
Supporting details	What are the supporting details for each major idea? How are the supporting details presented?
Aids	What aids does the author use to convey meaning? What information is included in the aids (major ideas, supporting detail, vocabulary)?
Vocabulary	What key vocabulary words are used to convey major ideas? What vocabulary words are used in the supporting details? What words should you understand to discuss or write about this book/selection?

Table 9.4
***The President's Cabinet and How It Grew,* by Nancy Winslow Parker**

Informational elements	Discussion questions	Possible answers
Author's purpose	Why did the author write this book/selection?	To teach us about how the Cabinet was formed and how it grew.
Major ideas	How are the major ideas presented?	The major ideas are presented in two ways—in relation to each president and each Cabinet secretary.
Supporting details	How are the supporting details presented?	Details about each president's Cabinet are discussed. The job of each Cabinet secretary is described.
Aids	What aids are used to help the reader learn about the Cabinet?	The aids are illustrations of the presidents and members of their Cabinets. There is also an illustration showing how the Cabinet sits at meetings.
Vocabulary	What key vocabulary words are used to convey major ideas? What key vocabulary words are used to convey the supporting details?	president, Cabinet secretary, job, chief

In the example given here, primary grade children read about animals in *Seashore Babies* by Kathy Darling (1997). *Seashore Babies* is an appropriate choice for such a discussion. In this colorful text, each double-page spread contains a brief description of several seashore babies along with a descriptive paragraph and an attribute box containing important characteristics about each animal.

The teacher presented the basic informational text map (on the board, on sentence strips, or on chart paper) and asked the students, "Why did this author write this book?" As comments from the children were gathered, the teacher recorded the children's responses. The teacher then pointed out that there were two major ideas in this text. As the children talked about the two major ideas, the teacher reminded them that they had read about two animals. As the children talk about the penguins and sea lions, the teacher recorded "Penguins" and "Sea Lions" under "Major Ideas" on the text map. Then the teacher guided the discussion to supporting details, aids, and vocabulary, adding the children's contributions to the text map (see Table 9.5).

Once the informational text map was completed, the teacher asked the children to find a partner. Using the informational text map, the teacher asked the children to share with their partner what they had learned about seashore animals and to use the informational text map to get ideas. Children can also be encouraged to use interesting text vocabulary as they discuss and write about the topic.

USING INFORMATIONAL TEXT ELEMENTS TO SUPPORT WRITING

Children as young as kindergarten age are not only capable of writing informational text but they do so naturally and spontaneously (Newkirk, 1989). Several studies indicate that the more children write, the more they differentiate among genres (Boscolo, 1996; Chapman, 1995; Donovan, 2001; Kamberelis, 1999). They begin writing informational text and the text they produce looks like the text found in informational books. There is, however, an important reciprocity between writing and reading. In order to engage in writing informational text, children must read and reread a wide variety of informational books.

Table 9.5
Text Map: *Seashore Babies*, by Kathy Darling and Tara Darling

Author's purpose	To share information about young seashore animals
Major idea	Penguin
Supporting detail	Baby animal is called a chick.
Major idea	Sea lion
Supporting detail	Baby animal is called a pup or calf.
Aids	Photographs, attribute boxes, symbols
Vocabulary	Birthplace, littermates, enemies

There is evidence of important benefits to be derived from having young children engage in informational writing. Researchers note the importance of nurturing the natural desire in young children to conduct research and write about their findings (Korkeamaki & Dreher, 2000). Analysis of the text created after a hands-on experience indicates that not only do young writers describe events and results but they do so using important text features such as descriptions, definitions, classifications, headings, and graphic representations (pictures, charts, etc.) (Pappas, 1986). Therefore, contrary to the argument that primary children are too young to engage with informational text, it appears these young writers make interstitial connections when reading and produce sophisticated informational texts during writing (Moss, Leone, & Dipillo, 1997). Finally, studies indicate that both overall writing proficiency and the number of texts produced increases when children are encouraged to write informational text (Donovan, 2001).

Writing also has been found to be an important support, or scaffolding experience, for discussion. Children have more positive attitudes toward nonfiction books and display deeper understanding of the material after writing in response to text (Moss, Leone, & Dipillo, 1997). In addition, Bobola (2003) found that discussions were richer and more specific if students engaged in writing prior to discussion.

Using Informational Pattern Guides

A pattern guide for writing can be created to provide additional scaffolding as readers prepare to write. An informational text map (see Table 9.5) can be transformed into a pattern guide when the teacher provides some element information. In the pattern guide for *Rosie: A Visiting Dog's Story,* by Stephanie Calmenson (1994) (see Table 9.6), the teacher provided the three major ideas (Rosie as a puppy, Rosie in training, and Rosie visiting), the children then filled in the supporting details.

Table 9.6
Pattern Guide: *Rosie: A Visiting Dog's Story,* by Stephanie Calmenson

	Rosie: A Visiting Dog's Story
Major idea	**Rosie as a puppy**
Supporting details **Details about Rosie as a puppy**	
Major idea	**Rosie in training**
Supporting details **Details about Rosie in training**	
Major idea	**Rosie visiting**
Supporting details **Details about Rosie visiting**	

Table 9.7
Summary Frame: *Rosie: A Visiting Dog's Story,* by Stephanie Calmenson

The following is a summary of ____.

This informational book is about ______________________________________.

Rosie: A Visiting Dog's Story is a special kind of informational book. It is a biography that describes the life and training of a visiting dog. The book is by

____.

It is illustrated with photographs by ____________________________________.

The first major idea tells about Rosie as a puppy. When she was a puppy, she ________

________________________________.

Another major idea describes her training as a visiting dog. When she was in training, she

________________________________.

The last major idea follows Rosie as she visits hospitals. When she visits, she

________________________________.

Rosie: A Visiting Dog's Story ends with an author's note. In the author's note, I learned ____.

After the children completed this activity, they used the pattern guide to generate their own written summary of the book.

Using Informational Summary Frames

A summary frame provides support for students as they generate informational text. Table 9.7 shows a summary frame for *Rosie: A Visiting Dog's Story.* In this case, the frame was used to model the construction of a summary. Summary frames can also support independent writing by younger children or children who would benefit from additional writing support. The example shown here uses informational elements to structure the frame. The major ideas and transition words were provided by the teacher. Children completed the summary by filling in supporting details from the pattern guide (see Table 9.6).

CONCLUSION

In this chapter, we stress the importance of choosing and using informational text in the primary grades. Most educators agree that young children are far more familiar and comfortable with narrative, or story, than they are with informational text. It is important to teach young readers the common elements found in most informational text (i.e., author's purpose, major ideas, supporting details, aids, vocabulary). Helping students read, discuss, and write using the elements is a critical step in preparing them to comprehend all types of informational text, including children's books, content area textbooks, newspapers, magazines, and the Internet.

Several practical instructional techniques have been presented in this chapter (e.g., interactive read alouds, text maps, and summary frames) as techniques that can be used during primary instruction. These instructional techniques familiarize children with the elements of informational text and afford them opportunities to read, write, and talk about books by using the language of informational text. Proficiency with informational text helps students build the skills they need to be successful in school, work, community, and everyday life (Pearson, 2003).

REFERENCES

Bobola, K. (2003). Children's minds at work: How understanding of rich narrative text emerges in fourth-grade classrooms that combine peer group discussion and journal writing. In *52nd Yearbook of the National Reading Conference* (pp. 66–84). Oak Creek, WI: National Reading Conference.

Boscolo, P. (1996). The use of information in expository text writing. In C. Pontecorvo, M. Orsolini, B. Burge, & L. Resnick (Eds.), *Children's early text construction* (pp. 209–227). Mahwah, NJ: Lawrence Earlbaum Associates.

Chall, J. (1983). *Stages of reading development.* New York: McGraw-Hill.

Chall, J., Jacobs, V., & Baldwin, L. (1990). *The reading crisis: Why poor children fall behind.* Cambridge, MA: Harvard University Press.

Chapman, M. L. (1995). The sociocognitive construction of written genres in first grade. *Research in the Teaching of English, 29,* 164–192.

Cooperative Children's Book Center. (2006). *Children's books by and about people of color.* Madison, WI: School of Education, University of Wisconsin–Madison. Retrieved September 2006, from www.education.wisc.edu/ccbc/books/pcstats.htm.

Donovan, C. (2001). Children's development and control of written story and informational genres: Insights from one elementary school. *Research in the Teaching of English, 35,* 394–447.

Duke, N. (2000). 3.6 minutes per day: The scarcity of informational text in first grade. *Reading Research Quarterly, 35,* 202–224.

Duke, N., & Bennett-Armistead, V. S. (2003). *Reading and writing informational text in the primary grades.* New York: Scholastic.

Gambrell, L., & Almasi, J. (1996). *Lively discussions: Fostering engaged reading.* Newark, DE: International Reading Association.

Gillett, J., & Kita, M. (1979). Words, kids and categories. *The Reading Teacher, 32*(5), 538–546.

Hall, K., Sabey, B., & McClellan, M. (2005). Expository text comprehension: Helping primary-grade teachers use expository text to full advantage. *Reading Psychology, 26,* 211–234.

Harris, T., & Hodges, R. (1995). *The literacy dictionary: The vocabulary of reading and writing.* Newark, DE: International Reading Association.

International Reading Association. (1999). *Providing books and other print materials for classroom and school libraries* (A position statement of the International Reading Association). Newark, DE: Author.

Kamberelis, G. (1999). Genre development and learning: Children writing stories, science reports, and poems. *Research in the Teaching of English, 33,* 403–460.

Kamil, M., & Lane, D. (1997, March). *A classroom study of the efficacy of using information text for first grade reading instruction.* Paper presented at the American Educational Research Association Meeting, Chicago, IL.

Kletzien, S., & Dreher, M. (2004). *Informational text in k-3 classrooms: Helping children read and write.* Newark, DE: International Reading Association.

Korkeamaki, R., & Dreher, J. (2000). What happened when kindergarten children were reading and writing informational text in teacher-and-peer-led groups? In T. Shanahan & F. V. Rodriguez-Brown (Eds.), *National Reading Conference Yearbook, 49,* 452–463.

McGee, L., & Richgels, D. (2003). *Designing early literacy programs: Strategies for at-risk preschoolers and kindergarten children.* (ERIC Document Reproduction Service No. ED 478237).

Menon, S., & Hiebert, E. (2005). A comparison of first graders' reading with little books or literature-based basal anthologies. *Reading Research Quarterly, 40*(1), 12–38.

Mohr, K. (2006). Children's choices for recreational reading: A three-part investigation of selection preferences, rationales, and processes. *Journal of Literacy Research, 38*(1), 81–104.

Moss, B., Leone, S., & Dipillo, M. (1997). Exploring the literature of fact: Linking reading and writing through information trade books. *Language Arts, 74,* 418–429.

Newkirk, T. (1989). *More than stories: The range of children's writing.* Portsmouth, NH: Heinemann.

Pappas, C. (1986, December). *Exploring the global structure of "information books."* Paper presented at the annual meeting of the National Reading Conference, Austin, TX. (ERIC Document Reproduction Service No. ED 278952).

Pappas, C. (1993). Is narrative "primary"? Some insights from kindergartners' pretend readings of stories and inform books. *Journal of Reading Behavior, 25,* 97–129.

Pearson, P. D. (2003). Foreword. In N. Duke & V. S. Bennett-Armistead (Eds.), *Reading and writing informational text in the primary grades* (pp. 8–9). New York: Scholastic.

Richgels, D., McGee, L., Lomax, R., & Sheard, C. (1987). Awareness of four text structures: Effects on recall of expository text. *Reading Research Quarterly, 22,* 177–196.

Snow, C., Burns, S., & Griffin, P. (1998). *Preventing reading difficulty in young children.* Washington, DC: National Research Council.

Williams, J. (2005). Instruction in reading comprehension for primary-grade students: A focus on text structure. *Journal of Special Education, 39*(1), 6–18.

Vygotsky, L. (1978). *Mind in society.* Cambridge, MA: Harvard University Press.

Yopp, R., & Yopp, H. (2000). Sharing informational text with young children. *The Reading Teacher, 53*(5), 410–423.

Zutell, J. (1999, July). *Word study and spelling instruction for elementary grade students.* Paper delivered at a meeting of the Central Dauphin School District, Harrisburg, PA.

Children's Book References

Calmenson, S. (1994). *Rosie: A visiting dog's story.* Boston: Houghton Mifflin.

Cole, J. (1990). *The Magic School Bus: Inside the human body.* Illustrated by B. Degen. New York: Scholastic.

Darling, K. (1997). *Seashore babies.* Photographs by T. Darling. New York: Walker Books.

Markle, S. (1996). *Outside and inside sharks.* New York: Atheneum.

Parker, N. (1978). *The president's cabinet and how it grew.* New York: HarperCollins.

Simon, S. (2002). *Fighting fires.* New York: Seastar Books.

Chapter Ten

EARLY LITERACY INSTRUCTION FOR LINGUISTICALLY AND CULTURALLY DIVERSE STUDENTS

Carmen M. Martínez-Roldán and Jeanne Gilliam Fain

In this chapter, we present a repertoire of instructional practices aimed at supporting the literacy development of culturally and linguistically diverse prekindergarten through 3rd-grade students. According to the U.S. Department of Education, National Center for Education Statistics (2004), the percentage of language minority youth in the United States (youth speaking other languages than English at home) has increased greatly in recent decades. The number of language minority individuals between 5 and 24 years old in the United States has more than doubled, growing from 6.3 million in 1979 to 13.7 in 1999, representing a 118 percent increase in this population. It is not surprising then that the number of teachers encountering language minority students or English language learners (ELLs) in their classrooms has also increased.

Language minority students include a wide range of diverse students; they do not represent a homogeneous group. They may be U.S.-born Americans who come from households where languages other than English are used or where more than one language or dialect is used. These students may have been identified by schools as limited English proficient or may have been removed from this classification. Language minorities also include recent immigrants. Some of them may have received formal literacy instruction in their first language, and even some instruction in English in their country of origin. They may also be students with little or no formal literacy instruction in their first language. Language minority students also include refugees. Unlike most immigrants, refugees for the most part have had little choice of where to go since they have been escaping from dangerous situations and have had little time to prepare for coming to a new country (Dien, 2004). When we refer to linguistically and culturally diverse students, we also include African American students, who because of their use of African American Vernacular English (AAVE) are also considered to be language minority students or bilinguals. Such diversity within language minority students challenges any notion of an idealized English language learner.

Although there are certain states that traditionally have had larger concentrations of language minority students, the U.S. Bureau of the Census (2000) reports that they are spread all over the United States, even in states like Maine, West Virginia, Vermont, Iowa, Georgia, Nebraska, and Washington, where the number of Latinos keeps increasing. They live in both rural and urban areas. They come from diverse socioeconomic backgrounds, although unfortunately, poverty is high among many of these groups (e.g., Latinos: Pew Research Center, 2005). This diversity in terms of backgrounds, residence status, and geographical location implies that one of teachers' primary roles is to know their students and learn about their backgrounds and communities, in order to be able to connect with them and address their needs. In this chapter, we highlight some literacy practices that have been documented as important for different communities. As we discuss later, there are intragroup differences within these communities; teachers need to attend to the local literacy practices of their students and to individual differences and needs. Attention to out-of-school culture and context is pivotal, given the ways that these conditions mediate learning, as highlighted by sociocultural theories of learning.

We begin our discussion by briefly reviewing the aspects of literacy that are brought to the forefront when literacy is viewed from a sociocultural perspective. We follow that discussion by focusing on the literacy practices of particular communities, and by describing literacy activities that different teachers have found effective to support early childhood literacy of language minority students in their classrooms. The chapter ends with implications for educators.

LITERACY FROM A SOCIOCULTURAL PERSPECTIVE

We approach literacy as embedded in sociocultural practices, not just as processes that take place inside a student's head. Vygotsky's (1934/1987) work reminds us that higher mental processes in the individual have their origin in social processes. This view of learning highlights the importance of cultural resources in the formation and development of thinking (Moll, 1990; Vygotsky, 1934/1987), by attributing to language a major role in this development. By language, we refer to the totality of the linguistic resources that children possess, including both their home language and the social languages learned outside of their homes, in their communities and in schools.

Research on language socialization (Heath, 1983) has shed important light on the roles of social context, families, communities, and schools in language and literacy acquisition. As Zentella (2005) points out, researchers examining immigrants' literacy practices go beyond thinking that "the problem is they don't speak English" to the idea of "ask which language and literacy practices do immigrant families keep and pass on to the next generations and why, which do they leave by the wayside or transform, and which new practices do they adopt?" (pp. 13–14).

Widely recognized is the importance for the success of language minority students and students in general that teachers and curriculum designers develop deep understandings of the particular resources or funds of knowledge that their students have available outside of school. "Funds of knowledge" refers to the accumulated bodies of knowledge and skills essential for household and individual functioning or well-being; for example, family members' knowledge of business, agriculture, form filling, and so on, and any other knowledge that is relevant for their lives (Moll, Amanti, Neff, & González, 1992). Usually, that knowledge and expertise is shared with other members of the family and the community, creating social networks in which people exchange their resources and expertise with one another. These bodies of knowledge and skills include the literacy practices that people engage in at home and in their communities. For students living in poverty (as is the case with many language minority students), educators' and curriculum makers' expectations involve assumptions about the kinds of literacy that these students possess or lack. Not surprisingly, many researchers have expressed concerns about the fact that the local literacy practices of language minority students and students of color are overwhelmingly ignored in school curricula. As Mercado (2005) asserts: "because of their lower social value, local literacies . . . often go unrecognized in dominant discourses about literacies" (p. 238).

One reason for this situation may be that these practices are not aligned with the mainstream literacy practices valued at school (Heath, 1983). Another reason is the difficulty that educational institutions have in viewing working-class or poor minority students as emerging from households rich in intellectual and social resources (González, Moll, & Amanti, 2005). For these reasons, the research conducted collaboratively by teachers and researchers to document families' funds of knowledge has much potential to help teachers gain a more accurate picture of the resources their students have at home. This work has the potential to make the students' and their families' hidden literacies visible. Those involved in documenting the funds of knowledge of their communities have proposed that to find those literacies, researchers need to go beyond searching what kinds of things people read, to observing how literacy operates in their daily lives (e.g., Mercado, 2005).

A major goal in examining the funds of knowledge of language minority students' households is transforming the relationships among students, teachers, and families and providing teachers access to these social and cultural resources so that they can develop curricula that successfully integrate this knowledge, as some teachers have already done (Moll et al., 1992). A major question is: "How can teachers support the literacy and biliteracy development of their students when their students' home languages are different than their teachers'?" We believe that part of the answer is found when we learn about the cultural and linguistic resources students bring to the classroom and when we begin to learn about each individual student. Although this is not enough, it is a critical component of effective teaching for linguistically and culturally diverse students. The next section aims to support teachers in learning more about the cultural and linguistic resources of children from various communities, as well as to give some important highlights of the collective experience of these groups in the United States.

LITERACY AND FUNDS OF KNOWLEDGE IN VARIOUS AMERICAN COMMUNITIES

We reject any attempt to describe language minority children from specific cultures as a monolithic group, that is, a group that shares the same characteristics, styles of learning, or styles of interactions. We agree, however, with McCarty and Watahomigie (2004) when they state that "children from diverse ethnolinguistic backgrounds do bring to the classroom unique learning dispositions developed in the context of their socialization within families and communities" (p. 91). Members of these groups are bounded not only by their language or cultural practices but by their place of origin and their collective experience, which includes the circumstances of their arrival in the United States.

Some groups, such as Mexicans from what became the U.S. Southwest, Puerto Ricans (who are citizens of the United States by birth), African Americans, and Native Americans, have survived a long process of Anglo-European colonization. This process involved a systematic effort to eradicate their languages. Other groups have arrived in the United States either searching for better opportunities for their families (including recent Mexican immigrants and Latinos from other Central and South American countries), or as refugees (including people from El Salvador and Vietnam). We need to stress, though, that given the intragroup differences within each of these communities, there are no typical Puerto Rican, Mexican, or Vietnamese households (Mercado, 2005).

Literacy Practices and Funds of Knowledge within Latino/a Communities

We use the name Latino to refer broadly to female and male youth of Latin American or Caribbean heritage with roots in 21 Spanish-speaking nations

(Zentella, 2005). In 1999, about two-thirds of the almost 14 million language minorities in the United States between 5 and 24 years old (or 65 percent) were Latinos. Puerto Ricans and Mexicans form the two largest Latino communities in the United States, and researchers have documented the literacy practices of some of their communities. The number of Dominicans and immigrants from Central and South America is also increasing rapidly, and their literacy practices and funds of knowledge are beginning to be documented as well.

When receiving language minority students in the classroom, it is important to find out whether they are U.S.-born students or recent immigrants. The length of time they have lived in the United States plays a major role in their use of language. For example, for many Mexican American children, their home language may be English or a combination of English and Spanish or an indigeneous language. In fact, in studies on the funds of knowledge of both Puerto Rican homes in New York City and Mexican American homes in the Southwest, one of the main findings involved the way English and Spanish (and any variants of the two) were interwoven into the day-to-day activities of households (e.g., Mercado, 2005). The alternation of the two languages, called code-switching, is not a sign of language deficiency or lack of vocabulary but a tool for thinking, and for some students the ability to code-switch and to use their home language represents an important part of their identity (Zentella, 1997).

In her home visits with teachers to document the literacy practices of their students, Mercado (2005) found that the families used reading and writing for a variety of purposes. Those purposes included, among others, their use of literacy for understanding everyday issues related to health, legal issues, the upbringing of children, and identity issues, and for satisfying the need for spiritual comfort and guidance. They also used literacy for social participation in different groups such as churches, clubs, and parents' associations; and for private leisure, reading about the lives of music, film, and TV personalities and documenting life through photos and souvenirs. Most of these uses of literacy have been also found in the homes of Mexican and Mexican American families in the United States. Teachers and researchers documenting the resources of families living in the Southwest found extensive knowledge of agriculture and mining, business and construction, contemporary and folk medicine, household management, and religion (Moll et al., 1992). These funds of knowledge have great potential for supporting learning and literacy development in classrooms.

Language and Literacy Practices in American Indian and Alaska Native Communities

There are about two million American Indians and Alaska Natives living in the United States. These are people with diverse backgrounds, representing more than 175 languages (McCarty & Watahomigie, 2004). According to

McCarty and Watahomigie (2004), nearly one-quarter of this population consists of school-age children who attend a variety of schools, most of them located on reservations. Nevertheless, "56% or more than 250,000 Indigenous students attend public schools with less than 25% Indian/Alaska Native enrollment" (U.S. Department of Education, National Center for Education Statistics, 2000, as cited by McCarty and Watahomigie, 2004, p. 79.)

Researchers have found that people in indigenous communities respect their elders and value the collective or the group over the individual. This emphasis on the collective may be reflected in Indigenous students' preference for cooperating in small groups. Another important aspect of Indigenous communities is the strong way in which language and identity are intertwined. Also important to American Indian and Alaskan native communities (and for Latinos and African Americans) is the tradition of oral storytelling (McCarty & Watahomigie, 2004). These cultural resources have implications for classroom instruction that is organized to support literacy.

Language and Literacy Practices in African American Communities

There are clear group distinctions among African Americans, depending on their geographical locations and shared experiences, which help create unique African American communities with distinctive customs, traditions, and dialects (Smith, 2004). African American scholars have documented the respect for adults and parents and the importance of oral practices and oral traditions within African American communities. Many of these literary traditions find their roots in various oral performance genres found in Africa, such as praise songs, formal speech, epics, and stories. For African Americans, storytelling, with the use of double-entendre, exaggeration, and religious-based phrases, is part of the literacy practices shared in their everyday life (Smith, 2004).

Because African American students' home language has been for the most part stigmatized or devalued in schools, many scholars are concerned about the fact that African American students "are overly represented in the lower reading groups for reasons other than ability" (Smith, 2004, p. 229). It is important that teachers value African American children's home language as they try to socialize them into the academic and standard discourse of schools. African American Vernacular English (AAVE, or Ebonics) is an important linguistic resource. This language has been described as a rule-governed language, highly structured, and with meaning-laden patterns (Smith, 2004).

Language and Literacy Practices in Asian American Communities

Asian Americans represent a diverse group. They may have arrived in the United States either as refugees, as in the case of Vietnamese Americans, or as voluntary immigrants, as in the case of Chinese Americans. Wealthy families as well as families living in poverty can be found within Asian American communities. Some Asian American students are doing very well in schools, but others are considered at risk (Dien, 2004). It has been argued that the needs of Vietnamese American students, in particular, have been neglected by our educational system (Dien, 2004).

According to Dien (2004), Vietnamese students seem to thrive in a noncompetitive environment and seem to prefer collaborative work and peer-group discussions. Some Vietnamese American students have been described as valuing accuracy over speed and as worrying about writing personal experiences that could be misinterpreted. Like Latino parents, parents of Asian American students teach their children respect for adults and teachers. Even in situations where parents cannot help their children with their homework, they support their students by monitoring their homework and their school attendance even when they do not make school visits.

PRACTICES AIMED AT SUPPORTING ELLS' LITERACY DEVELOPMENT

As Smith (2004) and other researchers have emphasized, it is crucial for students' success that teachers believe in their students' potential and ability to learn, and that they have high expectations for all students. Teachers demonstrate high expectations as they organize a curriculum that engages students intellectually. There are as many ways of organizing intellectually challenging and responsive curricula as there are teachers. One type of curriculum that has been documented as effective in supporting minority students is a curriculum that is organized around the local knowledge of students' communities and is based on students' inquiries.

Integrating Local Knowledge from Students' Communities

Teachers working with children from different communities have provided examples of how to integrate students' funds of knowledge and local literacy practices into the curriculum. For example, McCarty and Watahomigie (2004) described how Navajo 2nd-grade students engaged in learning and literacy through a unit on the government created in response to students' questions related to the presidential elections. The students prepared a mural by using butcher paper to illustrate events in their community that reflected the processes and procedures of government. The teachers worked in partnership with parents, grandparents, and other community elders. This partnership involved home visits as well as parental visits to the classroom. The teachers explored the community together with parents, elders, and children and became learners themselves.

Similarly, in an Alaskan community, teachers, teacher assistants, and elders came together to develop a curriculum by using the mathematics and scientific concepts embedded in everyday fish-camp experiences (Lipka, 1994, as cited in McCarty & Watahomigie, 2004). This was a collaborative effort to co-create a curriculum that integrated Indigenous knowledge. Another example of how to develop a curriculum based on the local knowledge of students and their communities came from a 2nd-grade teacher and researcher, Sandoval-Taylor (2005), who after visiting her Yaqui and Latino students' homes in the Southwest of the United States learned that many of the families had construction experience. So, she decided to create a curriculum around the concept of construction, to increase her students' reading, writing, and mathematics proficiency. The teacher incorporated the students' questions and interests with regard to construction into her planning. The students became inquirers and researchers into a topic in which their parents were consulted as experts, and so the parents were also integrated into this learning experience. Writing assessments at the beginning and the end of the unit documented the students' learning.

An integrated curriculum across the content areas of such subjects as language arts and mathematics supports language minority and culturally diverse students in many ways. This type of curriculum has the potential to offer prolonged engagement with literacy without rushing learning (Dien, 2004). This has been said to contribute to language minority students' learning. Students have more time to think about and focus on one issue by making connections across subject areas and knowledge from different sources. Such a curriculum also enables extensive and meaningful uses of literacy and language, as we show next.

A Curriculum for Primary Grade Minority Students

The belief that students first learn to read in the primary grades and then later use reading to learn is still pervasive in many primary classrooms. This belief is harmful for language minority students, especially when teachers also believe that students need to begin to speak standard English before engaging in meaningful literacy learning, and believe that decoding precedes comprehension. Julia López-Robertson's 2nd-grade classroom in a primarily Mexican American community was organized around a different belief—the belief that reading is a meaning-making process from the very beginning (Lopez-Robertson, 2003). This teacher believed that her students would benefit from engaging in learning to read by reading, by learning about reading, and by using reading to learn about life and about themselves, as Short (1997) proposed in applying Halliday's (1979) work on language learning. This principle applies to writing as well. We extend this idea by introducing in the next section some ways to engage learning found in classrooms designed to support second-language literacy development.

Drop Everything and Read (DEAR): Learning to Read by Reading:

Drop Everything and Read (DEAR) in Julia's 2nd-grade classroom was conducted during a 45-minute period that was part of the language arts block. In this period, the students experienced DEAR by choosing their own reading materials, including audio books, and by reading alone or with others for their own enjoyment and for their own purposes. DEAR offered multiple alternatives for children to engage with books and served several purposes, supporting the students in becoming lifelong readers. The main purpose of DEAR in Julia's classroom was to promote reading for the enjoyment of reading and to establish the habit of reading. DEAR was used to develop a wide background in reading, in story structure, and in literature. Students developed ownership of their learning and reading since they had many choices of reading materials.

DEAR also supported students' reading fluency and confidence. The students chose the books that they wanted to read, so that their level of reading difficulty was not imposed on them. Finally, DEAR supported second-language acquisition as students chose reading materials written in both their first and second languages, and as they participated in buddy reading with a student whose dominant language was not the same as theirs. Students also used puppets to enact stories and drama. It was during this time that Julia held individual reading and writing conferences with the students to offer individual support.

Guided Reading: Learning about Reading

Guided reading took place during the language arts block. A small group of students met with Julia to read the same book aloud together. These books were chosen by the teacher based on the students' reading abilities. Since this was a bilingual classroom, small groups were organized by language dominance (English or Spanish) and reading proficiency. The groups met for 20–30 minutes with the teacher while the rest of the class was involved in DEAR. Each group met two to four times per week according to the needs of the students. Guided reading was done to support students' learning about the reading process; to increase the students' repertoire of reading strategies; and to increase the students' confidence as readers. The practice of guided reading communicated messages to the students that reading involves knowing different strategies to construct meaning, and that reading is not just done for accuracy but is a process that involves trial and error.

Literature Discussions: Learning through Reading

Julia organized her curriculum in such a way that she alternated guided reading groups with literature discussion groups. Literature discussions can benefit all children, especially ELL students and bilingual students. There were two kinds of literature discussions in Julia's classroom—whole-class discussions and small-group literature discussions. Students would sometimes discuss the books read aloud during story time. The students shared their ideas about the books by making comments about the stories, their illustrations, and the connection between the stories and the illustrations and between the stories and their own experiences. Julia also posed questions, not to evaluate comprehension but to help the students predict, to help them think about specific parts of the stories, and to make meaning.

Small-group literature discussions or literature circles consisted of groups of four to five students who read or listened to the same book, and who then met to discuss their understandings of the story, as well as their connections to and ideas about the book. The literature discussion groups differed from the guided reading groups because the students had a choice in the selection of literature. The groups were not organized by reading proficiency or language dominance but were mostly heterogeneous groups organized by students' book choices (from texts offered by the teacher). Small-group literature discussions in Julia's classroom were considered mainly a curricular engagement suitable for encouraging meaningful and critical discussion about books with all of the children, regardless of their reading proficiency or language dominance. All students participated in the literature discussions by sharing their ideas about the texts and by putting questions to their peers about their interpretations. They helped each other when people needed assistance with their second language. Even students who could not read the books independently engaged enthusiastically with the written text and worked at different points to read the texts by themselves, because the stories were interesting and culturally relevant for the children.

Literature discussions offer opportunities to young children to talk about texts and support students' identities as readers and as persons, especially when teachers include multicultural literature. Even when teachers do not speak the language of their students, they can still honor their students' languages and cultures. One effective way to accomplish this is through the use of multicultural literature. Some texts are even published as bilingual editions. It is important to examine these texts' cultural authenticity. Day (2003, pp. xvii–xx) proposes the following criteria to examine books for cultural biases:

- Omission (exclusion of minority characters and experiences)
- Illustrations (stereotypes, tokenism, characters' roles)
- Story line (whose standards lead to success, resolution of problems, role of females)
- Lifestyles (oversimplified, exotic depictions?)
- Relationships between people (which people possess the power?)

- Heroines/Heroes (whose interest is the hero/heroine serving?)
- Effects on a young person's self-image
- Author's or illustrator's background and perspectives
- Use of loaded words
- Copyright date

The following Web sites are sources for quality multicultural literature. The American Library Association's website (http://www.ala.org) has information about the Coretta Scott King Award and the John Steptoe Award, two awards that honor authors and illustrators of African descent. It also includes information about the Pura Belpré Award, offered to Latino/a writers. The Americas Award honors work that authentically and engagingly portrays Latina America, the Caribbean, or Latinos (see http://www.uwm.edu/Dept/CLACS/outreach_americas.html). Another Web site includes information about an Asian-Pacific American award for literature, which is presented biennially (http://www.uic.edu/depts/lib/projects/resources/apala/laward). The Oyate On-Line organization reviews Native American children's literature for cultural authenticity (http://www.oyate.org). The National Council of Teachers of English has many resources available online on the use of literature, and provides information about effective strategies to support the literacy development of language minority students (www.ncte.org).

FAMILY LITERATURE DISCUSSIONS

Robin, a 1st- and 2nd-grade teacher, also used the engagement of literature circles in her sheltered English immersion classroom, where English only is used for instruction and students' languages are used for clarification. She emphasized parental participation. The second author of this chapter conducted collaborative research with Robin and documented her use of literature circles (Fain & Horn, 2006). Prior to involvement in the literature circle, each child self-selected a book in Spanish or English and then the children read and talked about these books with their families in their homes. Parents were invited to participate through a bilingual letter and by attending an informational meeting on literature circles. Robin also invited families to respond to the literature the children were reading, using a family-response notebook. Robin recognized that her students spoke two languages and although her classroom was not bilingual she emphasized that all responses were welcomed in whatever language the family chose.

Robin and the second author intended this invitation to discuss books to be open ended. They wanted to provide parents with the freedom to construct and facilitate conversations abut the books from their own perspectives and insights, and to conduct the discussion in the languages spoken at home.

Because the sheltered English immersion model emphasizes just English, Robin and the second author felt that the children's bilingual backgrounds needed to be supported by encouraging families to discuss in their first language at home before having to discuss the books at school in English (Fain & Horn, 2006).

Each of the families then constructed a format that was meaningful and purposeful in their specific family context. The families' conversations were initially influenced by school discourse, such as occurs when teachers dominate the talk by initiating questions to which students respond and then teachers evaluate the responses (Cazden, 2001) Three families used questioning strategies to facilitate the discussions, but their conversations progressed, gradually moving toward meaning-based dialogue about the literature. Each family carefully and purposefully constructed its literature conversations from a different perspective. Table 10.1 summarizes the various ways in which three bilingual families created meaningful dialogue connected to children's literature.

Families used these discussions as a part of maintaining their first language and practicing their second. The family discussions created a language-rich literacy activity by using the discussions to promote the families' first and second languages. Families made conscious linguistic choices that deepened the level of their talk connected to the children's literature.

Storytelling

Another important literacy activity found in the homes of many culturally diverse American communities is the practice of storytelling. Research on

Table 10.1
Family Discussion Formats

Rafael	Elena	Kristina
• His mom and sister used question strategies	• Her mom and sister discussed the books	• Read books together
• Included all siblings in discussions	• Spanish books had longer discussions	• Discussed books
• Started with broad questions	• Asked questions within discussions	• Then taped discussions
• Moved to wanting his opinion	• Made sense of both languages with questions	• Wrote in response journal
• Reflected on family's heritage	• Used 30–60 second wait time as a way of allowing time for response	• Made sense of books using knowledge in Spanish and English
• Encouraged written response and she wrote her response as well	• Wrote and responded in response journal	• Used Spanish dictionary

the literacy practices of Latinos, American Indians, and African Americans has described storytelling as part of students' funds of knowledge (Martínez-Roldán, 2003) and as a very valuable literacy practice that in the case of African Americans has been used in families and communities for multiple purposes, including "entertaining, education, working through problems, sharing history, and recording community events" (Smith, 2004, p. 221). When recognized as a valid literary experience in classrooms, storytelling supports students' ethnic and academic identities. Teachers can use students' stories to build a bridge from oral to written language.

Writing Workshops

Included in Julia's language arts instruction was a 40-minute writing workshop period, in which students engaged in prewriting, creating a rough draft, editing, revising, and sharing with their peers a piece of writing sometimes about self-selected topics and other times responding to an assigned focus. Sometimes the students did group writing. Each day, four or five students signed up to share their writing with the class by reading it aloud. The writings were kept in each student's writing folder. At the end of the month or trimester, students went though their folders and chose a piece of writing that they wanted to expand into a poem, a story, or a published book. There was an authors' celebration at the end of the trimester when the students shared their written and published pieces with their parents.

The writing workshop also seemed to support students in the process of becoming readers. The students were learning genre conventions and letter-sound relationships. There was a great deal of rereading as the students went through the editing process. As part of this process, Julia had conferences with the students on an individual basis to discuss selected pieces of writing. With the less experienced readers and writers, she tried to conference every other day. Only the pieces that were going to be published were edited and revised for grammar or spelling. The messages that the writing workshop sent to students about reading and writing point to the interconnections between these processes and to the variety of purposes that writing serves. For example, one message students received from the experience was that writing promotes learning about reading and reading promotes learning about writing. Another message that the students received was that people read and write for different purposes and use different genres.

Today's Page

Another literacy activity intended to support literacy in Julia's classroom was called "Today's Page." The day always ended in this classroom with a five-minute shared writing experience where the students recorded the most important events of the day. After the students brainstormed as a class the events of the day, they chose five or six events that were written down by Julia on a single sheet in big letters. As Julia wrote what the children were dictating, she slowly read aloud each word, giving the children an opportunity to focus on letter-sound relationships and other aspects of language conventions, such as letter formation, syntax, representation of meaning, and genre formats. After finishing the writing, the whole class read each sentence with the teacher and a student illustrated the page in a space that was left for a drawing. At the end of the month, Julia put together all the pages in a book, which became the history of the class as well as reading material for DEAR. Through this activity, the students could learn that reading and writing are ways to record history, and through this recording, a sense of community was being strengthened.

Addressing Differences through Grouping

Teachers of culturally and linguistically diverse students organize their literacy curriculum in such a manner that students have opportunities to participate in different kinds of groupings, including homogeneous and heterogeneous groups, and individual work. Homogeneous language or reading groups in which teachers can check for understanding and assist learners are vital to support language minority students' learning. These groups are reconstituted periodically as individual needs are addressed, and as new reading and writing strategies are learned. Heterogeneous groups are formed on the basis of students' language, literacy, and content expertise. These grouping patterns help all students to contribute something to the group's learning. These groups are also crucial in providing students with opportunities to negotiate different perspectives and identities. Working in groups develops students' sense of community, which in various language minority communities is valued over a sense of competition.

Finally, one-on-one interaction with students through reading and writing conferences provides teachers with opportunities to follow up on students and provide the specific support each student needs. These individual conferences can be distributed over one or two weeks. Teachers may conference with individual students while the rest of the class is engaged in other learning activities. Over time, this pattern develops into a predictable routine.

Assessment

The topic of the assessment of linguistic and culturally diverse students deserves a chapter of its own. Many scholars have raised concerns about the negative impact of standardized assessments on language minority students and about the limitations of evaluating English language learners only in

English. Here, we want to focus more on assessment that can inform teaching. We highlight some ideas that can help teachers reflect upon their current assessment practices.

When assessing the literacy development of language minority students, teachers would benefit from the use of a range of assessment strategies to get the most comprehensive picture of their students' learning. A major assumption of this assessment is that teaching and learning should not be separated. The most informative and useful assessment is that which uses children's processes and products to document their learning and progress over time, such as Hudelson's (1999) close observation of the literacy development of a bilingual girl across time or Peyton and Reed's (1990) development of profiles of individual writers. By collecting samples of students' work and systematic notes on students' work and participation in literacy activities, these authors were able to present a more complex picture of the students' learning than any test or card report can offer. Peyton and Reed developed profiles of nonnative English speakers based on the analysis of students' journals. These examples offer teachers an indication of the types of writing, patterns of development, and kinds of changes that teachers might expect from their students.

Another important point to remember when assessing language minority students is not to confuse students' ability to express their learning in English with their actual learning. In reading, for instance, students may be able to comprehend English texts far better than they can show through retellings or tests in English (Martínez-Roldán & Sayer, 2006). Therefore, teachers will be in a position to do a more accurate assessment of their students if they take into account the role of language, and particularly the ways in which students may use their first language to mediate and support their reading and writing in English.

Pérez and Torres-Guzmán (2002) offer a variety of examples of assessment strategies that can help teachers document their English language learners' and bilingual students' literacy development. These authors describe and show examples of assessment strategies in chapter 7 of their book. For example, they describe the development of a portfolio system, the use of emergent literacy checklists, and the use of reading assessment strategies. Assessment strategies include the cloze procedure in which every fifth word is deleted and students fill in the blanks; the teacher then checks students' responses to see if they are grammatically appropriate and make sense in the context, resulting in a determination of students' ability to read the material. Another assessment strategy is the informal reading inventory. This measure consists of short reading passages at various difficulty levels followed by comprehension questions; students' responses result in a determination of their independent reading level (their ability to read on their own), their instructional level (their ability to read with some assistance), and their frustration level (the level at which reading is too difficult).. Other writing assessment strategies include journal writing, rubrics for scoring writing, peer-group assessment, and self-assessment.

IMPLICATIONS FOR EDUCATORS

Because there is no typical Puerto Rican, Mexican, Asian American, Native American, or African American community, it is imperative that educators examine their own assumptions about minority students and engage in a process of learning by acknowledging intragroup differences among their students. It is crucial that teachers' and policy makers' decisions reflect an understanding of the fact that children with different proficiency skills and contrasting orientations to literacy and books can be found in the same classroom, community, or family (Zentella, 2005). An implication of this diversity is the need to consider the individual linguistic and cultural backgrounds of each learner within the classroom and the linguistic resources and funds of knowledge that they bring to the classroom. Teachers can learn about these funds of knowledge through home visits designed to learn from the families, not to teach them.

The use of scripted programs in primary classrooms leads often to curicula that overlook and ignore students' cultural and linguistic resources. We argue that educators must begin to creatively build upon their students' local literacies by constructing and implementing literacy teaching that invites all students to learn and to become competent, literate members of different communities in and out of school. Family and community literacy practices can be incorporated in the classroom if teachers make conscious space for authentic learning experiences that involve inquiry, as well as reading and writing for real purposes. Teachers can look for resources, artifacts, multicultural literature, and family and community members to create a curriculum that honors multiple voices within the classroom while socializing students in the use of the genres and social languages that they will need to succeed at school.

Even if teachers do not know their students' languages, teachers can still help their students in many ways. As Cummins (2007) noted, regardless of institutional constraints, educators have individual choices. Educators have choices in how to interact with students, in how to engage them, in how to activate their prior knowledge, in how to use technology to amplify their imaginations, in how to involve parents, and in what to communicate to students regarding home language and culture. As Cummings noted, our society needs all of the intelligence, imagination, and multilingual talents of all of our students.

REFERENCES

Cazden, C. (2001). *Classroom discourse: The language of teaching and learning* (2nd ed.). Portsmouth, NH: Heinemann.

Cummins, J. (2007, February).Teaching for transfer: *Challenging monolingual instructional assumptions in educating bilingual students.* Paper presented at the 36th Annual International Bilingual/Multicultural Education Conference, San José, CA.

Day, F. A. (2003). *Latina and Latino voices in literature: Lives and works* (updated and expanded). Westport, CT: Greenwood Press.

Dien, T. T. (2004). Language and literacy in Vietnamese American communities. In B. Pérez (Ed.), *Sociocultural contexts of language and literacy* (2nd ed., pp. 137–177). Mahwah, NJ: Lawrence Erlbaum Associates.

Fain, J. G., & Horn, R. (2006). Family talk about language diversity and culture. *Language Arts, 83,* 310–320.

González, N. L., Moll, L. C., & Amanti, C. (Eds.). (2005). *Funds of knowledge: Theorizing practices in households and classroom.* Mahwah, NJ: Lawrence Erlbaum Associates.

Halliday, M.A.K. (1979). Three aspects of children's language development: Learning language, learning through language and learning about language. In Y. Goodman, M. Hausser, & D. Strickland (Eds.), *Oral and written language development research: Impact on schools* (pp. 7–19). Newark, DE: International Reading Association.

Heath, S. B. (1983). *Ways with words.* Cambridge, UK: Cambridge University Press.

Hudelson, S. (1999). Evaluating reading, valuing the reader. In E. Franklin (Ed.), *Reading and writing in more than one language: Lessons for teachers* (pp. 81–94). Alexandria, VA: Teachers of English to Speakers of Other Languages.

Lipka, J. (1994). Culturally negotiated schooling: Toward a Yup'ik mathematics. *Journal of American Indian Education, 33,* 14–30.

Lopez-Robertson, J. (2003). Tomas and the library lady: A call to social action. *Arizona Reading Journal, 39,* 10–17.

Martínez-Roldán, C. M. (2003). Building worlds and identities: Case study of the role of narratives in bilingual literature discussions. *Research in the Teaching of English. 37*(4), 491–526.

Martínez-Roldán, C. M., & Sayer, P. (2006). Reading through linguistic borderlands: Latino students' transactions with narrative texts. *Journal of Early Childhood Literacy, 6*(3), 297–326.

McCarty, T. L., & Watahomigie, L. J. (2004). Language and literacy in American Indian and Alaska Native communities. In B. Pérez (Ed.), *Sociocultural contexts of language and literacy* (2nd ed., pp. 79–110). Mahwah, NJ: Lawrence Erlbaum Associates.

Mercado, C. (2005). Reflections on the study of households in New York City and Long Island: A different route, a common destination. In N. González, L. C. Moll, & C. Amanti (Eds.), *Funds of knowledge: Theorizing practice in households, communities, and classrooms* (pp. 233–255). Mahwah, NJ: Lawrence Erlbaum Associates.

Moll, L. C. (Ed). (1990). *Vygotsky and education: Instructional implications and applications of sociohistorical psychology.* New York: Cambridge University Press.

Moll, L. C., Amanti, C., Neff, D., & González, N. (1992). Funds of knowledge for teaching: Using a qualitative approach to connect homes and classrooms. *Theory into Practice, 31,* 132–141.

Pérez, B., & Torres-Guzmán, M. (2002). *Learning in two worlds: An integrated Spanish/English biliteracy approach* (3rd ed.). Boston: Allyn & Bacon.

Pew Research Center. (2005). Hispanics: A people in motion. In *Trends 2005*, pp. 71–89. Retrieved February 26, 2007, from http://pewhispanic.org/reports/report.php?ReportID = 40.

Peyton, J., & Reed, L. (1990). Profiles of individual writers. In J. Peyton & L. Reed (Eds.), *Dialogue journal writing with nonnative English speakers: A handbook for teachers* (pp. 81–107). Alexandria, VA: TESOL.

Sandoval-Taylor, P. (2005). Home is where the heart is: A funds of knowledge-based curriculum mode. In N. Gonzalez, L. C. Moll, & C. Amanti (Eds.), *Funds of knowledge: Theorizing practice in households, communities, and classrooms* (pp. 153–165). Mahwah, NJ: Lawrence Erlbaum Associates.

Short, K. G. (1997). *Literature as a way of knowing.* York, ME: Stenhouse.

Smith, H. L. (2004). Literacy and instruction in African American communities: Shall we survive? In B. Pérez (Ed.), *Sociocultural contexts of language and literacy* (2nd ed., pp. 207–245). Mahwah, NJ: Lawrence Erlbaum Associates.

U.S. Census Bureau (2000). *Census of population and housing.* Washington, DC: U.S. Department of Commerce, Bureau of the Census.

U.S. Department of Education, National Center for Education Statistics. (2004). *Language minorities and their educational and labor market indicators—Recent trends.* NCES 2004–009, report by S. Klein, R. Bugarin, R. Beltranena, & E. McArthur. Washington, DC. Retrieved February 4, 2007, from http://nces.ed.gov/pubs2004/2004009.pdf.

Vygotsky, L. S. (1934/1987). Thinking and speech. In R. W. Rieber and A. S. Carton (Eds.), *Collected works of L. S. Vygotsky: Vol. 1. Problems of general psychology* (pp. 39–289). New York: Plenum Press.

Zentella, A. C. (1997). *Growing up bilingual: Puerto Rican children in New York.* Malden, MA: Blackwell.

Zentella, A. C. (2005). Premises, promises, and pitfalls of language socialization research in Latino families and communities. In A. C. Zentella (Ed.), *Building on strength: Language and literacy in Latino families and communities* (pp. 13–30). New York: Teachers College Press & CABE.

Chapter Eleven

THE IMPACT OF DISABILITIES ON THE ACQUISITION OF LITERACY

Kathleen M. McCoy

WHO IS LITERATE?

Children and adults who read and write are demonstrating conventional literacy. Students who enjoy reading and learning from print are typically excellent readers and writers. Some children, however, even though they are involved in the same reading programs as their more skilled peers, fail to develop literacy or continue to be nonresponsive readers and writers. Some children with disabilities have difficulty accessing meaning from print.

Many children with disabilities become literate, but exceptions frequently occur. Most often, children with neurological or perceptual disabilities remain emerging readers—they can use language to describe important events in their lives, interact well with others, and appear to have very active imaginations, but do not develop the same level of reading and writing fluency as their peers. Less often, some children with mild and severe disabilities will be unable to demonstrate conventional literacy; these children are nonresponsive to reading and writing instruction.

Children who are eligible for special education services can still become literate. For example, children with Down Syndrome have achieved reading competencies equivalent to 5th-grade levels, and Down's children as young as three and four years old, although lacking all the typical preskills of reading readiness, including alphabetic knowledge, have been able to able to learn sight words. Many, but not all, children with disabilities can read and write.

Difficulty in acquiring reading literacy skills is a predominant characteristic of many individuals with disabilities. Most of the approximately 2,887,217 school-aged children in the United States who are receiving special education services have qualified for those services because of poor reading ability (Lyon et al., 2001).

Problems acquiring reading are not limited to students with high-incidence disabilities, such as behavior disorders, learning disabilities, and mild mental retardation, autism, or speech and language impairments. Students who do not qualify for special education services may have reading problems, due to a variety of conditions, such as ineffective instruction, cultural background, and insufficient opportunities to develop reading skills. Both students with and without disabilities can be reading below grade level. Achievement differences in literacy are particularly noticeable in children from urban areas among specific ethnic populations (National Assessment of Educational Progress, 2000). Students' reading scores have not significantly improved over the last three decades. .

WHO ARE THE POOR READERS?

Children with low levels of literacy have difficulty completing assignments in school and taking tests and do not view themselves as bright and capable individuals. No one knows for sure why not all children develop conventional literacy, but many theories have been developed. The most popular theories include causes such as auditory disabilities, visual difficulties, rate or time-processing issues, anxiety ,or combinations of these behaviors, for example, poor visual processing or slow auditory processing coupled with anxiety when approaching a reading task. Ironically, some children with these problems do become literate; some children with documented disabilities learn to read and write at the same level as their peers or beyond their peers'.

Most students with disabilities who also exhibit poor literacy skills desperately want to be good readers. They want to be like their peers who can sound out words and understand and remember what they have read. Many students with disabilities cannot sound out words, and cannot comprehend or remember many of the words they can decode. Some children who do not demonstrate conventional growth in literacy are said to exhibit a condition called dyslexia.

DYSLEXIA

The term dyslexia has multiple meanings, but they all imply that an individual cannot read or write very well. Dyslexia and related reading disabilities have been attributed to neurological problems, such as a limited capacity for storing, manipulating, or processing information, an inability to recall speech-based sounds, or a difficulty retaining the visual-spatial information found in letters and words. Reading disabilities have also been attributed to ineffective or inappropriate teaching practices.

Determining the cause of reading disabilities is challenging at best and frustrating at worst. If, however, specialized programs designed to address reading problems are not successful, then most likely the problem is inherent in the way the students are processing the information needed to acquire reading literacy. The results of various reading studies strongly suggest that reading difficulties resulting from problems in language are more difficult to remediate. One simple measure that suggests processing difficulties is listening to the sequence of events in a story while trying to understand what the story means. Children with certain types of intrinsic language-processing problems have difficulty keeping information in their memory while dealing with incoming ideas. This measure can be used to distinguish typical from atypical processors and to develop appropriate literacy programs early in a student's program.

NEED FOR LITERACY

Without belaboring the obvious, the ability to read is a critical factor in successful school achievement. Not surprisingly, a strong correlation exists between poor reading ability and school failure. Students with disabilities who do not have access to the information contained in textbooks and related materials are at a significant disadvantage in acquiring the knowledge contained in the school curriculum. Hence, the search for techniques to raise literacy levels for students with disabilities such as behavior disorders, learning disabilities, mild mental retardation, autism, and speech or language impairments, who constitute about 85 percent of the approximately 5 million school age youth classified with disabilities, is a high priority for educators.

Improving early reading instruction is an important goal for general and special educators alike. "Matthew effects" is a phrase used to identify the theory that small problems in reading ability in the primary grades spiral to huge gaps by the elementary and upper grades, resulting in some children being placed in special education classes. Students' poor reading skills are magnified at every successive grade level as opportunities for intervention diminish.

Although many extensive and praiseworthy efforts to develop techniques to prevent reading problems have been attempted, an overwhelming number of middle and high school students with disabilities read significantly below grade-level expectations. Only 26 percent of students who display literacy disabilities in 3rd grade will be successful readers; 74 percent of students with reading disabilities will continue to struggle to access print in 9th grade and beyond (Lyon, 1995).

LITERACY DURING PRIMARY YEARS

Developing literacy during the primary years has received strong emphasis. Many children with disabilities entering kindergarten and 1st grade, however, have not developed physiologically and cognitively to the point at which they are able to learn the relationships between abstract symbols and meaning. Fine motor skills involving the hands and the eyes may not be well developed in these early years. Some five- and six-year-old children with disabilities have not developed sophisticated language concepts. Some young children with disabilities have not yet learned how to communicate with others. Although most children with disabilities have been exposed to print, not all are ready to learn to read effectively through traditional approaches.

The reading methods to which a learner with disabilities has been exposed may be excellent for typical students but be a poor fit for students with disabilities. For example, Reading Recovery is a reading program designed to raise the lowest-achieving readers in 1st grade up to the average of their class within four months. Children whose reading skills seem very similar at the initiation of the Reading Recovery program may show very different competencies after 16 weeks of instruction. One child may be reading at grade level, but another may have made no progress whatsoever. The reading program may be an excellent match for one student but a poor fit for another. For children with disabilities, the instructional solution is to find the best fit between students' strengths and the instructional method or combinations of methods.

BEYOND PRIMARY LEVEL INTERVENTION

Reading, writing, and thinking are interrelated processes that foster communication. Reading and writing are socially constructed communicative practices that grow in sophistication as students' skills become more refined. Intervention at the beginning levels of reading and writing may be able to create a sound foundation for more sophisticated literacy practices. Reading and writing are not an end product but an ongoing and lifelong developmental process. With a little assistance from a sound intervention, many floundering young readers can become literate. Some children with atypical communication may flourish with early intervention, while others may not develop age-appropriate skills from language intensive programs.

Even with instructional emphasis on early literacy, not all children with disabilities learn to read in grades K–3. Although the skill levels of beginning readers and older poor readers may look the same, a quick look at the physical differences between a 5-year-old and an 11-year-old suggests otherwise. Interventions for older children with disabilities need to take into account experiential interests, as well as the impact of past instructional strategies and the physical, emotional, or cognitive effects of a disability. Interventions for middle school and secondary school readers are often modeled on strategies used with much younger children. These approaches fail to take into account the impact of the disability on the acquisition, maintenance, and generalization of literacy skills.

By middle school, most struggling students with or without disabilities have made several failed attempts to become better readers and writers. They are not very receptive to beginning the reading process again, especially when most of the reading material is written at a very low level. Even when poorly skilled middle and upper level readers do attempt to read, they typically fumble through texts to the point where comprehension is compromised. Many nonresponsive readers over age nine would rather not engage in reading activities that promise more of the same embarrassing and uninteresting "little kid" materials that they have experienced over and over again.

Middle school students with literacy issues are given the almost impossible task of reading complex textbooks. These texts are built on the premise that middle and upper grade readers possess vocabularies and comprehension skills that are suitable for accessing curriculum content. Not all students, however, have highly developed language skills that are in tune with the language of the textbooks or related materials. Some children have language deficits caused by having a first language other than English, making the struggle for literacy with printed English overwhelming.

Many primary-aged students with literacy issues will continue to experience reading-based learning problems well into adolescence and beyond. Reading disabilities do not end with high school graduation. The good and bad news is that some students in college and even graduate school are dyslexic; their reading continues to take a lot of effort, time, and energy. Many older readers with serious skill deficits are so delayed that they struggle with remembering words, sounding out new terms, and comprehending simple information (Fletcher, Morris, & Lyon, 2003).

ACTIVE AND INTERACTIVE NATURE OF READING

Many definitions of reading propose that reading is an active and interactive process between the author and the reader or between the printed page and the past and current experiences of the reader. The most popular reading definitions are based on some variation of a cognitive-constructivist model. A cognitive-constructivist model is a view of the reading process as composed of many interrelated components, some of which are based on higher-level thinking processes usually associated with comprehension and some of which are grounded in lower-level mechanical skills usually associated with word recognition and sound-symbol correspondence.

Reading could be considered *thinking guided by print* or *print guided by thinking*. Realistically, however, a person can think with and engage in all kinds of comprehension activities, such as following verbal directions, or understanding the main ideas of stories read orally or videos, but not be able to read print. In turn, an individual can sound out symbols and recall whole words but not be able to comprehend. Reading from print requires the ability to engage higher-level skills with lower-level skills, but in different degrees of interaction depending on the nature of the reading material and the developmental, linguistic, and experiential sophistication of the reader.

With many instructional reading approaches, the first steps in acquiring reading ability typically focus on sounds and symbols and word recognition. Yet, these mechanical components of reading are meaningful only when the emerging reader can use mechanical skills and associate words or sounds and symbols with prior knowledge. For example, most five-year-old children are engaged in the act of reading as they carefully sound out words. They have been organizing their individual bodies of knowledge, called schemata, since the day of their birth. Stored in their brains are personally meaningful memories, some of which were experienced directly and others vicariously. All the objects, situations, events, and actions and their respective sequences that children have valued have been carefully stored and internalized in their young minds, and now they are matching their schemata with the print in front of them. Typical five-year-olds have many schemata; these may include a schema for animals, like birds and cats, for situations like being in kindergarten, at church, and at a best friend's house, for events like going to the movies or the mall, for smells like popcorn and chocolate, and for sequences of events, like preparing to go play with a friend.

Most five-year-olds are making sense of what they are reading by seeking meaning between the printed word and their schemata. When a match between the reading material and their schemata is found, they relate the new experience to similar experiences or concepts. When a match is not found, the information is put into a new category to be matched with future experiences. Students are organizing and networking concepts in their minds. Having rich and interconnected networks of schemata assists children in having almost instantaneous access to massive amounts of knowledge. Too many isolated categories negatively impact reading; a network-poor child will not be able to make matches between text and prior experience rapidly or efficiently with print. Some children with disabilities have difficulty relating past to current experiences. Some children with disabilities are network poor.

EFFECTS OF DISABILITY

The type of disability is a factor that forms experiences and is integral to the development of schemata. Disability affects schemata development. Children with disabilities, including many who have language and learning disabilities, often display expressive and receptive communication difficulties. Typically, children with language issues engage less in social interactions than students with more typical language skills. These children's experiences and resulting schemata are different from the norm and may be impoverished due to lack of social interaction—an important source for acquiring incidental knowledge. Incidental knowledge is gathered informally from life experiences in contrast to formal classroom-based instruction. Incidental knowledge is a powerful contributor to developing schemata. Children with various types of disabilities can learn to read, but they may need specialized techniques to access print.

The type of disability a child has shapes the number, kind, and quality of mental networks he or she develops. Children with visual impairments, for example, will have different experiences with sounds, letters, and words than children whose language deficits are distorted due to blocked access to hearing or saying letter sounds and words. Some children who are heavily medicated as a result of their disability either intermittently or continuously may lack focus, which in turn impairs the development of their schemata. Children who do not have access or who have limited access to sensory input develop schemata, but their references or networks are built upon somewhat different experiences than the schemata of children with more typical sensory and motor skills.

Disability labels do not and cannot identify the appropriate reading and writing approach for any child. Labels such as learning disabled, autistic, physically disabled, or hearing impaired, for example, do not determine a corresponding methodology for teaching reading and writing. For example, one child might have severe visual restrictions: the child is not blind, but does have low vision. Such children are partially sighted and typically require special aids, such as large type, magnifiers, and special lighting so they can complete work that requires detailed vision. Other children also labeled partially sighted can have different types of visual impairments, for example, visual issues involving ocular fine motor control impacting the ability to maintain near or far point focus. As their visual system tires, so does their ability to concentrate. They must use a great deal of energy to keep their ocular system focused, but eventually, depending on the level of involvement, after a time ranging from seconds to minutes, the letters on the page may become blurry, melt into each other, and/or eventually simply disappear.

READERS AT RISK

A phoneme is the smallest unit of sound in a language that differentiates one word from another; for example, the word *fat* involves blending three phonemes, /f/ /ae/ and /t/. Letter-sound knowledge and the ability to manipulate phonemes is an important predictor for growth in reading for children at risk for reading disabilities (Savage & Carless, 2004). Many ways to develop phonological awareness exist. Some children expand their phonological awareness informally by becoming sensitized to sound-related events in their daily lives. Without any formal instruction, some children understand the relationship between sounds and letters by experiencing nursery rhymes and songs, listening to stories read by relatives and teachers, or manipulating plastic letters on the front of the refrigerator. Television programs like *Sesame Street* also help students heighten letter-sound correspondence.

Some children with disabilities may also experience nursery rhymes and songs, listen to stories, and manipulate plastic letters, but unlike their counterparts, no matter how often they watch programs like *Sesame Street* they do not or cannot integrate such phonemic information when attempting to read. These children, especially those at risk for reading disabilities, become phonologically sensitive primarily through formal instructional approaches. The development of phonological awareness cannot be left to chance for most children with disabilities, because their disability puts them at risk for reading problems. For children with disabilities who are at risk for reading failure, phonological awareness must be explicitly taught. These children need to be taught how to identify rhyming and nonrhyming word pairs, how isolated sounds blend to form words, and how spoken words can be segmented into individual syllables.

EXPLICIT INSTRUCTION

In the last decade, many reading intervention specialists have concluded that some form of explicit and direct instruction in phonemic awareness/analysis and decoding skills is essential for students who are at risk for or those who already demonstrate reading difficulties This work was discussed in Torgesen, Rashotte, Alexander, Alexander, and MacPhee (as cited in Papalewis, 2004). Children with disabilities in language, hearing, and vision are usually categorized as students at risk for reading failure. The techniques most often associated with explicit instruction incorporate elements of direct instruction. Direct instruction includes direct explanation, modeling, and guided practice, with continual monitoring and feedback, review, and mastery learning. Letter sounds and names, syllable identification, and common vowel rules are explained, modeled, and practiced in a variety of reading situations, and are checked and rechecked for understanding and reviewed until the phonics skills are automatic and fluent.

Instruction in decoding can be a major boost for the acquisition of reading proficiency. This is the case for many at-risk readers with disabilities, but even explicit instruction will not be appropriate for all students. Some students can receive direct instruction in a phonics-rich reading environment, but in spite of instruction that specifies letter-sound relationships, practice in converting letters to sounds, and making words out of letters, some children show no gains in reading. About 30–50 percent of low-achieving children, despite exemplary and explicit instruction, never acquire sufficient language and decoding skills to become fluent readers (Fuchs et al., 2001).

FACTORS CONTRIBUTING TO VOCABULARY DEVELOPMENT

For nonresponsive primary-aged readers, the reading picture is indeed dismal. Even with special education services and after years of instruction, the techniques for improving reading and spelling skills for nonresponsive readers beyond the primary grades remain unclear. Repeating phonics instruction and expecting significant change in reading performance for nonresponsive readers is futile. Learners must be fluent readers before they can derive meaning from text, but most nonresponsive readers cannot develop enough fluency in applying what they have learned about letter-sound combinations to be able to derive meaning from the printed words. Students with phonological processing problems have difficulty with basic word recognition and reading comprehension.

A student's capacity for remembering words is also a predictor of who will be a good reader and who may need extraordinary means to access meaning from print. Even the most efficient readers probably have an upper limit to the number of new words that they can recognize and remember (Hiebert, Martin, & Menon, 2005). When asking children to read words in short, predictable books, the best readers remembered 30 to 160 new words; the middle ability readers recalled 15 words, and the lowest ability readers remembered only 6 words (Johnston, 2000). Children whose disability includes memory issues are likely to be considered nonresponsive readers.

Children's experiences play a large role in determining their vocabulary growth. Long before children come to school, they have developed word identification strategies. They use *picture cues* and *environmental cues*. They associate meaning with pictures or print in their everyday world. Children often develop a word recognition strategy called reading *by configuration*—figuring out a word by its shape, length, or even its significant letters, such as the first letter of a child's name.

For children who are experiencing physical, cognitive, or emotional issues or whose surroundings are print poor, access to environmental, picture, and configuration cues may be limited or distorted. Many children with disabilities are disadvantaged relative to their peers in acquiring words through environmental, picture, or configuration cue strategies. Children's visual, auditory, motoric, affective, or cognitive challenges in their everyday world may limit their contact with the environment. For some children, physical or emotional disabilities keep them in and out of hospitals during much of their early lives, and limit their experiences. Complications from the primary condition can create secondary issues, such as fatigue, lack of concentration, and distractibility, which have significant ramifications for the acquisition of literacy.

FLUENCY

Fluency, speed, and accuracy are significant characteristics of reading. Speed and accuracy are developed as readers start to internalize letter-sound correspondence, word patterns, and matching the pronunciation of the word to its spelling. Fluency is the development of speed after accuracy has been established (Spinelli, 2006). Repeated reading of words is usually the final step that anchors words in the reader's memory and speeds sight word recognition during reading. The more quickly the reader can recognize a word, the more quickly communication is gathered from print. An appropriate level of fluency provides the reader with more cognitive space for processing the meaning of the word or text.

Beginning readers rely heavily on phonics to learn new terms and commit words to memory. Children's mental resources, which have been focused on sounding out letters at the beginning reading stage, can as they progress be redirected to tap into their schemata, their interconnected and multiple networks of meaning. A reader's schemata, phonics awareness, and word recognition cannot be separated, but play different parts at different developmental levels.

Nonresponsive readers cannot construct meaning from the text and do not develop oral or silent reading fluency. Beginning readers and less-skilled older readers typically read aloud slowly, haltingly, and with little or no expression. These readers are not likely to develop a high level of literacy.

A variety of fluency levels have been established, identifying appropriate reading rates at each grade level. Systems based on broad guiding principles for minimum oral reading fluency rates, like the one provided by Guszak (1985), also include grade level criteria: (a) 60 words per minute for grade 1; (b) 70 words per minute for grade 2; (c) 90 words per minute for grade 3; (d) 120 words per minute for grades 4 and 5; and (e) 150 words per minute for grades 6 and 7.

As with any generalization, exceptions will be common, especially for children who have disabilities. Many children with disabilities will read at the same rate as their nondisabled peers, but the effects of disabilities on some children may interfere so strongly that a particular number of words per minute may be irrelevant or may never be achieved. Children whose speech and language skills are affected by motoric issues, significant intellectual challenges, and visual and auditory processing difficulties are unlikely to demonstrate minimum oral reading fluency rates. The reading rates of many children with disabilities will be influenced by the nature of their problem.

Since the goal of word recognition is to establish communication from print between the reader and the author, teachers must monitor word recognition development by assessing the reader's ability to comprehend text. Rate will play a factor, but rate is not sacrosanct. Forcing readers with disabilities to meet the expected norms for their peers without disabilities may be damaging at best and lethal to word recognition at worst.

DIFFERENTIATING INSTRUCTION

Children with disabilities, even more so than their typically developing peers, need differentiated programs of instruction. Program development must be based on the needs of the student. Progress in learning to read and write is, among other factors, strongly related to individual differences in language, phonological skills, listening comprehension, and vocabulary knowledge. A child's disability may or may not affect his or her reading progress, but must be analyzed relative to the child's strengths and weaknesses. To provide effective instruction, programs must address the development of fluency and comprehension in accordance with the child's intellectual, emotional, and sensory repertoire.

BALANCED READING PROGRAMS

Most instructional theories recognize aspects of text-based and reader-based models. In text-based models, the reading process is presented through explicit and direct instruction with words and word components, practice, and correction. Text-based models place instructional focus on processing skills in a sequential and systematic manner.

Proponents of reader-based models generally believe that reading begins with the reader making a hypothesis about the author's intentions. Readers read to verify or refute their hypothesis and do so by selecting words or passages to validate their thoughts. In these models, readers use the *lower units* of reading, such as letters, only to a limited extent. Instructional reading programs must incorporate a differentiated approach in which text-based and reader-based lessons are complementary and fit the instructional needs of the student.

As students become more proficient with low-level strategies, such as sounding out words, most will advance to word recognition and meaning. Most students, when given the opportunity, will move back and forth between high- and low-level reading strategies, blending techniques provided through text-based and reader-based models.

All students are unique in their literacy attainment and development. To develop literacy, students with disabilities need a balanced program. *Balance* refers to providing students with differentiated instruction according to their level of achievement and their cognitive, affective, and sensory abilities. Larger amounts of instructional attention and time spent with students who have reading deficits are characteristic of a balanced literacy program (Rasinski & Padak, 2004). A fundamental source of differentiation in a balanced, comprehensive, and equitable reading program is time. For some students, the balance will tilt toward more time spent on acquiring phonics skills; for others, the balance can lean more toward whole-word acquisition. Struggling students need more time in instruction than students who are developing literacy with ease, and that time must take account of the unique levels of cognitive, affective, and sensory abilities found in children with disabilities.

MODIFICATIONS

Not all students are going to be able to use textbooks without major modifications to the text. Many learners, especially those who are eligible to receive special education services, are struggling readers. Readers who do not make reading progress even with well-crafted programs may need extraordinary means to access print. Accessing print is the key to literacy. Technology may provide the way into text content for some children previously locked out of meaningful use of print.

Fortunately, assistive technology offers an affordable means of using the text for those students who will not be able to access print in a meaningful manner. Compensatory approaches involving technology can be provided if learners' persistent performance deficits are directly addressed. These approaches may reduce or eliminate the effect of the disability and allow struggling readers to use textbooks as information sources.

Technological resources that help students with disabilities to access texts include (a) text to speech capability; (b) varying text size; and (c) reference resources, such as online dictionaries. These are found in electronic books (e-books), online publications, and digital libraries. Students can also access print through the use of specialized hand-held pens that can scan, store, and transfer printed text.

The advantage of many assistive technology devices is that they provide audio feedback. The devices allow the learners literally to hear the message encoded in print. Assistive technology can open the floodgates of knowledge for students previously trapped in a nonmeaningful world of print.

The overarching focus of all literacy instruction is the reader. Each child is actively constructing new meaning based on comparisons he or she is actively making with his or her prior knowledge and experiences. Children, regardless of disability, are engaged in constructing meaning. They need the support and guidance of teachers who eliminate learning barriers and build on children's prior experiences and knowledge to enable the children to read meaningful content.

REFERENCES

Fletcher, J. M., Morris, R. D., & Lyon, G. R. (2003). Classification and definition of learning disabilities: An integrative perspective. In H. L. Swanson, K. R. Harris, & S. Graham (Eds.), *Handbook of learning disabilities* (pp. 30–56). New York: Guilford Press.

Fuchs, D., Fuchs, L. S., Thompson, A., Al Otaiba, S., Yen, L., Yang, N., et al. (2001). Is reading important in reading-readiness programs? A randomized field trial. *Journal of Educational Psychology, 93,* 251–267.

Guszak, F. J. (1985). *Diagnostic reading instruction in the elementary school.* New York: Harper and Row.

Hiebert, E. H., Martin, L. A., & Menon, S. (2005). Are there alternatives in reading textbooks? An examination of three beginning reading programs. *Reading and Writing Quarterly, 21,* 7–32.

Johnston, F. R. (2000). Word learning in predictable text. *Journal of Educational Psychology, 92,* 248–255.

Lyon, G. R. (1995). Research initiatives in learning disabilities: Contributions from scientists supported by the National Institute of Child Health and Human Development. *Journal of Child Neurology, 10,* 120–126.

Lyon, G. R., Fletcher, J. M., Shaywitz, S., Shaywitz, B., Torgeson, J. K., Wood, F., et al. (2001). Rethinking learning disabilities. In C. Finn, A. Rotherha, & C. Hokanson (Eds.), *Rethinking special education for a new century* (pp. 259–287). Washington, DC.: Thomas B. Fordham Foundation.

National Assessment of Educational Progress (NAEP). (2000). *The Nation's Report Card on Reading—2000.* Washington, DC: National Center for Education Statistics.

Papalewis, R. (2004). Struggling middle school readers: Successful, accelerating intervention. *Reading Improvement, 41,* 24–37.

Rasinski, T., & Padak, N. (2004). Beyond consensus—Beyond balance: Toward a comprehensive literacy curriculum. *Reading and Writing Quarterly, 20,* 91–102.

Savage, R., & Carless, S. (2004). Predicting growth of nonword reading and letter-sound knowledge following rime- and phoneme-based teaching. *Journal of Research in Reading, 27,* 195–211.

Spinelli, C. G. (2006). *Classroom assessment for students in special and general education* (2nd ed.). Upper Saddle River, NJ: Pearson.

Part Three

FOUNDATIONS FOR EARLY LITERACY DEVELOPMENT

Chapter Twelve

CHALLENGING THE READINESS MYTH: PARENTS' INVOLVEMENT IN EARLY LITERACY DEVELOPMENT

Christine Walsh

We knew that our six-year-old son, James, was really thinking like a reader or a writer when he participated in the following exchange after spontaneously hitting his father: "Why did you hit Dad, James?"

"It wasn't a hit; it was an exclamation point!"

My husband, Brian, and I looked at each other with huge grins on our faces, both thinking, "Did he really say that?"

The instant at which James compared a nonverbal gesture (hitting Dad) to a punctuation mark (an exclamation point) told me so much about his level of understanding of language. It showed his ability to think abstractly and symbolically; we know he can linguistically use one object or idea to represent another, and he can draw comparisons. In his mind, the hit reminded him of a heavy punctuation mark or "hit" at the end of a sentence.

In most cases, a child learns spoken language before he learns to read or write; oral communication is the basis for all other language processes (Cambourne, 1988). I believed in this assumption for many years as a literacy educator. There was no reason not to believe it until I began closely watching a real language learner in my own home. In James's case, and possibly in many other children's cases, this was not the route literacy took. James, diagnosed with autism and global developmental delays at age three, did not speak before he could read and write. Until he was three and a half years old, we waited impatiently to hear "Mama" and "Dada," but heard nothing. We wondered if he would ever have expressive language. Instead, James learned to read, write, and then speak.

Much has been written in past years about reading readiness, a theory that suggests there is a stage children pass through before they become readers (Leu & Kinzer, 1995), and that nonreaders really have no reading skills or abilities. If this is true, then if a child exhibits certain preacademic literacy behaviors now, can you predict how well he will read later? I laugh when I think about what this theory suggests. How can anyone really know for sure what literacy behaviors are going to lead to others, especially with children for whom language development is atypical? Literacy development is recursive and more complex than this; there are no lockstep stages or steps that all children must pass through. Even parents can't understand all the thinking that takes place for a child who is nonverbal. In James's case, he was more than ready to read even before kindergarten; he was already reading and we would have never known it had we not watched and listened carefully to what he was "telling" us.

LISTENING AND WATCHING, MOVEMENT AND GESTURES

We need to listen to children to learn how to teach them. But how does a parent listen when a child doesn't have a voice? How is James's early language development similar to and different from other children's because of his autism, because of the absence of oral communication, and because of his different way of "reading the world"?

There was really no consistently workable communication system for this very bright little boy who wanted to hear his own voice and see that it was being heard. Clearly, he wanted to make things happen but could not figure out how. So we learned and signed (using American Sign Language) a handful of words (e.g., "yes," "no," "please," "more," "thank you," "stop," "open," "all done," "play," "yellow," "blue," "stop"). In addition to signing, James and I would also touch the boldly printed word labels on particular objects I had placed around the house (e.g., TV, chair, door, cart, books, computer) and use flash cards with objects around the house to reinforce the idea that each thing has a series of letters (a word) that represents it. He was passing my "quizzes" with flying colors, and that is how I know he learned to read before he learned to speak. When I held up the card that said "door," he'd touch the door. When I showed the card for "computer," he would touch the computer. At three and a half, James spelled "books" out loud with no prompting as soon as he started talking because it had been written on every bookcase in the house.

Pointing and showing are two milestones in literacy, though these expressions are often taken for granted and neglected in literacy education textbooks. Most young children exhibit both as forms of purposeful communication. Pointing to objects, near and far, pointing to observations made, then looking to see if the parent/caregiver notices, is a highly complex skill. Bringing, sharing, and showing objects that they find is another way children demonstrate their interpersonal literacy skills and understandings, even before solid oral communication patterns are developed. James did neither. No checking with us to see if we saw what he saw. No excitement over a toy or other object to the point where he'd bring it to us. At five, he began repeating the same phrase or word again and again, each time waiting for a response from the listener. He gets upset when there is none. In the car, he now points at and identifies all the signs and places as we pass by them. He is still developing the reciprocity of language that most children develop between two and four years of age. Literacy is happening, just not in the same order or in the same fashion as with other children.

James could nod "no," but nodding "yes" presented a problem. He still moves most of his upper body when nodding "yes," a more global body gesture instead of just a head bend from the neck. The up and down of "yes" for some reason is more difficult than the side to side of "no." So we decided to wear lanyards around our necks with signs/pictures for YES/NO on one side, and MORE/ALL GONE on the other. This became a constant in our communication exchange each day. He would point to the symbol that represented his desired response. We would also offer him choices throughout the day by showing our fists: one fist for milk, one fist for juice. Again, he would point to the fist that represented his desired choice. It served as a breakthrough in helping James find a voice he could use for real purposes in life. Thank you, early intervention!!

When I really watch carefully, I see that James's mind always seems to be more engaged when his body is also engaged (tactile, kinesthetic). I suspect this might be the case for most children. As adults, think of how much easier it is for us to exercise when we're conversing with a friend. We often walk longer distances when we partner walk and engage our minds in some kind of stimulating activity. Bodies and minds really need each other, a fact that some of us tend to forget after we leave childhood. Each morning before school starts, James and I dance and sing to at least one Wiggles song on the TV or CD player. His teacher thinks this helps him concentrate better once he gets to school. It literally "gets the wiggles out"!

WE LEARN TO READ BY READING

The single most important thing I have done as a parent is reading to James every day since shortly after he was born. I made sure to begin by telling him the title and the author of each book before starting it, and I would usually read two or three different books each time we read, such as *Goodnight Moon* (Brown, 1947) and *The Runaway Bunny* (Brown, 1942). These books are still his favorites and have the worn pages to prove it. Shortly after learning to speak, James began reciting favorite titles and their authors like a seasoned reader. Even before learning to speak, he would choose a few books before bedtime each night, or he would find the books that he was asked to find in the book basket. It was probably a combination of the illustration and color and the words on the front cover that allowed him to remember authors and titles so quickly. I made sure to change the books in the book basket regularly so that he would be exposed to a variety of texts, but not so often that he wouldn't have a chance to fall in love with one or two or ten.

James could identify letters and spell and read words long before he could make his mouth produce sounds. We know this because as soon as he did begin speaking, he was uttering two, three, and four syllable words, spelling words, and reading words from picture books. I had barely heard my son's voice when one day, he looked at my coffee creamer on the kitchen table during breakfast, pointed to the words and said, "Coffee-Mate." I had to look at the label to believe it myself. I looked back at James in disbelief, "James, you're a reader!!" How in the world did that happen?

How did James learn to read? I am in awe at how invisible this process really was. If I had to attribute it to one thing, I would have to say that he learned to read simply by reading. Like the rest of us, he still is learning to read, the process still evolving at a good pace. But young readers literally learn language patterns, letter sounds, and relationships among ideas very naturally by participating in frequent, enjoyable reading events with more capable readers. We have always maintained and asked his teachers and therapists to maintain high expectations for him, to always assume he will be able to do something as opposed to starting with a deficit model, or believing that, because of his disability, he probably cannot accomplish something. James has far exceeded our expectations.

When teachers and parents encourage children to use picture/text connections in books they enjoy, by pointing to the picture and then the word as we read aloud to them, over time they will do the same. Taking picture walks or wonder walks with young readers is a great way to orient them to books. Young children often think in pictures, as do many autistic individuals (Grandin, 1995). Allowing James to create meaning with text through pictures was a motivational step that sustained his interest throughout his nonverbal years, so that by the time he began speaking, he was already hooked on reading and books.

I never allowed his disability to interfere with the idea that James would be literate, despite his inability to speak until almost age four. Now he jumps in bed each night ready with his favorite storybooks: *Curious George,* Jan Brett's *The Mitten* (1989), and the old standbys, *The Tale of Peter Rabbit* (Potter, 1991) and *The Poky Little Puppy* (Sebring, 1945). He still loves *The Runaway Bunny* (Sebring, 1942), because now he knows how to decode the words instead of just reading the pictures and memorizing the words we have read over and over again. He loves Alexander's "no-good very bad day" books (Viorst, 1972), and just about all of Mem Fox's books, especially the rhymes in *Sleepy Bears* (1999) and the beautiful expression of love between mother and child in *Koala Lou* (1988). As 1st grade progresses, he is also branching out into nonfiction and informational stories: *Icky Bug Shapes* (2003) by Jerry Palotta and *Stellaluna* (1993) by Janelle Cannon are new favorites. All of this could not have happened in a split second, or even over the course of a week or a month, as soon as he learned to speak at almost four years old. It must have been gestating for some time!

All the while we were under the impression that maybe James's literacy skills and abilities were not going to emerge, that they might not even exist, his literacy development was alive and well, hard at work, probably working double time, trying to find a voice, meaning, purpose, and audience in his quiet little world. Why do we sometimes assume, when someone cannot express himself well, that he must have little of value to express?

James's wonderful speech therapist, Kristen, had a firm belief in repetitive, isolated drills in phonics, which challenged my long-standing philosophy in teaching literacy using a purely holistic approach. "He needs to know sound/symbol correspondence first in order to learn to read." I disagreed. Did she know from her years of working with autistic kids that he probably was already learning to read even though he wasn't speaking much yet? I felt it a waste of time to focus on letter sounds when he hadn't yet found his own voice.

James had many pre-reading skills before having this phonemic awareness. Thus, over the years, James was exposed to a variety of literacy activities, both discrete skills-based (e.g. applied behavior analysis, as described in Maurice, 1993) and holistic/child-centered (e.g., Greenspan's floortime model, 2006). Without Kristen's rigid instruction in letter sounds, I wonder if James would be reading as well as he does now. That combination of both approaches seemed to be a key, at least for one language learner. Children are "excellent critics of our theories" (Kane, 1995) once we stop and look and listen.

LEARNING TO WRITE AND DRAW: THE POWER OF VISUALS

Emergent readers often embed much of their meaning of stories and communicate many of their ideas in pictures before they learn to represent meaning in sound/symbol correspondences (letters and words). For many autistic people, too, seeing and thinking in pictures is much more powerful than just hearing language (Grandin, 1995). Simply put, some people create meaning more readily through patterns and visuals. When the members of James's kindergarten class were asked to draw a picture of their family standing in front of their house, then add and color the clothes that each family member might be wearing, I was heartbroken for James, who was just learning how to draw a circle with eyes, nose, and mouth on the paper. In his mind he was likely thinking of Mom and Dad and James and our dog, Khemo; however, given his delayed fine motor and motor-planning skills, he could only eke out a huge happy face with two eyes. I remember being amazed at the detail in other children's illustrations.

Calkins (1994) encourages us to "read" our children's drawn stories as much as we listen to their spoken stories and to encourage them to add more detail and embellish upon the good ideas. "How much was it?" "What color were they?" "How long did it take?" "What were YOU doing when this happened?" By asking probing questions like these, we are first and most importantly telling our children that their ideas are interesting and important to us and we want to know more about what and how they are thinking. In addition, we are getting them to think more laterally and more deeply about each thought they are sharing with us. We are giving them tools they will need to add description and detail to their written work later, when writing becomes a viable communication tool for them. Adding detail to pictures now will lead to more vivid detail and description later. If we make it a game and probe regularly, they will begin asking us and then themselves the very questions we ask them: except when the child cannot draw what he is thinking.

Instead of James's kindergarten teacher asking him over and over again to draw these pictures on large blank pieces of white paper all year long (which other children loved and he dreaded!), she could have fostered his sense of story through oral language first, since he was talking by then. She needed to show him that his language does count, that it does have a shape to it. She needed to help him get the detail down somehow if that was the objective, then later attempt to teach him to draw what he was saying and thinking. Doing it in a way that reversed the order in which his language processes were acquired might have helped James progress more as a literacy learner.

LEARNING TO SPEAK: LAST BUT NOT LEAST

Communication and interaction with others are what form and sustain our relationships in life. But parents and teachers cannot make the assumption that for all people these abilities simply develop; they are neither a natural progression nor an effortless event for all children. I am often reminded about Greenspan's "communication circles" and how they changed my way of thinking about early literacy. Greenspan suggests, after years of researching hundreds of young children of varying abilities and ages, that in one act of communication between a sender/speaker and a receiver/listener, there can be 30 or more completed circles, depending on the relationship between the two persons. Saying one thing and getting a response back is one circle. Nonverbal gestures, such as sharing a toy, a quizzical look, or a wave signifying "hi," are also parts of one circle. An example of a completed circle would be saying "Hello!" to someone and receiving a "Hello!" in return, or giving someone an object and getting a smile in return.

When I started taking a closer look at James's communication patterns at the time when he was three and four years old, I was counting maybe one or two circles at any one time, meaning that if I said something to him and he acted on my comment or question (first circle), then I would initiate a second circle by making a comment or asking a question and receive a response of some kind back (second circle). And that would be the extent of our social interaction. It happens in a matter of seconds. Ideally, we want to continually increase the number of consecutive circles that occur between the parent and child. Often people with autism will not respond after the first or second initiation, or their response will not relate directly to the speaker's content, which means it takes much longer for one circle to be completed. After many years of therapy and good modeling, James is now able to complete up to 10 communication circles, again depending on with whom and about what he is interacting.

We were encouraged by a behavior consultant to withhold granting James's requests until he made good enough approximations in signs or pointing or with pictures that communicated what he wanted (picture exchange communication system). Even though I knew instinctively what he wanted, I had to pretend I did not know, until he was able to show me/us somehow what it was. This was one of the hardest things I had to do as a mother. We are so quick to react, to give, to nurture, even if it means our child is becoming more and more dependent on us. I needed to be reminded that our goal was for James to become more independent, more skilled at communicating his own needs.

Interestingly, as soon as James began speaking, he went around the house taking down each and every word label! He also could orally spell any of those words without looking at them, if quizzed. He still can. His visual memory is simply amazing. He can sometimes recite much of a 30-page book verbatim after seeing it and reading it aloud with me only four or five times. So while we remained under the impression that maybe James's literacy skills and abilities were untapped or nonexistent, his literacy development had progressed immeasurably. His young brain was probably working very hard, trying to find a voice, meaning, purpose, and audience for language in his quiet little world. Finally, after years of worrying that he would never speak, the first words we heard were: "mud puddle" as he pointed to one outside. Then "purple" the same day. Hooray!

EARLY LITERACY AT HOME AND SCHOOL

Nothing can replace reading with a child at home. Pamela Michel, in *The Child's View of Reading* (1994), explains that children's perceptions of reading at home are very different from their perceptions of reading at school, and that "the child's perspective is critical to understanding how children learn to read" (p. 11). This was clearly illustrated when I was helping James choose a book to read before bed one night. I picked up a book we had not yet read, one that came from his school library. (I often wonder how James goes about choosing books during library time.) "No, Mom, I don't want a school book; I want this one." Each week he has a few school library books in his backpack, but none of them ever make it to the top of the read-aloud pile at home. Most times they are returned without being opened.

Likewise, elementary school reading instruction too often moves children away from seeing reading as a meaning-making activity and instead gives children the idea that reading in school is "stand up, sit down," "fill in the blanks," and "too much seatwork" (Michel, 1994). Sadly, paper and pencil activities and teacher directions have replaced pleasure and engagement in the process of learning to read in these classrooms. We desperately need to give our children a more hopeful and purposeful version of what reading really is, by doing it at home with them every single day and letting them be in charge.

Parents need to create a print-rich environment in their homes that models for children the literacy they are expected to acquire in their world. This will help them learn from what they read and plan their behavior according to what the signs say to them. As we play at home, we put up railroad crossing signs, store signs (Home Depot, Target, etc.), stop and go signs, end of the road signs, North, South, East, and West signs. He loves the fact that "JCT" stands for "junction," then he looks for that sign when we drive around. Now he says that "W" stands for "West" and "N" stands for "North," which I never mentioned to him.

As parents, we can teach so much about language to children by taking them for a ride in the car and using our language to describe how and where we are going. New vocabulary words abound, including directions such as "left," "right," and "yield." "Yellow means caution!" James yells from the back seat. Prepositions are also easy to teach when you are doing something fun: "under" the bridge," "over" the hill, "next to" the farmhouse, swinging "up" high, "behind" the building! The colors red, yellow, and green coordinate with the "red light, green light" game played in physical education class and at swim lessons at the YMCA: kick hard for green, slow down for yellow, stop kicking for red. This is all purposeful, authentic communication consistently and happily modeled by adults in real contexts. "Children benefit when we establish literacy in the social and cultural contexts of their everyday lives" (Taylor & Strickland, 1989, p. 275).

Though at home each night James reads 20- and 30-page books independently, at school he is unable to focus on text for more than a few pages at a time. When asked to choose a book for free choice reading, rather than selecting a text on his true reading level, James chooses *Chicka Chicka Boom Boom* (Martin, 1989), a preschool favorite that tells more about his social/emotional age than it does about his actual literacy development. His teachers do not fully know yet what James's literacy successes are. I need to stay in touch with them, with him, so we all get to know the complete James. We will all nudge him toward literature choices that will challenge him, while giving him some measure of control over books he loves to read just for fun.

James's 1st-grade teacher has already found out that when she puts her arm around him during reading group time, he laces his arm around hers, and he is able to sit and pay attention for longer periods of time than when he is sitting on his own without that tight comforting feeling. She is creating for him that homey feeling that he gets every night as we lie in his bed with our heads on the pillow taking turns reading a page at a time.

LOVING GOOD LITERATURE

An important question for literacy teachers and parents is what kinds of texts motivate children to read? James reacts to storybooks quite differently than to what I would call nonsense literature. Despite his relatively well-developed sense of humor, he doesn't seem to be greatly motivated by texts with which he cannot make meaning. It seems as though texts whose primary purpose is to reinforce the interesting sounds and spelling patterns of our language do not turn him on. While the characters are silly, the silliness does not hold his interest.

Tonight we barely made it through another lengthy nonsense text that asks the reader to consider a similar scenario on just about every page. James's legs were up in the air, his feet hitting the book, his humming clearly telling me that he was done. When I asked him if we should stop reading, he first said "no," but then when I paused a few pages later, he quickly threw the book to the bottom of his bed. I am secretly happy he has graduated from this stage of development! James rarely abandons a book once we've started reading it. But this one had no plot, no real meaning. And he wasn't going to be fooled. It's okay to let children abandon a book if it has little interest for them. There are so many books available that will be motivating; let's not waste our time on ones that are not. Good teachers allow the child to determine and let us know which are right for them at certain times.

Likewise, James has no interest in reading photocopies of stories that are sent home every Friday night, with a homework assignment to read them again and again and keep them at home. They contain contrived sentences with no flow and characters that are not real. I don't blame him for not wanting to read these books when he has hundreds of really exciting stories to listen to and read and look at, books with interesting sounds and spelling patterns. He is getting more from books of high interest, books that have characters he can really relate to, books that have sentences that relate to each other, books that have a variety of words to roll off his tongue like real English language, all of this combining to form a story with meaning that a young reader can think about, learn from, and enjoy. Imagine having a discussion about something other than the short "a" and short "i" sound after reading Harcourt's *Ham? Hat?* (Williams, 2005) the purpose for which is also to teach the short "a" sound.

I don't know about James, but I was having trouble keeping all the names straight myself! I had to turn back a page or two to make sure I kept the characters' names straight. Too many words with similar sounds made fluency and comprehension nearly impossible even for an experienced reader. Plus, I couldn't have cared less about who had the ham and who had the hat at the end.

I allowed James to skim over these books when I saw his lack of engagement. I can focus on the short vowel sounds in so many other, more fun books if need be. If, and only if, James were having difficulty decoding words like a 1st grader, I might consider pulling these fake (oops!) books out over the weekend, but that is not the case. James is an excellent decoder. When I begin reading these books with him, I see his anxiety increase. I try to get him to say why he doesn't like what we are reading, but I don't think he quite knows why he doesn't like it. It seems hard for him to make his mouth twist around to fit all of these sounds that usually do not go together. It's English, but no one speaks or writes this way in real life. He knows it. He understands language enough to know this. Why do teachers continue to spend valuable instructional time making strong readers sound out words and read artificially created texts, just to teach the skills they have already mastered? What is the effect on student motivation when they do this?

I watch and listen and respect James's wishes. We last about two pages into the basal story when he runs to get something better, like this one, from H. A. Rey's (1941) timeless picture book, *Curious George:*

> George wanted to get out.
> He climbed up to the window to try the bars.
> Just then the watchman came in.
> He got on the wooden bed to catch George.
> But the watchman was too big and heavy.
> The bed tipped up,
> the watchman fell over,
> and, quick as lightning,
> George ran out through the open door. (Rey, 1941, p. 34)

James is glued. This story has suspense, a funny and interesting story line that is easy to follow, a character children can relate to, and text that challenges young readers to develop their decoding skills while they are comprehending and learning new (not artificially selected) vocabulary. Children deserve to escape to the worlds offered to them through good literature. So do adults. Why not do it together? Imagine the rich discussions you can have together after reading about George and all of his curious antics! Now when we go to the local library, James looks for other *Curious George* books, videos, CDs, and so on. We hold his stuffed Curious George monkey from the 1960s while we read about George!

I will tell James that there are many kinds of reading, and that the little nonsense books are just one type of reading. They are different, but that they can teach us things. I do not want him to think that his teacher can make up a homework assignment and we can simply choose not to do it. Just as Jeanne Reardon (1990) teaches her 1st graders that reading tests are just another genre, I also need to show James that reading these texts serves a purpose, too. Maybe I will tell him we are practicing reading words with the short "a" sound, and that we aren't going to be looking for a story or funny characters. Or maybe I'll just have him read the list of high-frequency and decodable words at the end of the story, and if he is successful, I'll say we've done the homework for tonight. He does feel like such a big boy when it's homework time, always glad to do it before playing. There are so many different purposes for reading and it's never too early to point them out.

CONCLUSION

Until now I assumed all children needed to learn literacy in the same order: speak, then read, then write. James is a perfect example of our need to revisit our beliefs about language acquisition and language learning, as educators who are prepared to teach all children, not just children who fall into the neat mainstream of education. How many other parents and teachers are attempting to help their children speak, then read, and then write, in that order? Just as the writing process is recursive, so, too, is the process of learning all language. It is very individual, nonsequential, and nonlinear. It cannot be taught in a formulaic way to all children with identical results.

What kind of literacy support do teachers and parents, who teach children for whom the "normal" progression of developmental steps is out of order, need? What do we do with the children who challenge our assumptions about how children learn to read, write, speak, and listen for a variety of purposes? As James has taught us, contrary to the readiness theory, there is no one natural way to get ready to read or learn to read. Children's progression through literacy processes may not follow a neat, logical order, and might instead result in something completely unique. Our scaffold must support the process, whatever shape it takes.

James has also taught us that when there is a voice, there is literacy in one form or another. With any luck, James will have teachers who empower him to use his own voice to make his own decisions and to show the world who he is and what he is capable of. When we stop more often, look more closely, and listen more carefully, parents and teachers alike can use what our children teach us to make critical literacy decisions that can influence them for a lifetime.

REFERENCES

Calkins, L (1994). *The art of teaching writing.* Portsmouth, NH: Heinemann.
Cambourne, B. (1988). *The whole story: Natural learning and the acquisition of literacy in the classroom.* New York: Scholastic.
Grandin, T. (1995). *Thinking in pictures and other reports from my life with autism.* New York: Doubleday.
Greenspan, S. (2006). *Engaging autism: Helping children relate, communicate and think with the DIR Floortime Approach.* Englewood, NJ: Prentice Hall.
Kane, S. (1995). My children became my teachers: Developing a philosophy of reading. *The Reading Teacher 48*(6), 530–531.
Leu, D., and Kinzer, C. (1995). *Effective reading instruction K-8.* Upper Saddle River, NJ: Merrill Publishing.
Maurice, C. (1993). *Let me hear your voice.* New York: Knopf.
Michel, P. (1994). *The child's view of reading: Understandings for teachers and parents.* Boston: Allyn & Bacon.
Paley, V. (1990). *The boy who would be a helicopter: The use of storytelling in the classroom.* Cambridge, MA: Harvard College: President and Fellows.
Reardon, S. J. (1990). Putting reading tests in their place. *The New Advocate, 1*(1), 29-37.
Taylor, D., and Strickland, D. S. (1989). Learning from families: Implications for educators and policy. In J. B. Allen and J. M. Mason (Eds.), *Risk makers, risk takers, risk breakers* (pp. 251–280). Portsmouth, NH: Heinemann.
Vygotsky, L. (1986). *Thought and language* (A. Kozulin, Ed. and Trans.). Cambridge, MA: MIT Press. (Original work published in 1962).

Children's Literature Cited

Brett, J. (1989). *The mitten.* New York: Scholastic.
Brown, M. (1942). *The runaway bunny.* New York: HarperCollins.
Brown, M. (1947). *Goodnight moon.* New York: Harper and Row.
Cannon, J. (1993). *Stellaluna.* New York: Scholastic.
Fox, M. (1988). *Koala Lou.* New York: Trumpet Club.
Fox, M. (1999). *Sleepy bears.* New York: Harcourt Brace.
Martin, B. (1989). *Chicka chicka boom boom.* Aladdin Picture Books.
Palotta, J. (2003). *Icky bug shapes.* New York: Scholastic.
Potter, B. (1991) *The tale of Peter Rabbit.* Lakewood, OH: Smarty Pants Audio and Video.
Rey, H. A. (1941). *Curious George.* New York: Scholastic.
Sebring, J. (1945). *The poky little puppy.* New York: A Golden Book; Racine, WI: Western Publishing.
Seuss, Dr. (1960). *Green eggs and ham.* New York: Beginner Books.
Viorst, J. (1972). *Alexander and the terrible, horrible, no good, very bad day.* New York: Aladdin.
Williams, G. (2005). *Ham? Hat?* New York: Harcourt Brace.

Chapter Thirteen

PLAY AND EARLY LITERACY IN THESE TIMES

Kathleen Roskos and James Christie

Play has long had a key role in early childhood education, where it has been viewed as an efficient medium for promoting all aspects of child development (e.g., Van Hoorn, Nourot, Scales, & Alward, 2007). Preschool programs have routinely allocated large blocks of time to play-related activities. Play has indeed been at the center of the early childhood curriculum.

Recently, major policy shifts in early childhood education, including the standards movement and the new science-based perspective on early learning are threatening to erode play's stellar curricular status. Zigler and Bishop-Josef (2004, p. 1) warn:

> In recent years, children's play has come under serious attack. Many preschools and elementary schools have reduced or even eliminated play time from their schedules.... Play is being replaced by lessons targeting cognitive development and the content of standardized testing, particularly in the area of literacy and reading.

Long-standing beliefs about play as the antithesis of work and a lack of strong evidence linking play with academic outcomes have worked together to marginalize play as a context for learning school readiness skills. In today's pragmatic climate, if an activity is not directly linked with the skills needed for school success, that activity can be quickly forced out of the early childhood curriculum.

Play is resilient and its defenders steadfast, however. Even as current policy initiatives threaten play's role in early childhood education, these same policies also open up new possibilities for understanding and promoting the play-literacy interface. Recent curriculum guidance in the UK, for example, sets out a *pedagogy of play,* broadly defined as providing play-based activities, designing play-learning environments, and using play-supportive teaching techniques (Wood & Attfield, 2005). Movement in this direction is also occurring in the United States. At the Play = Learning conference held at Yale University in 2005, a number of play scholars argued convincingly for play-learning links at home and school (Singer, Golinkoff, & Hirsh-Pasek, 2006).

Over the past decade, we have reviewed play-literacy studies through different lenses, observing the strengths of the relationship and the yet unknown. Given the rapid changes in early education at the start of this century, we think it is useful to revisit this area of research again, to benchmark what we know and still do not know about the play-literacy interface. We have organized our review of play/literacy studies around three perspectives: (a) what play does for the child's developing mind; (b) how it contributes to the literacy learning environment; and (c) its role as social activity that scaffolds literacy performances and mediates literacy practices.

THE PLAYFUL MIND

Is play biological or cultural in origin? There is a long-standing debate about this issue. Although no clear answer is in sight, neuroscience is unearthing new data showing that the young brain is amazingly versatile and a "jungle of potentials" (Sutton-Smith, 1999, p. 246). Play may be a biological necessity in early childhood because it supplies the brain with what it needs to grow: exploring, testing ideas and skills, combining materials and actions, repeating actions to the point of automaticity, inventing, and pretending. This playful mind perspective opens up new avenues of thought about the play-literacy interface.

Examining the play-literacy relationship from the perspective of what is going on the child's mind addresses the question, "Does play promote cognitive growth that lays the foundations for literacy learning?" In a recent review, Smith (2007) cited three sources of evidence of play's role in cognitive growth: (a) the evolutionary history of play, which suggests that play may be a general-purpose learning mechanism; (b) cross-cultural evidence that pretend play is always present in young children and thus is likely to be useful; and (c) evidence on the extent to which play is designed to provide opportunities develop specific cognitive skills, such as narrative skills and theory of mind, that in turn may promote literacy learning.

Smith examined the "design" research studies in more detail, focusing on evidence that pretend play contributes to the development of theory of mind, the awareness of one's own and other people's knowledge and beliefs. Results from both correlational and experimental studies suggest that make-believe play may increase children's theory of mind, which may later help them with planning, guiding, and monitoring their own intellectual activity, including reading and writing (Flavell & Hartman, 2004). Smith points out a number of methodological limitations of both types of research, however, such as the difficulties that "third factors" can create in correlational studies and a multitude of issues that can confound the findings of experimental research (e.g., inappropriate controls, experimenter bias).

Smith concludes that evidence supports that pretend play may *help* to bring about theory of mind and other cognitive skills, but the current evidence does not support the contention that make-believe play is *necessary* for their development. Make-believe play appears to be one avenue for developing the cognitive equipment that will lay the foundation for successful literacy acquisition, but these same skills can be also learned through direct instruction. Smith does point out that play has one advantage over instruction—play is highly motivating and enjoying, giving it an important advantage with young children. Little research has been done to explore this potential motivation advantage, however.

Along these lines, a recent study conducted by Sawyer (2002) focused on the "design features" of pretend play that may lead to the development of narrative competence, the ability to express and make sense of experiences through stories. He points out structural similarities between pretend play and narrative. Both make-believe play and narrative (a) are framed as alternative worlds, distinct from everyday life; (b) have fictional characters; (c) involve decontextualized language; and (d) have plot elements (characters, goals, actions to attain goals, and resolutions). When pretend play becomes social and occurs in groups of children, another even more important parallel arises. Group make-believe play and narrative both involve *collaborative emergence,* in which the outcome of the activity is not determined by an individual; rather it results from the collective contributions of each member. Sawyer proposes that group make-believe provides children with experience of a form of improvisation. When children collaborate in play, their contributions are evaluated and sometimes accepted and other times rejected by playmates. Each contribution builds on the prior turns of others, resulting in the gradual emergence of an improvised narrative. To successfully participate in group pretend play, children must negotiate with each other and coordinate their actions and symbolic transformations (e.g., everyone needs to know that the rope is a pretend hose to be used to fight fires). This negotiation draws children's attention to the features of narrative and also requires them to make judgments about what other players know and understand—the theory of mind discussed in Smith's (2007) review. The collaborative nature of this play improvisation creates mutual enculturation, in which children learn to construct meaning in conventional ways that can be understood by others, building a foundation for writing.

Rowe conducted two related studies, one with her colleagues and one alone: (a) a nine-month naturalistic study of two- and three-year-old children's book-related play in a preschool classroom (Rowe, Fitch, & Bass, 2003); and (b) a case study of her own child's literacy learning from ages two to four (Rowe, 1994). Data from both studies showed that the young children's book-related play involved a number of cognitive activities that may promote literacy acquisition. For example, the young children used book-related toys to connect book content to concrete objects (e.g., miniature dinosaurs) and to express personal responses to books (e.g., the use of a toy to punish another toy that represents a "bad" character in the story). This type of play has the potential to bolster the development of symbolic representation. Rowe also discovered that children engaged in play that appeared to clarify the author's meaning and build new concepts. She gives an example of how her son was confused about the concept of a steam engine in the book *Mike Mulligan and His Steam Shovel* (Burton, 1939) and used play to sort this out. He pretended that his closet was the boiler and that a wooden spoon was a coal shovel.

Our view of the play-mind connection is that it appears likely that pretend play *can* lead to the development of cognitive skills that promote early literacy learning. It is also likely, however, that these same early literacy skills can be learned just as well, if not more efficiently, through other means such as interactive storybook reading, shared writing, and age-appropriate forms of direct instruction. As Smith (2007) pointed out, play does appear to have some potential advantages as a learning medium for young children, such as high interest, engagement, and motivation. Yet these features of literacy-related play have not yet received much attention from researchers. We think back to the excitement that was initially generated by Sylva, Bruner, and Genova's (1976) finding that play has a facilitative effect on children's problem-solving abilities. In this study, children had to solve a problem that involved clamping sticks together in order to retrieve a marble or piece of chalk that was out of reach. Children who were allowed to play with the clamps and sticks did just as well at solving this lure retrieval problem as the children who were directly trained to solve it. In addition, the play condition had an *advantage*. The children who played with materials were much more persistent in their attempts to solve the problem than those who were taught to solve it. Failed attempts did not appear to frustrate them, because they were just playing around with the materials. Later research indicated that these results may have been partially due to experimenter bias (Simon & Smith, 1983), but the notion that play has a motivational edge warrants further study.

Our point is that in this new era of early literacy "basics," it is going to take more than studies to show that play *can* result in children engaging in activities that are *likely* to promote early literacy. Research is needed to show that play experiences or curricula that have a strong play component are at least as effective as, if not more so than, alternative means of instruction.

THE PLAY-LITERACY INSTRUCTIONAL ENVIRONMENT

Are playful early experiences with print and books beneficial? That question has been asked often in the play-literacy research—and the answer is yes. Literacy-enriched play environments encourage more play with print, support book-reading, develop language skills, and motivate children to read and write (Roskos & Christie, 2004). What remains unanswered, however, is the question as to whether playful experiences with literacy result in meaningful improvements in children's later academic achievement? If so, how do language and literacy-rich play experiences and the play environment help shape literacy development in different ways at different times?

We have recently examined the relationship between play, literacy, and instruction at the curriculum level by focusing on the concept of *networked play* and its role in helping children learn the new preschool academic basics (Roskos & Christie, 2007). Our review examines the rise of three megatrends in early education and their impact on play: (1) the new science-based approach to early education; (2) the movement toward early childhood learning standards and standards-based education; and (3) the view that early literacy is the cornerstone of school readiness. We view the impact of these trends as less dire than do many play advocates, provided that early educators expand play's role to complement and enhance the new pre-K basics. In the past, play has functioned as a stand-alone activity, isolated from the rest of the curriculum. Play themes and materials were chosen on their own merit to elicit rich play, with little regard for how this play was connected to what went on during large-group circle time and small-group instruction. This needs to change. We believe that if play is to thrive in the current educational environment, a considerable amount of classroom play needs to be closely connected or *networked* with the academic curriculum. This can be accomplished by linking play environments and activities with the standards-based content taught in large- and small-group settings. In addition, teachers need to take an active role during play periods and guide children's play activities toward instructional goals.

As a case in point, Han's (2004) recent research examines the play-literacy instructional environment at a more specific level by looking at how child characteristics—play style and literacy ability—relate to children's access to the play environment and supportive teacher interactions. Previous research on literacy-enriched play environments has tended to be unidirectional, focusing on the effects of the environment and teacher scaffolding on children's play and literacy behavior. Han examines these interactions from a multidirectional, bioecological perspective: the environment affects the child and the child influences the environment. Han's findings suggest that children's play preferences appeared to influence their choice of play setting, which, in turn, influenced their access to play materials and opportunities. Children's play predispositions also appeared to affect the amount and type of interaction that children had with teachers. Dramatists, who expressed a keen interest in people and group pretend play, spent more of their time in the dramatic play and art centers and were exposed to richer oral language, interactive storybook reading, and other supportive teacher interactions. Patterners, who were interested in objects and their design possibilities, spent most of their time in the block and computer areas and received less attention from teachers. Han interpreted her findings to indicate that the literacy-enriched play strategy, as it is commonly implemented, may be more effective for dramatists than for patterners. She pointed out the need to develop literacy play strategies that accommodate the interests and abilities of children with diverse play interests.

We believe that current research offers a ray of hope for the future of play in the current science-based early education environment. However, there is difficult work to be done. In an earlier review, we have pointed out the need for connecting many (but not all) play activities with the academic curriculum, so that play directly supports standards-based educational outcomes (Roskos & Christie, 2007). There is great need for carefully controlled experimental studies to compare this type of networked play curriculum with programs that rely mainly on direct instruction and tiered interventions (i.e., skill-and-drill curriculums). It's not enough to argue that play is beneficial for the whole child. We need evidence that play-based curricula are as effective as programs that do not include play, if not more effective. Our hunch is that, if given a fair test, programs that connect play and instruction will do just as well as instruction-only programs in terms of learning the basics. In addition, networked play programs should produce some extra benefits in the areas of child engagement, motivation, and self-regulation.

Han's research (2004) points out the importance of taking individual differences into account when designing curricula and doing evaluation studies. Effective curricula should include activities that appeal to the interests of different genders, cultural backgrounds, and basic personality characteristics such as play predisposition. For example, curricula that network play and instruction should include literacy-enriched, theme-related activities in all centers—dramatic play, blocks, manipulatives, art, and computers. This will help ensure that *all* children get the academic, social, and emotional benefits of play activity. Evaluation research should always use designs that allow subject by treatment interactions to be examined.

THE PLAY-LITERACY SOCIAL CONTEXT

Can social relationships and local literacy-in-play practices shape literacy development? We have only scratched the surface on this question, which shifts the focus of attention from *what's going on in there* (inside the head) to *what's going on out there* (outside the head in the social milieu). Fundamentally the sociocultural perspective seeks to understand the influences of social participation and human relationships, whether in peer-led or adult-led situations. It attempts to describe children's participation in local literacy events, their position or role in these events, the ideological assumptions that literacy events hold, and the literacy objects and spaces used to engage in literacy activity (Rowe, 2006). A sociocultural focus expands the agenda for play-literacy research by broadening the scope of the *who, what, when,* and *where* of investigation. It broadens the lens on literacy development, attempting to trace change from its earliest roots, and urges new prospective theoretical models to capture this dynamic, as in microgenetic studies (Yaden, 2006). The study of the play-literacy interface from this perspective is moving forward, but in many ways it is a slow go due to the methodological challenges of documenting multiple, interacting systems.

Three studies are noteworthy here. Neuman and Gallagher (1994) investigated the effectiveness of an intervention program designed to help teenage mothers enhance the quality of their communicative interactions with their children during everyday home literacy activities and routines. This everyday literacy approach differs from that of previous family literacy programs that have attempted to train parents to provide school-like experiences for their children. The Neuman and Gallagher intervention used a guided participation strategy, derived from Rogoff's work (1990), that prods children use their imaginations, make plans, and take personal responsibility for accomplishing everyday tasks. In short they try their hand at mental work that holds much in common with that of literacy. Mothers are taught a four-step strategy: (a) Get Set, in which the mother adjusts her level involvement to match the child's abilities; (b) Gives Meaning, in which she focuses the child's attention on certain aspects of activity through labeling, comparing, contrasting, and/or elaborating; (c) Build Bridges, in which she helps connect the current activity to her child's prior knowledge and experiences; and (d) Step Back, in which the mother phases out her support so that the child takes control of the task.

Neuman and Gallagher investigated the effectiveness of the four-step strategy in three contexts: storybook reading, instruction, and play. Findings revealed that the storybook reading context provided the most opportunities for mothers to give meaning to experience. In the play context, mothers were more likely to build bridges, helping children employ their imaginations. This can promote distancing, the ability to separate one's thinking from concrete here-and-now reality. Instruction appeared to provide a situation in which mothers could step back and hand over responsibility to their children.

Examining the sociocultural side of play-literacy connections from another angle, Hall (2007) approached the in-school/out-of-school dichotomy from a more critical perspective that draws heavily on a social literacy, a view that emanates from anthropology and sociology. Social literacy emphasizes how literacy is used in everyday life outside of school settings. Hall uses the distinction between *ideological* (everyday life) versus *autonomous* (school) literacy as the rationale for a new type of adult involvement in play. Hall argues that teachers should set up situations that require children to use *ideological* forms of literacy in connection with their play. This involves setting up problems or obstacles that children need to overcome before they can continue with their play (e.g., getting planning permission to build a play garage). This is quite different from the play facilitator role that is typically advocated in the play-literacy literature (Roskos & Neuman, 1993; Enz & Christie, 1997). Rather than simply assisting children's play efforts, Hall recommends that teachers stretch children's literacy skills by presenting them with challenges that link play with real life. Here the teacher acts as a gadfly or provocative stimulus, presenting children with situations and problems that link play with real-world *ideological* literacy activities. Further research is needed to understand the promise of this strategy in literacy-enriched play settings.

Deeply rooted in a Vygotskian perspective, Bodrova and Leong (2006) have investigated the play-literacy connection in a series of formative field studies. Make-believe play, according to Vygotsky, creates its own zone of proximal development for acquiring the mental tools (e.g., symbolic representation, metalinguistic awareness, and self-regulation) that are needed to learn to read and write. Bodrova and Leong have developed a *play-planning* strategy that promotes the acquisition of these mental tools. The teacher leads a 10-minute, play-planning period prior to center time in which each child makes his/her own plan for what he/she will do in centers. Teachers guide children to use these plans to manage their own behavior and to resolve conflicts with other players. Initially, children's play plans consist of meaningful scribbles. In time, the plans progress to drawings and then to emergent writing. When children are ready to use writing in their plans, teachers support the process with scaffolded writing. They teach children to write lines that serve as placeholders for the words the child wants to write. Initially, the child dictates words, and the teacher writes them on the child's lines. Soon, children begin writing their own words using invented spelling. Again, the teacher provides a support tool:

picture alphabet charts. Eventually, children begin reading each other's writing, providing social motivation to use more conventional forms of spelling to represent words.

One theme that connects all of these sociocultural-based studies of the play/literacy relationship is that each expands the definition of literacy beyond traditional academic boundaries and recognizes that literacy is a social practice in which children create meaning with the help of others. Neuman and Gallagher's family literacy intervention is embedded in everyday interactions between mother and child. Hall's approach to literacy-enriched play is connected with real-life literacy activities such as dealing with planning permits, help-wanted ads, and job applications. Literacy in Bodrova and Leong's play-planning intervention involves meaning-laden scribbles, drawings, and scaffolded writing used to plan and manage play activities. Another common thread found in the sociocultural perspective is adult scaffolding. Parents or teachers supply temporary assistance to promote children's play, language, and early literacy. This scaffolding takes several forms: guided participation (Neuman), play challenges and hurdles (Hall), and play planning (Bodrova and Leong). In each of these strategies, the adult raises the bar, while at the same time providing temporary assistance that helps children progress to the next level of development.

RESEARCH TO PRACTICE

So where are we now in this endeavor to understand the zone of convergence between play and literacy? From our at-a-glance survey, we can see clearly the cognitive processes that merge in play and literacy (e.g., using symbols to convey meaning), especially in the renewed emphasis on children's developing theory of mind. But we lack the benefit of basic neuroscience research that goes to the core of the neural mechanisms that play and early literacy precursors may share (e.g., self-regulatory abilities). The developing mind, after all, is housed in a developing brain that organizes core processes at a neural level. Basic research along these lines has the potential to add a new dimension to our understanding of the playful mind.

Some new studies show that we are gaining ground in learning about the external environments that support the transfer of play's processes and skills to the demands of literacy. Environments differentially support individual play propensities with consequences for early literacy exposure. We are also making headway in understanding the role of instructional resources as capacity builders in the educational environment for linking play and literacy in more productive ways. Networked play curricula and more knowledgeable teachers, for example, increase the potential of the learning environment for connecting play and literacy activities. Future studies should attempt to unbundle (and reassemble) the key components of instructional capacity in the early childhood classroom environment, including the factors of teacher knowledge, quality of materials and play objects, and overall culture of learning.

Too little attention, however, has been paid to the digital turn at the play-literacy interface, which is surprising given the rapid expansion in modern societies of new technologies such as televisions, DVDs, computers, handheld computers, cell phones, and computer games (Larson & Marsh, 2005). Clearly this is an area ripe for new studies that examine the links between play processes (e.g., engaging in semiotic activity) and new concepts of print involving nonlinear, nonsequential, multilayered negotiations of multimodal texts (Hassett, 2006). Early literacy learning in a new media age, in fact, may spur a resurgence of social play in early education because its demands for complex, abstract thinking (e.g., imagining, negotiating, improvising) are closely related to those needed for negotiating multimodal texts (navigating screens, interpreting images, parallel processing).

While the research base on the play-literacy connection is relatively thin, there is enough evidence that specific play strategies may yield early literacy learning benefits. Providing for book-related dramatic play and group collaborative pretend play has important implications for children's narrative competence. Creating high-quality, literacy-rich environments that appeal to children's different interests and preferences supports literacy engagement. Coaching play by scaffolding play sequences and introducing challenges into play scenarios can make a difference in literacy play quality. Play, in sum, earns its place in a strong preschool and kindergarten curriculum, even in this era of accountability and early childhood content standards.

REFERENCES

Bodrova, E., & Leong, D. J. (2006). Vygotskian perspectives on teaching and learning early literacy. In D. Dickinson & S. B. Neuman (Eds.), *Handbook of research in early literacy development.* New York: Guilford Press.

Burton V. L. (1939). Mike Mulligan and his steam shovel. Boston: Houghton Mifflin.

Enz, B., & Christie, J. (1997). Teacher play interaction styles: Effects on play behavior and relationships with teacher training and experience. *International Journal of Early Childhood Education, 2,* 55–69.

Flavell, J., & Hartman, B. (2004). What children know about mental experiences. *Young Children, 59*(2), 102–109.

Hall, N. (2007). Literacy, play and authentic experience. In K. Roskos & J. Christie (Eds.), *Play and literacy in early childhood: Research from multiple perspectives* (2nd ed.). (pp. 169–184). Mahwah, NJ: Lawrence Erlbaum Associates.

Han, M, (2004). *A bioecological view of play and literacy: interaction between play predisposition and environment.* Unpublished doctoral dissertation, Arizona State University.

Hassett, D. (2006). Signs of the times: The governance of alphabetic print over "appropriate" and "natural" reading development. *Journal of Early Childhood Literacy, 6*(1), 77–104.

Larson, J., & Marsh, J. (2005). *Making literacy real: Theories and practices for learning and teaching.* Thousand Oaks, CA: Sage Publications.

Neuman, S. B., & Gallagher, P. (1994). Joining together in literacy learning: Teenage mothers and children. *Reading Research Quarterly, 29,* 382–401.

Rogoff, B. (1990). *Apprenticeship in thinking: Cognitive development in social context.* New York: Oxford University Press.

Roskos, K., & Christie, J. (2004). Examining the play-literacy interface: A critical review and future directions. In E. Zigler, D. Singer, & S. Bishop-Josef (Eds.), *Children's play: The roots of reading* (pp. 95–123). Washington, DC: Zero to Three Press.

Roskos, K., & Christie, J. (2007). Play in the context of the new preschool basics. In K. Roskos & J. Christie (Eds.), *Play and literacy in early childhood: Research from multiple perspectives* (2nd ed.). Mahwah, NJ: Lawrence Erlbaum Associates.

Roskos, K., & Neuman, S. (1993). Descriptive observations of adults' facilitation of literacy in play. *Early Childhood Research Quarterly, 8,* 77–97.

Rowe, D. (1994). Learning about literacy and the world: Two-year-olds' and teachers' enactment of a thematic inquiry curriculum. In D. Leu & C. Kinzer (Eds.), *Forty-third yearbook of the National Reading Conference* (pp. 217–229). Chicago: National Reading Conference.

Rowe, D. (2006, April). *A social practice perspective on two year-olds' learning about writing.* Paper presented at the annual meeting of the American Educational Research Association, San Francisco.

Rowe, D. W., Fitch, J. D., & Bass, A. S. (2003). Toy stories as opportunities for imagination and reflection in writers' workshop. *Language Arts, 80*(5), 363–374.

Sawyer, R. K. (2002). Improvisation and narrative. *Narrative Inquiry, 12*(2), 321–351.

Simon, T., & Smith, P. (1983). The study of play and problem solving in preschool children: Have experimenter effects been responsible for previous results? *British Journal of Developmental Psychology, 1,* 289–297.

Singer, D., Golinkoff, R., & Hirsh-Pasek, K. (Eds.). (2006). *Play = learning: How play motivates and enhances children's cognitive and social-emotional growth* . Oxford, UK: Oxford University Press.

Smith, P. K. (2007). Pretend play and children's cognitive and literacy development: Sources of evidence, and some lessons from the past. In K. Roskos & J. Christie (Eds.), *Play and literacy in early childhood: Research from multiple perspectives* (2nd ed.). Mahwah, NJ: Lawrence Erlbaum Associates.

Sutton-Smith. B. (1999). Evolving a consilience of p lay definitions: Playfully. In S. Reifel (Ed.), *Play and culture studies* (Vol. 2, pp. 239–256). Stamford, CT: Ablex.

Sylva, K., Bruner, J., & Genova, P. (1976). The role of play in the problem-solving of children 3–5 years old. In J. Bruner, A. Jolly, & K. Sylva (Eds.), *Play and its role in development and evolution* (pp. 244–257). New York: Basic Books.

Van Hoorn, J., Nourot, P., Scales, B., & Alward, K. (2007). *Play at the center of the curriculum* (4th ed.). Upper Saddle River, NJ: Prentice Hall.

Wood, E., & Attfield, J. (2005). *Play, learning and the early childhood curriculum* (2nd ed). London: Paul Chapman Publishing.

Yaden, D. (2006, April). *Developing a prospective, developmental theory of early writing ability: Applications from dynamic skill theory, indeterministic constraints modeling, and probabilistic epigenesis.* Paper presented as the annual meeting of the American Educational Research Association, San Francisco.

Zigler, E., & Bishop-Josef, S. (2004). Play under siege: A historical overview. In E. Zigler, D. Singer, & S. Bishop-Josef (Eds.), *Children's play: The roots of reading* (pp. 1–14). Washington, DC: Zero to Three Press.

Chapter Fourteen

MEDIA, POPULAR CULTURE, AND LITERACY LEARNING IN THE TWENTY-FIRST CENTURY

Donna J. Grace

At the very moment when children's literacy learning in school is increasingly dependent upon a narrow, skills-based curriculum focused on decoding and encoding print, their out-of-school literacies encompass communicating and meaning making in multimodal worlds composed of sound, symbols, images, and interactivity. In addition to books, children are growing up interpreting and making sense of a multitude of texts that include film, television, videos, DVDs, computer and video games, and Internet Web sites. Electronic images have as much, or more, presence in students' lives as printed texts. As David Buckingham (2003) contends, the media have become the major means of cultural expression and communication.

Print literacy is no longer adequate to address the realities of children's experiences or to prepare them for life in a rapidly changing world. Yet the classroom continues to privilege the printed word. Children learn much from the media they engage with in their everyday lives, yet there is much more they could and should learn. The need to broaden school definitions of literacy and bring children's out-of-school interests and communicational practices into the classroom is long overdue.

In this chapter, I draw from research and the results of a two-year project with six-to eight-year-old children in an elementary school in Hawaii to argue for the inclusion of media and popular culture in the school lives of children (Grace & Tobin, 2002). This research contributes to a growing body of evidence demonstrating that incorporating students' out-of-school interests and experiences in the classroom provides (i) pathways into classroom literacy practices for reluctant readers and writers; (ii) opportunities for the transfer of children's knowledge of the media and popular culture to literacy in school; (iii) spaces for children to rework some of the messages of the media; (iv) sites for the exploration of identities; and (v) contexts for developing critical literacy skills necessary for analyzing and evaluating media. I begin with a discussion of the obstacles to this process.

PERCEPTIONS ABOUT CHILDREN'S RELATIONSHIP WITH THE MEDIA

In 1984, Patricia Greenfield wrote that "Television, video games, and other computer technology are here to stay, and . . . their growing pervasiveness makes it all the more urgent that we discover how best to use them" (p. 3). Yet, more than two decades later, the potential to build upon and expand children's knowledge of and experience with the media and popular culture lies largely untapped in the classroom. There are at least three underlying reasons for this: perceptions about the detrimental influence of the media and popular culture on children; teachers' lack of familiarity with and knowledge about children's interests in these areas; and the blurring of boundaries between the high (traditional academic content) and the low (popular culture) in the classroom.

Television, more than any other medium, has been blamed for numerous social ills. It is seen as seducing children away from reality and contributing to delinquency, amorality, acts of aggression, obesity, and declining literacy skills. Liberals and conservatives converge in their condemnation of this medium. The former have blamed television for transmitting particular worldviews, values, and lifestyle choices, and creating unnecessary wants and desires. Concerns have centered around war toys, stereotyping, consumerism, materialism, and the promotion of poorly made products and unhealthy food choices. On the other hand, those with more traditional and conservative political views have criticized television for violent and deviant content, for the destruction of American morals and values, and for generally turning children's brains to mush. Representative of this conservative position, Neil Postman (1985) has blamed the negative influence of television for what he sees as a decline in literacy, rational and analytical thought, and public discourse. In all of these positions, the child viewer continues to be seen as essentially passive, helpless and manipulated, and viewing pleasures are considered to be a form of deception, depravity, or a mindless waste of time.

A second reason for the failure to build upon children's knowledge of the media and popular culture in school is that students often have more knowledge about the media and popular culture than do their teachers. As noted by Chris Richards (in Buckingham, 1998, p. 142), school knowledge is typically considered to be what teachers possess and students do not. Students, unlike most of their teachers, have grown up in a media-saturated world. Thus, they are often the experts in this area, leaving teachers on unsafe and unfamiliar ground. Teachers no longer have the upper hand, and therefore they avoid using the media and popular culture in the classroom.

The third reason for resistance to popular culture in the classroom relates to the deprecation of popular pleasures. Since the advent of comic books, the radio, and film, the media have been at the center of middle-class moral panics. Consequently, these areas of students' experience have typically been banned or frowned upon in the classroom. Considered to be a low form of culture, the popular is seen as lacking in worth and importance. It is rarely regarded as knowledge worth knowing.

What have we learned from the research regarding the impact of the media on children's literacy learning and academic achievement? After more than a half century of studies, there is actually little convincing research to back up the theories and speculation about the dangers of the media (Buckingham, 1993). There have been several studies, dating as far back as the 1950s, that found a negative association between television viewing and the development of reading skills and abilities. However, an association does not prove causation. In other words, one factor does not necessarily cause the other. Children who do not engage with their schooling, for various reasons, may prefer to watch television rather than read or do their homework. It might be another factor, or combination of factors, that causes their poor reading performance. In fact, when IQ is controlled for, the negative association between television viewing and academic achievement is greatly reduced or eliminated (Koolstra, van der Voort, & van der Kamp, 1997). In other words, it appears that children's basic levels of intelligence may have more to do with the development of reading skills than does television viewing. In addition, many of the studies that found a negative relationship between television viewing and academic achievement have been criticized for bias and flawed methodology. A major limitation of these studies has been the focus on a single factor, the number of viewing hours, without taking into consideration the context of the viewing or the type of programs viewed (Tyner, 1998).

Several longitudinal studies conducted in the United States have concluded that television viewing has no effect on the development of reading skills (Gaddy, 1986; Gortmaker, Salter, Walker, & Dietz, 1990; Ritchie, Price, & Roberts, 1987). A 1998 U.S. Department of Education review found no conclusive evidence that television viewing has any association with or correlation to reading scores (Tyner, 1998, p. 143). As asserted more recently by Alphie Kohn (2000), "The conclusion that emerges from a review of more than a hundred empirical studies [is that] there is very little about television viewing, per se, that is cause for alarm, according to the available evidence" (p. 168). Other more important influences impacting children's literacy learning include the home environment, parents' education, parenting characteristics, socioeconomic status, the community in which students live, peer social group affiliations, and students' intellectual abilities.

Although positive research findings about the media do not make the headlines as often as negative reports do, there is a growing body of evidence that not only dispels many of the fears about adverse effects but also suggests that the media may actually contribute to children's literacy learning. Earlier research in the area of cultural studies demonstrated that children are active viewers and do not absorb the messages of the media like sponges. For instance, children and youth have demonstrated their ability to interpret televisual texts in varying ways including acceptance, negotiation, and resistance to the texts' intended meanings (Hall, Hobson, Lowe, & Willis, 1980).

The findings of Hodge and Tripp (1986) have provided further evidence that television is not necessarily time out from thinking, as is commonly assumed. These researchers state that children need a diet rich in explicit fantasy cartoons, because such programs can help them to discriminate between reality and fantasy rather than confusing the two. Hodge and Tripp found that by the ages of eight or nine, children were able to interpret ideological messages in cartoons and identify contradictions and gaps in the story lines. The researchers conclude that children use television to think, and that their thinking is shaped by their stage of development.

The work of Hodge and Tripp is reinforced by Howard's findings (1998), which demonstrate that the three- and four-year-old children in Howard's study were intellectually stimulated by their favorite television shows and used these programs to think and talk about how the images related to reality. Roberts and Howard (2005) also found that the children participating in their research, two years old or younger, were active meaning makers when watching the television program *Teletubbies*. These children's attention levels were high and they frequently joined in with the action on the show. They were also able to make inferences and predictions, and put into practice language that they learned from the program.

Neuman (1988) found that young children who watched television between two and three hours per day had higher reading scores than those who watched one hour or less. Browne (1999) reported two studies with similar results. The first is a 1995 survey study conducted by the National Foundation for Educational Research (Brooks, Schagen, & Nastat, 1997), involving approximately 5,000 young students, in which the researchers found that children who watched little or no television were not necessarily better readers than children who watched moderate amounts. In fact, the children who watched television sometimes achieved higher scores than the children who never watched television. The second study, in India (Shasti & Mohite, 1997), concluded that the average reading achievement scores of children who were heavy, moderate, and light television viewers were not significantly different on tests of listening, comprehension, and silent reading. Heavy viewers did, however, score lower than light viewers in the area of oral reading. Gentzkow and Shapiro (2006) found that students who watched television during their preschool years scored well on standardized verbal and reading texts later in life, especially children from homes where English was not the primary language, children whose mothers did not complete high school, and nonwhite children.

Hence, there is ample research refuting the view that television viewing is inherently detrimental to the development of children's academic skills. There are also research findings disputing the commonly held belief that children's use of the media displaces reading as an out-of-school activity. Browne (1999) reported an Australian study in which children with access to two television channels read more books than children in communities with one channel or no television. Margaret Mackey (2001) found that spin-off products from popular books such as the Harry Potter series, including movies, video and computer games, board games, Internet sites, and toys, do not replace the reading of the books but actually support it. Mackey contends that children's interests in popular cultural products accompany rather than undermine their interest in reading. Marsh and Millard (2000, p. 50) reference a 1997 study by Robinson in which Robinson notes that although the Thomas the Tank Engine books have been around a long time, book sales increased after the television series appeared. The fact that children are frequently motivated to buy books related to their favorite shows and movies demonstrates that the media and popular culture may enhance rather than diminish children's interest in reading. Although the media and popular culture are frequently seen as being in competition with books, the research suggests that they more often coexist, and may even be mutually supportive of one another.

Video games have also been the subject of recent research. The findings of several studies call into question the commonly held assumption that children's involvement in this activity is basically mind numbing and without redeeming value. Greenfield (1984), one of the first researchers to investigate this topic, asserted that playing video and computer games held the potential to positively impact retention, spatial skills, parallel processing, motivation to learn, critical viewing, problem-solving skills, eye-hand coordination, cognitive development, motor skills, and an understanding of the narrative genre. Gee (2003) has produced what is probably the most comprehensive investigation of young people's use of video/computer games, and has identified more than twenty principles of learning that can be developed through engagement with them. These principles will be explained in a later section.

Hence, there is a lack of evidence to support the view that the media have supplanted reading and writing in children's out-of-school lives. In fact, the results of numerous studies suggest that children's experiences with the media and popular culture may actually sustain or enhance their literacy-related interests and skills. Although the media may contribute negatively to school achievement for *some* children, in *some* environmental contexts, the media are only one of many potential influential factors on literacy learning and academic achievement. Other conditions must be taken into consideration.

When children lead a balanced life and are involved in a variety of different activities, television can provide relaxation, entertainment, and education, just as it does for many adults. Needless to say, it is the responsibility of family members to monitor how much and what kind of TV is viewed by children in their households. Children's understanding of television programs is enhanced when parents watch and discuss the shows with them. In the process, the skills needed to analyze and evaluate media can also be developed. Children also benefit from seeing the enjoyment of reading in the home. Heavy television viewing, or other forms of media consumption, may have a negative effect on their academic progress. Parents need to trust their judgment about the amount of time their children spend with popular media in contrast to other activities, and be aware of research that provides evidence that the media is not an inherently bad part of children's lives.

INTEGRATING STUDENT VIDEO PRODUCTION IN THE PRIMARY GRADES IN HAWAII

In the study by Grace and Tobin (2002), children's interests in and knowledge of the media and popular culture were brought into the classroom through the process of student video production. The study was part of a school-university partnership, headed by Joseph Tobin, who was a faculty member at the University of Hawaii. I was part of a team formed to assist the classroom teachers in integrating technology into the literacy curriculum. Although the overall project involved eight classes of students in the 1st through 6th grades, I focus primarily on our work with four classrooms of six- to eight-year-old children.

The objective of the project was to integrate reading, writing, speaking, and visual literacy through technology, while developing the children's skills as communicators and meaning makers. Media education has typically been structured around a deficit model of teaching, with children positioned as passive, vulnerable, and endangered in their relationship with the media. Our intent was to implement a strengths-based model of media education by building on students' knowledge of and experiences with the media in ways that were positive and educationally sound. The emphasis in such a model is on preparing children for life in our media-oriented society, rather than protecting them from it (Buckingham, 2003). In this project, we found that even six- and seven-year-old children were able to use the video camera and equipment with practice and guidance from the teachers. As discussed by Tyner (1998), video is an excellent tool to help students explore narrative structure in the video stories they produce. The equipment is sturdy and simple to use, and they are able to view their videos immediately after taping them (p. 184).

The Hawaii teachers were enthusiastic about the video production project but wondered about the possibility of a negative response from the parent community. Over half of the parents expressed concerns about the amount of time their children spend engaged with the media, but they were overwhelmingly supportive of the project. In their survey comments, parents commented that the project held potential to motivate children, enhance self-confidence, develop oral speaking skills, instill responsibility, increase understanding of television productions, provide experience in using technology, and make learning more relevant and fun.

The parents seemed to believe that much could be gained through enabling students to produce videos, rather than merely viewing them. Assured of parental support, the video curriculum was subsequently developed by the teachers and the university team. After introducing the children to the basic roles and jobs involved in video production (writers, actors, camera person, and director), to the technical terms, and to hands-on work with the cameras and equipment, the first project involved small-group work where the children were helped by the teacher and university team to script, storyboard, and tape a video version of a favorite storybook.

The use if a familiar story allowed the children to move relatively quickly to the production stage, where they still needed much assistance. It was, thus, a good way to support the children's learning as they moved to the next project, in which the groups collaboratively wrote and taped short stories. In some ways, the experience was similar to that of producing a school play. There were differences as well. Plays are associated with books, the written word, and the literary canon. They are considered to be a higher form of art, more socially approved and educationally sound. In contrast, video production is linked to the media and popular culture. We found, however, that video production provided children with the tools to enter into the genre and use it for their own purposes.

When the children were given free choice in story topics, it quickly became apparent that many of the characters, plots, and themes were drawn from the movies, videos, and television shows that the children enjoyed. Their scripts were filled with X-men, ninja warriors, cartoon characters, Disney heroes and heroines, monsters, and superheroes. Tensions arose for the teachers as popular culture crept into the curriculum. The teachers expressed concerns about the influence of the media and video games on the children, the appropriateness of the content of their stories, and the intermingling of the "high" and the "low" in the classroom (see Grace & Tobin, 2002, for discussion of these issues).

Over time, however, the teachers found value in creating a space for the children's popular-cultural interests within the curriculum. As state and national literacy and technology standards were being met, the children were actively engaged in a curriculum that blended their out-of-school interests with school literacy learning. During the course of the project, data were gathered from observations, field notes, teacher and student questionnaires, and teacher interviews. The results of integrating the media and popular culture into the literacy curriculum through student video production are summarized in five general categories and discussed below.

PATHWAYS INTO CLASSROOM LITERACY PRACTICES

The video production project created interest and generated enthusiasm for the literacy curriculum. The teachers frequently commented on the self-motivation and excitement they observed in many of the students throughout their video work, as well as their eagerness to use the equipment. On a student questionnaire, 96.6 percent of the children in the 1st through 6th grades reported enjoying producing videos in school.

We found, as have other researchers, that bringing popular-cultural texts into the literacy curriculum has a strong motivating effect on the children. Jackie Marsh (Marsh & Millard, 2000) reports on a study in which preschool children who were not confident or interested in literacy were motivated to engage in reading and writing activities when a superhero area was set up in the classroom. Leonie Arthur (2005) found that four-year-old boys who were reluctant readers and writers became actively engaged in these processes when Pokemon cards, magazines, and toy catalogues were added to a literacy center.

Comic books, typically considered to be a less valued form of reading, have also been reported to provide entry points into literacy for students. John Lowe, department chair at the Savannah College of Art and Design, recalls that as a young boy, he "started reading comics and then got into other types of fiction and literature," and that he would not "have made the leap into literature if it weren't for comics" ("Council Chronicle," 2005, p. 2). In a similar vein, Jason Ranker (2004), writes about his work with an eight-year-old boy who lacked confidence and interest in writing. When allowed to pursue his interest in superhero comics, the child turned a corner in his writing, producing his own series of comics. As his writing drew the attention and appreciation of several of his peers, he developed confidence and a positive identity as an author.

In the video project, we also observed struggling readers being motivated to read and write through the use of popular culture in the curriculum. Ronny, for example, was a 3rd-grade boy who had a history of failing to engage with his schoolwork. In the initial stages of the project, he showed very little interest in his group's efforts to develop and write a video story. Ronny was usually found sitting at the back of the group, rarely paying attention, and often distracting anyone near to him. However, when one of the children suggested writing a scary story, Ronny immediately perked up. He suggested they base it on "the Chucky movie" (*Child's Play*), which he then began to retell with great enthusiasm. His teacher and I were both surprised by his level of interest and involvement in creating this story. Although the teacher had hesitations about the potentially violent content of the story, Ronny's eagerness to participate convinced her to wait and see how the story actually turned out:

Chucky II

There was a boy named Chucky who went to a park and had some fun. At the park, Chucky saw a boy and his name was Justin. Then Chucky made friends with the boys and Chucky said, "Let's play hide the needle." Justin said, "Okay." Then, Chucky said, "Close your eyes." Justin closed his eyes while Chucky went to hide the needle. When Chucky came back, Justin went to look for the needle. When he was looking behind a tree, he saw an ugly, horrible monster! Justin screamed and Chucky came to save him. Chucky tried to kill the monster with a knife, but the monster said, "Wait! I want to help you. I want to be your friend." So Chucky, Justin, and the monster became friends. They lived in a really beautiful house together. And they never fought again.

The teacher's initial fears about the content of the story were clearly not realized. In fact, the resulting script bore little resemblance to the horror movie that it was based upon, and ended with the monster being nice and becoming a friend. Whether or not it was appropriate for Ronny to have watched the movie *Child's Play* is another issue, but, as will be discussed in a following section, writing this story may have offered Ronny a means for working out some of his fears associated with the movie, while at the same time providing an inroad to reading and writing in the classroom.

In addition to providing an entryway into literacy for students like Ronny, the teachers in this study also saw the video project lead to impressive growth in literacy skills and self-confidence in other children, including those who were typically shy and quiet, those who were easily distracted, and especially those who were identified as special education students. As one teacher commented, "The video project was particularly good for the special ed. students. It's something they can all participate and feel successful in." Another added, "When I think of the self-esteem, for once they [the special ed. children] are really shining."

Others have also suggested that popular culture provides topics for children to talk about and to base play upon, and thus can be particularly beneficial for language development, vocabulary building, and confidence in language use, especially for children for whom English is not their first language (Arthur, 2005; Marsh & Millard, 2000). In this context, popular culture can potentially serve to bridge cultural diversity in the classroom by offering children a common ground upon which to interact and socialize.

TRANSFER OF CHILDREN'S KNOWLEDGE OF THE MEDIA AND POPULAR CULTURE TO LITERACY IN SCHOOL

In addition to being motivated to engage in classroom literacy, children also gain knowledge from the media and popular culture that can transfer to reading and writing in school. Gee (2003), for example, has documented more than twenty high-order learning principles, developed in good video games, that can be applied to classroom learning. These include critical, metalevel, strategic, and reflective thinking; predicting, hypothesis testing, risk taking, logic and problem solving; eye-hand coordination, effort, and perseverance.

Comic books, like video games, have also been found to contribute to children's literacy learning in several child-friendly ways. In "The Council Chronicle" (2005), teachers share how comics and graphic novels can be effectively used in the classroom. Since pictures are more prominent than text in comics, Hong Xu (p. 2) uses them to help students learn about inferences, and sees this transferring to book reading. Sawyer-Perkins (p. 2) adds that comics provide an excellent vehicle for teaching writing, as a story has to be pared down to its most basic elements: beginning, middle, and end. Sawyer-Perkins also uses comics to teach paragraphing, punctuation, and the use of dialogue (p. 8). In addition, comics have been shown to be useful in developing understanding of genre, characterization, and plot (Pahl & Roswell, 2005).

Students also learn a great deal about genre, plot, character development, setting, and narrative structure from the films, television shows, and videos that they watch; this can transfer to print literacy (Braggs, 2002; Browne, 1999; Neuman, 1997). Evans (2005) reports on a study in which students learned about structuring and sequencing stories from their engagement with media; this also transferred to the classroom. In addition, Linda Sheldon (1998) found that the five- to twelve-year old children in an Australian study understood many codes and conventions of television shows, including the use of flashbacks and dream sequences, that can be applied to creative writing in the school setting.

Similarly, the teachers in the video project frequently commented that the children's familiarity with popular media facilitated their production work. Drawing from favorite television shows, movies and videos provided the students with a sense of narrative structure that helped in the writing of their collaborative group stories. Their knowledge of different media genres was also evident when they created their own news, cooking, and quiz shows in the classroom. The teachers all reported that student growth had been demonstrated throughout the project in reading, writing, vocabulary, sequencing, and story grammar. The gains in sequencing skills were particularly impressive. A test was administered at the beginning and again at the end of the first year of the project. In these assessments, the children had to sequence scenes in a clip taken from a popular children's movie. Not only did the posttest results greatly surpass the pretest results for each grade level, but the posttest scores were all consistently higher than the pretest scores of the *succeeding* grade level, indicating that the growth in sequencing skills was over and above that which would be expected to occur during the course of the school year without the intervention.

The Hawaii teachers also commented that the video project promoted collaborative learning and problem solving. Janet Evans (2005) cites a similar study by Reid, Burn, & Parker (2002), which also found that, when digital filming and editing were integrated into the school curriculum, "problem-solving, negotiation, thinking, reasoning and risk-taking" were developed (Evans, 2005, p. 34). These examples all demonstrate how students' popular-cultural interests can transfer to classroom literacy learning, while bridging the worlds of home and school.

SPACES FOR CHILDREN TO REWORK SOME OF THE MESSAGES OF THE MEDIA

Due to the prominence of the media and popular culture in the Hawaii children's video products, we initially feared that they would lack creativity and imagination. We expected to see little more than empty reproductions of the television shows and movies that they had viewed. However, these fears did not materialize. Rather than merely mimicking existing media texts, the students used them as springboards to develop their own inventive stories. As others have noted, borrowing from other texts, or imitating them, is an essential part of literacy learning (Browne, 1999; Buckingham, 2003).

When incorporated into student scripts, the themes, characterizations, plots, and scenes drawn from the media and popular culture were reshaped through the students' own childlike lenses. Rather than replicating the remembered plots and themes, the children adapted, modified, and transformed the media texts from which they drew.

Superheroes, ninjas, and X-men also prominently figured in the students' video stories. Through video production, the students were able to experience power and pleasure in portraying these strong, bold, and brave characters. The 3rd graders were asked to write in their journals about how they would feel if they were ninja warriors. Not everyone responded approvingly, but for those who did, the most common adjectives listed were cool, great, awesome, radical, strong, fast, brave, tough, and powerful (Grace, 2003). As Browne (1999) suggests, children may "seek to overcome their feelings of anxiety and vulnerability through identification with superheroes," and this identification may contribute importantly to their emotional development (p. 164).

In addition, ghosts, monsters, and other scary creatures were frequently featured in the students' videos. Carol Clover (1992) tells us that the appeal of horror has long been explained by its association with repressed fears and desires. Evidence of this was provided when the members of a class of 3rd graders in our project were asked to describe a scary dream they remembered. Many of the elements that were turning up in their videos were found on their lists. Anna Freud (in Turner 1969) explains that by identifying with terrifying objects (fierce animals or monstrous beings), children are able to symbolically rob them of their power. Browne (1999) adds that "adopting a role and playing it out enables the child to take control of it and, in so doing, work toward a resolution in terms of the fear or anxiety induced by the character or the situation or the video or TV program" (p. 110).

The students' "scary" stories contained little, if any, evidence of the frightening or violent aspects of the real movies or television shows from which they were drawn. Instead, they had much more to do with everyday childhood concerns such as being teased or bullied, being friendless, or not being believed by grown-ups. In their re-creations, the children selected the parts of the movies to which they could relate, and made sense of them in their own ways. The majority of their stories ended with everyone making up, being friends, and living happily ever after together.

These examples suggest that through video production, the students were provided with the opportunity to incorporate their interests and pleasures into the curriculum, explore their fears and fantasies, make their own meanings, and mediate some of the messages of the media in the safety of the group.

SITES FOR THE EXPLORATION OF IDENTITIES

As the children explored different roles in the video project, the possibilities for thinking about their ways of being in the world were expanded. As Davies (1989) asserts, when children talk, write, and play, they are "making conscious and unconscious investments of themselves in particular storylines, subject positions and readings of the social world" (p. 66). Identities are constructed socially, in numerous ways, in our day-to-day interactions. Student video production provided a safe space for the Hawaii students to try out and experiment with different roles and identities. In their performance of gender, the students sometimes reaffirmed traditional roles and relationships, and sometimes reworked them.

We were pleased to find that the girls, particularly the younger ones, showed a strong interest in working with the video cameras and equipment, along with the boys. It may be that with computers, DVD players, digital cameras, and MP3 players becoming increasingly commonplace in children's home lives, girls are growing up feeling more familiar and comfortable with technology. In addition, as discussed elsewhere (Grace, 2003), the girls often took on aggressive and action-oriented roles that are typically reserved for males. Although some girls opted for traditional female roles such as mother, wife, or girlfriend, many of the girls chose to play superheroes, "bad guys," or aliens from outer space. The reverse was rarely the case. Although a boy once played a waitress, and another dressed up as a female teacher, most boys gravitated toward typically masculine roles. The fact that it is more socially acceptable for girls to move into male roles than it is for boys to swing away from them may explain why the girls seemed to experience more freedom in breaking with tradition in this area.

Similarly, in another study, Marsh (Marsh & Millard, 2000) found many of the young girls taking on assertive roles as Batwoman. These examples of girls exploring alternative identities are encouraging, particularly as they try on strong and powerful roles. However, much work remains to be done in broadening identities for boys, particularly in supporting and validating more sensitive, caring, and nurturing behaviors typically considered to be feminine.

CONTEXTS FOR DEVELOPING MEDIA LITERACY SKILLS

In developing literacy skills and abilities, children need be offered a variety of modes for communication and meaning making including sound, images, and new information and communication technologies involving computers and the Internet. They should have choice and ownership over decisions about which modes to use and how to use them, depending upon their goals and purposes. Working in multimodal forms of literacy can and should start in preschool. Children are naturally inclined toward active, tactile, multimodal, and experiential learning. As demonstrated by Evans (2005), children as young as three and four years old can learn to use computers, webcams, and editing software. And, as found in the Hawaii project, even 1st graders can become adept at using video cameras and equipment.

The very notion of literacy itself needs to be broadened, if we are to prepare students with the critical, analytical, and technological skills needed for life now and in the future. As Victoria Carrington (2005) argues, students should be involved in literacies that enable them to produce and disseminate texts "that engage meaningfully with the world outside the classroom" (p. 24). The Hawaii project took steps in that direction.

Bringing students' interests in the media and popular culture into the curriculum through video production motivated the children to read, write, speak, and perform, while broadening the terrain for student expression. In the process, the students became producers rather than merely consumers of media. Through hands-on learning they developed technical skills, understanding of the production process, and awareness of key concepts of the media, including a sense of audience and issues of representation. Today's youth are the media makers of tomorrow. Thus, they need to become informed and astute in creating and evaluating media, and we need to encourage them to hold high standards for its quality.

CRITICAL LITERACY SKILLS

Literacy today needs to encompass far more than reading and writing. As Nikki Gamble and Nick Easingwood (2000) contend, literacy must involve "access to ideas that challenge our thinking and promote new ways of looking at our world" (p. 4). Critical literacy involves developing in students the skills needed to analyze and assess the media. Although students are often more media-savvy than their teachers, they have rarely spent much time in thinking critically about the media with which they engage. Given the prevalence of the media and popular culture in the lives of children and youth, they have both a need and a right to develop these skills in school.

The media are not neutral carriers of content. Without a doubt, they convey many stereotypical, derogatory, and discriminatory messages regarding gender, ethnicity, culture, class, age, body-ableness, and body size and type. Furthermore, children will not all come away from their media experiences with the same meanings. Thus, there is a need to provide time in school for structured reflection upon the media, evaluation, dialogue, and the consideration of multiple perspectives.

In conclusion, we need to move away from viewing children's engagement with the media and popular culture as a problem. Instead, we need to utilize and build upon these experiences in the classroom. This can serve to democratize the classroom by making a space for students' everyday interests, while providing a foundation for helping them to acquire new skills and abilities. As stated by Gamble and Easingwood (2000), failing "to harness children's emerging capabilities or to offer a progression and continuity to them" results in "a clear waste of both potential and opportunity" (p. xii). The media and popular culture have a prominent and ever-growing place in the lives of children and youth. They are here to stay. If we are to have an active, informed, and critical future citizenry, new literacies must include a knowledge of how to use, integrate, evaluate, interpret, and produce various media forms in school.

REFERENCES

Arthur, L. (2005). Popular culture: Views of parents and educators. In Marsh, J. (Ed.), *Popular culture, new media and digital literacy in early childhood* (pp. 165–182). New York: Routledge.

Bragg, S. (2002). Wrestling in wooly gloves: Not just being critically media literate. *Journal of Popular Film and Television, 30* (1), 42–52.

Brooks, G., Schagen, I., & Nastat, P. (1997). *Trends in reading at eight.* Slough, UK: National Foundation of Education Resources.

Browne, N. (1999). *Young children's literacy development and the role of televisual texts.* New York: Routledge.

Buckingham, D. (1993). *Children talking television.* London: Falmer Press.

Buckingham, D. (Ed.) (1998). *Teaching popular culture: Beyond radical pedagogy.* London: UCL Press Limitied.

Buckingham, D. (2003). *Media education: Literacy, learning and contemporary culture.* Cambridge, UK: Polity Press

Carrington, V. (2005). New textual landscapes, information and early literacy. In Marsh, J. (Ed.). (2005). *Popular culture, new media and digital literacy in early childhood* (pp. 13–27). New York: Routledge.

Clover, C. (1992). *Men, women, and chain saws: Gender in the modern horror film.* Princeton, NJ: Princeton University Press.

The Council Chronicle. (2005, September). *Copy Editor, 15* (1). Urbana, IL: National Council of Teachers of English.

Davies, B. (1989). *Frogs and snails and feminist tales: Preschool children and gender.* Sydney, Australia: Allen & Unwin.

Dyson, A. H. (1993). *Social worlds of children learning to write in an urban primary school.* New York: Teachers College Press.

Evans, J. (2005). *Literacy moves on: Popular culture, new technologies, and critical literacy in the elementary classroom.* Portsmouth, NH: Heinemann.

Gaddy, G. D. (1986). Television's impact on high school achievement. *Public Opinion Quarterly, 50*(3), 340–349.

Gamble, N., & Easingwood, N. (2000). *ICT and literacy: Information and communications technology, media, reading and writing.* New York: Continuum.

Gee, J. P. (2003). *What video games have to teach us about learning and literacy.* New York: Palgrave Macmillan.

Gentzkow, M., & Shapiro, J. (2006). *Does television rot your brain? New evidence from the Coleman study* (Working Paper No. 12021). Cambridge, MA: National Bureau of Economic Research.

Gortmaker, S. L., Salter, C. A., Walker, D. K., & Dietz, Jr., W. H. (1990). The impact of television viewing on mental aptitude and achievement: A longitudinal study. *Public Opinion Quarterly, 54*(4), 594–604.

Grace, D. (2003). Gender, power and pleasure: Integrating student video production into the elementary curriculum. *Curriculum Perspectives, 23*(1), 21–27.

Grace, D., & Tobin, J. (2002). Pleasure, creativity, and the carnivalesque in children's video production. In Bresler, L., & Thompson, C. M. (Eds.). *The arts in children's lives: Context, culture, and curriculum* (pp. 195–214). Boston: Kluwer Academic Publishers.

Greenfield, P. (1984). *Mind and media: The effects of television, video games, and computers.* Cambridge, MA: Harvard University Press.

Hall, S., Hobson, D., Lowe, A., & Willis, P. (1980). *Culture, media, language.* London: Hutchinson.

Hodge, B., & Tripp, D. (1986). *Children and television.* Cambridge, UK: Polity Press.

Howard, S. (Ed.). (1998). *Wired-up: Young people and the electronic media.* New York: Routledge.

Kohn, A. (2000). *What to look for in a classroom, and other essays.* San Francisco: Jossey-Bass.

Koolstra, C., van der Voort, T., & van der Kamp, L. (1997). Television's impact on children's reading comprehension and decoding skills: A 3-year panel study. *Reading Research Quarterly, 32*(2), 128–152.

Mackey, M. (2001). The survival of engaged reading in the internet age: New media, old media, and the book. *Children's Literature in Education, 31*(3), 167–187.

Marsh, J. (Ed.). (2005). *Popular culture, new media and digital literacy in early childhood.* New York: Routledge.

Marsh, J., & Millard, E. (2000). *Literacy and popular culture: Using children's culture in the classroom.* London: Paul Chapman.

Neuman, S. B. (1988). The displacement effect: Assessing the relation between television viewing and reading performance. *Reading Research Quarterly, 23,* 414–440.

Neuman, S. B. (1997). Television as a learning environment: A theory of synergy. In J. Flood, S. B. Heath, & D. Lapp (Eds.). *Handbook of research on teaching literacy through the communicative and visual arts* (pp. 15–22). Mahwah, NJ: Lawrence Erlbaum Associates.

Pahl, K., & Rowsell, J. (2005). *Literacy and education: Understanding the new literacy studies in the classroom.* London: Paul Chapman.

Postman, N. (1985). *Amusing ourselves to death: Public discourse in the age of show business.* New York: Viking Press.

Ranker, J. (2004). *Responding to student-authored. popular cultural fictions: Rethinking the literature studies–writing workshop connection.* Unpublished doctoral dissertation, University of Iowa.

Ried, M., Burn, A., & Parker, D. (2002). *Evaluation report of the BECTA digital video pilot project.* London: British Film Institute. In J. Evans (Ed.). *Literacy moves on: Popular culture, new technologies, and critical literacy in the elementary classroom.* Portsmouth, NH: Heinemann.

Richards, C. (1998). Beyond classroom culture. In D. Buckingham (Ed.), *Teaching popular culture: Beyond radical pedagogy* (pp. 132–152). London: UCL Press.

Ritchie, D., Price, V., & Roberts, D. F. (1987). Television, reading, and reading achievement: A reappraisal. *Communication Research, 14* (3), 219–315.

Roberts, S., & Howard, S. (2005). Watching Teletubbies: Television and its very young audience. In Marsh, J. (Ed.), *Popular culture, new media and digital literacy in early childhood* (pp. 91–107). New York: Routledge.

Shastri, J., & Mohite, P. (1997). Television viewing pattern of primary school children and its relationship to academic performance and cognitive skills. *International Journal of Early Years Education, 5* (2), 153–160.

Sheldon, L. (1998). The middle years: Children and television—Cool or just plain boring? In Howard, S. (Ed.), *Wired-up: Young people and the electronic media* (pp. 77–94). New York: Routledge

Turner, V. (1969). *The Ritual Process.* Chicago: Adeline Press.

Tyner, K. (1998). *Literacy in a digital world: Teaching and learning in the age of information.* Mahwah, NJ: Lawrence Erlbaum Associates.

Chapter Fifteen

COMPUTER TECHNOLOGY AND DIGITAL LITERACY IN THE EARLY GRADES

Linda D. Labbo

Over twenty years ago, the Head Start Bureau, a national government initiative to provide preschool children from poverty backgrounds with early literacy instruction, banned federally funded programs from purchasing computers in the early grades (Cuban, 2001). At the time, the Head Start administrators made a wise decision, because computer applications for children were sparse, dull, and derived from a behaviorist learning perspective, a learning approach based on the idea that human beings learn by getting positive or negative feedback that shapes behavior, and the applications consisted of boring skill and practice exercises. In the 1990s, the Head Start Bureau lifted the ban, because computers became more portable, less expensive, and developmentally appropriate for young children. In addition, national professional literacy–related organizations circulated position statements recognizing the critical need for better use of computer technologies in the early grades (see National Association for the Education of Young Children, NAEYC, 1996).

More recently, the National Educational Technology Standards (NETS), which have been made available online by the International Society for Technology Education in 2002, set out guidelines and performance indicators for what educators and caregivers can expect pre-kindergarten through 2nd-grade students to learn about technology. In addition, NETS includes six pre-K- to 2nd-grade performance indicators: (1) Youngsters will be able to use computer input devices, such as the mouse and the keyboard, as well as output devices, such as monitors and printers, to operate computers; (2) Young children will use various types of media for both directed and independent learning activities; (3) Children in the primary grades will be able to talk about technology using developmentally appropriate terminology; (4) Young students will be able to use multimedia resources such as interactive books, software, and electronic encyclopedias to support learning; (5) Pre-kindergarten through 2nd-grade children will be able to work cooperatively with classmates and family members to use technology; (6) Young children will demonstrate positive ethical and social behaviors when using computers; (7) Youngsters will be respectful, demonstrating responsible use of computers; (8) Young students will be able to create developmentally appropriate multimedia presentations with support from peers or adults; (9) Young children will be able to use technology resources such as digital cameras and creativity programs for solving problems; (10) Students in the early grades will be able to gather and communicate information in collaboration with others using electronic communication methods such as e-mail and the Internet with the support of peers or adults.

Therefore, in the first decade of the twenty-first century, the Internet and computers are present in primary grade classrooms across the United States (National Center for Educational Statistics, 1999). Standards are in place to support the use of computers in the early grades. Unfortunately, educators of young children are sometimes hard pressed to determine how to use the available computers wisely. For example, recent data indicate that only one out of five teachers feels well prepared to use computers for instruction in classrooms (Irwin, 2003).

Other challenges facing educators are the changing definition of literacy and changing approaches to literacy instruction that are inherent in new communicative technologies. In the past, traditional notions of literacy acquisition and development focused primarily on the ability to read and write in a print-based environment. Approaches to traditional literacy instruction in the early grades have also been primarily focused on helping children learn print-based literacy skills and strategies, such as phonics, sight word recognition, letter recognition, and comprehension of fictional and narrative text. It is clear that these print-based skills continue to provide the foundation for children's reading achievement and academic success. The introduction of computer technologies into the early grades, however, requires an understanding of the nature of the new forms of reading and writing that occur on computer screens. These new literacies are frequently referred to as digital literacy.

DIGITAL LITERACY

Gilster (1997) noted that "[d]igital literacy is the ability to understand and use information in multiple formats from a wide range of sources when it is presented via computers" (p. 1). Digital literacy "encompasses the abilities required to use computer technologies to read, write, and interact with multimedia symbols on computer screens" (Flood & Lapp, 1995, p. 1). New literacies include traditional skills and strategies but also include other abilities, such as being able to compose and publish with word-processing and desktop-publishing programs, to exchange messages using e-mail and Web postings, to assemble knowledge from various multimedia resources, to understand visual components of literacy, to be able to read critically, to access hypertext and linked information on the Internet, and to express meaning in multimedia forms.

Digital literacies are becoming more important in an increasingly global workplace that requires employees to search the Internet for information, problem-solve with a team that may be distributed across many distant locations, publish reports online, create Web pages, and so forth. Not only must workers in the present and the future be able to gain the skill of using computer technologies to locate information, but they must also gain the skill of using this information in their lives (Gilster, 1997).

It is clear that parents, caregivers, and educators need to select software, Internet sites, and activities that introduce young children to digital literacy in ways that are appropriate for their ages and early literacy abilities. It is worth noting that the most effective use of computer technologies in the early grades involves social contexts for shared, interactive meaning making. The goal for effective use of computers is *not* to sit a child in isolation in front of a computer screen for extended amounts of time. The goal is to skillfully craft computer experiences that integrate the child's ability levels with the curriculum and instructional goals.

GUIDELINES FOR SELECTING APPROPRIATE SOFTWARE AND INTERNET SITES

Given the above caveat, it still behooves educators to have guidelines for sorting through the growing profusion of available, commercially prepared software programs for young children. Not all commercial programs are effective in supporting young children's literacy development. Early childhood software programs and Internet sites can support children's development of both traditional and digital literacies if they include a core set of features that are developmentally appropriate. Effective early childhood literacy-related computer programs and sites include multimedia tools that allow children to interact with and learn the content presentedwithout a great deal of adult supervision, because the children receive the scaffolding, or support, they need from the multimedia tools that appear on-screen to make the programs work. For example, if a child is not able to read print he may be able to click on an on-screen button that allows him to hear the text read aloud. Another case in point occurs when a child is given a choice between a right or wrong response to a question posed by a program. If she selects the wrong answer, she will be prompted to try again.

This section briefly highlights the features that are most effective across various types of software programs and Internet sites. It bears repeating: educators must keep in mind that the most effective use of computers for literacy instruction in the early grades is not likely to consist of a child or even pairs of children simply sitting in front of a computer. The most effective computer activities will involve connections to the classroom culture and literacy curriculum The following guidelines for evaluating the developmental appropriateness of on-screen programs take into account multimedia features that are likely to scaffold children's independent computer interactions. These guidelines are adapted from the suggestions of educators who are interested in computer technologies and include ease of use, child control, auditory/speech support, clear and appealing graphics, motivating and engaging activities, and feedback.

Ease of Use

Children should be able to use the software easily because the directions are clear and the way to interact with the program is intuitive. The way to navigate through different parts of the program should be clear and supported. For example, the skills necessary to run the program should be within the range of the child. Children should be able to work with the program independently after a brief introduction that uses audio narrative on demand. It should also be easy for a child to move in or out of an activity at any given time.

Child Control

Children are actively involved in learning. They are not passive recipients of knowledge or mere observers of on-screen activities. Interactions with on-screen activities should require children's decision making; effective sites or programs should provide feedback and offer new directions if children encounter difficulties. When children interact with the program, there should be a clear response to their actions.

Auditory/Speech Support

The program should provide guidance to children who are not yet able to read independently in the form of brief, easy-to-follow narrated directions or offers of pronunciation of unknown words on demand. As children listen to text as it is read aloud, they should receive narrated directions or they should be able to click on a word to hear it pronounced.

Clear and Appealing Graphics

Children should encounter graphics in the program that align with, complement, and support textual information. Artistic illustrations should not be so abstract that children cannot understand their meaning. The graphics should not distract from the program objectives or the content.

Motivating and Engaging Activities

Children should find the activities and multimedia features to be engaging and motivating. They should receive appropriate feedback on interactions that keep them wanting to continue. The program should be appropriately challenging and fun to use.

Feedback

The type of feedback children receive should be clear and should prompt ongoing exploration or rethinking of a task. Children who make errors or mistakes should not be left to keep practicing and reinforcing their wrong responses. Effective feedback should be corrective.

LEARNING *FROM* COMPUTERS VERSUS LEARNING *WITH* COMPUTERS

Goldberg and Sherwood (1983) identified five categories of computer use that are helpful in understanding the role of computer technologies in fostering both traditional and digital literacy. In particular, two categories of computer use, ranging in focus from traditional literacy to new literacy skills, are important in the early grades and include learning from computers and learning with computers. The following section describes each category.

Learning from computers is an approach that uses the computer as a type of drill instructor or electronic worksheet. The purpose of the program is to reinforce discrete, traditional literacy skills that have already been taught in the classroom. Software programs in this category may consist of a game-playing format with a behaviorist orientation to learning. Behaviorist learning theories are based on the notion that children learn through practice and immediate feedback on isolated skills practice. Some drill and practice programs require a child to sign in at the start of the session. In this way, the software program can keep track of and report each child's score on each literacy game he or she has played.

Even though the focus of skill and drill programs is to help children develop traditional literacy skills, some minimal digital or new literacy skills are required. For example, children need to be able to interact with the computer monitor by controlling the mouse, using a touch pad, using the keyboard, or touching a touch-sensitive monitor screen. Children must also know how to drag and click a cursor, a pulsing arrow or line on screen that indicates locations for interactivity, across the screen to select a correct answer.

In most game-playing software formats, children are presented with a stimulus in the form of a task to complete or a question to answer. Each task or question has only one correct answer for children to select from among three to four possible answers. If a child answers correctly, most programs will offer some type of "bells and whistles" as a reward for the desired behavior. If a child answers incorrectly, some programs offer a prompt to try again. Other programs may provide the correct answer. Most programs, however, either ignore a wrong response or give an audio signal that the response was incorrect.

Many skill and drill programs have a branching feature. This feature tracks and follows the students' progress through a limited number of attempts to master a particular skill. If the skill is not mastered at the end of a series of on-screen lessons, children will be rerouted to more practice on the same skill. If students show mastery of a skill, they will be routed to another series of skill lessons.

Bailey's Book House (1996–2005) is representative of a type of software program that includes many different kinds of literacy activities. One game activity, "Letter Machine," focuses on helping children learn the names of letters of the alphabet. The opening screen presents an image of a large computer. In the question and answer mode, a digitized voice asks a student to find a letter by clicking on a keyboard. For example, if the child successfully selects the letter d on the keyboard, the message "D" for "Dinosaurs' Dance" appears on the screen along with an animation of dinosaurs dancing. Learning with computers requires children to interact in an open-ended way in the computer screen environment. Such an approach invites exploration, and trial and error. There is usually no *one* right answer or *one* right way to interact with the computer. Learning with computers in this type of open environment fosters diversity of thought and a disposition toward using the computer as a problem-solving and thinking tool.

Playing simulation games, models of events or situations, supports children's abilities to make decisions and see the results of their decisions. For example, in the early grades, when children play in the simulated neighborhood of *Richard Scarry's Busy Town* (1995), they have unique occasions to see the causes and effects of decisions. In one scenario, children use an on-screen delivery truck to pick up supplies and deliver them to the appropriate store. A delivery store manager orally states the name of the object and tells where it should be delivered. For example, bicycle tires need to go to the bicycle shop down the street. By controlling the mouse, a child navigates through a map that is a maze of streets and problem areas (e.g., construction work, a school zone, a fire hydrant). If a child accidentally runs into a construction area, she will be met with a policeman on a siren-wailing motorcycle who offers a warning. Children who play in this open-ended environment learn the digital literacies required to navigate through the program. They can also click on words to hear them pronounced, an early skill that is related to learning how to access hyperlinks, links to additional information that are included in digital text and typically highlighted and underlined in blue.

Learning with a computer may also involve using on-screen tools found in word-processing programs (e.g., pencils, keyboard displays, stamp pads, electronic erasers, cutting and pasting functions) as devices for making meaning. Children may also learn with a computer when their interactions support their comprehension, as in the case of CD-ROM talking books.

SOFTWARE TYPES THAT SUPPORT CHILDREN'S DEVELOPMENT OF DIGITAL LITERACY WHEN LEARNING *WITH* A COMPUTER

Two types of computer software are especially supportive of young children's digital literacy development, multimedia talking books and multimedia authoring programs. The sections that follow describe the features of each type, briefly discuss their educational benefits, and provide examples of the technology in use.

Multimedia Talking Books

Commercially produced talking electronic books are interactive, digital versions of printed books that are pressed onto CD-ROMs or accessed via the Internet and then displayed on computer monitors. CD-ROMs are storage devices that hold a large amount of multimedia information. They also allow users to access information that is stored on any part of the disk.

Looking at most talking books is like looking at two pages of an open book being displayed. In on-screen versions, however, storybook characters can literally come to life through animation and multimedia effects. Most talking books come prepared with varying types of multimedia features that include an oral narration of the text, digital graphics, animations, music, and sound effects. Phrases of text are usually highlighted as they are read aloud. Children also have on-demand access to the digitized pronunciation of each word through the simple click of a mouse on the text. These features allow young students to control the learning and reading processes.

McKenna (1998) has noted the compensatory function of electronic talking books in supporting beginning readers' development of traditional literacy. Children who are unable to recognize printed words independently benefit from reading talking books that pronounce unknown words. The child is in control of the amount of support that is needed to "read" the story. Over time, as children recognize more words automatically, their need to access unknown words lessens. The underlying assumption is that children's word recognition improves through multiple exposures to words.

Many CD-ROM talking books offer language options. Children who do not speak the language spoken at school may access talking book stories in their home language. Immigrant children learn new vocabulary words in a fairly short amount of time when they hear a story unfold simultaneously with animations that reflect the story's events (Verhallen, Bus, & de Jong, 2003). For example, the CD-ROM of *Little Monster at School* (1994) presents the adventures of Little Monster's school day (e.g., getting ready for school, riding a school bus, eating lunch, playing in the playground, studying a map, going home). Children who speak Spanish may simply press the #2 key on the keyboard to see and hear the story in Spanish. The CD-ROM of *Just Grandma and Me* (1992), the story of a day at the beach, allows children to select English, Japanese, or Spanish versions.

Some CD-ROM talking books present the story on the screen in a way that allows children to view animations while simultaneously listening to the story read aloud. The CD-ROM version of *The Ugly Duckling* (1993) displays the text and an illustration of a duck sitting on eggs. During the narration of the text, the illustration dramatizes the story content through animation. The mother duck appears to be upset when the ugly duckling emerges from his egg. Bus, de Jong, and Verhallen (in press) note that in these types of talking books, the combinations of multimedia effects are more cartoon-like than they are book-like.

Parents, caregivers, and teachers can help children use CD-ROM talking books in different ways to support literacy development at the following four levels: an initial interaction level, enjoying the story experience and appreciating the multimedia effects; a fluency and story comprehension level, reading along with the story narration, or echo reading (reading phrase by phrase); a word-interaction level, from looking for rhyming words to pointing to words known by sight; and a strategic interaction level, talking about how one screen page relates to another screen. These types of activities are likely to support students' ability to draw conclusions or make important story connections. Children who read talking books have opportunities to learn digital literacies related to accessing multimedia effects. Many talking books include "hot spots" related to illustrations. Clicking on a part of an illustration brings it to life through animation. Hot spot animations may relate to the central story line or may be incidental or even unrelated to the story line at all. Children require new digital literacy skills to comprehend talking books. They learn how music and sound effects help them interpret the mood or plot of a story. They learn how animations help them understand a character's emotional state. They learn to control how they navigate, or move through, various multimedia resources in ways that support their story comprehension.

Multimedia Authoring

When children learn to write on paper with pencils, they learn that they can use a tool, the eraser, to make revisions. Multimedia authoring/applications software programs allow children to compose in a different way, which requires new digital literacy skills. For example, they learn to express and publish their ideas on screen by using various types of symbols. Children gain digital literacy skills as they learn to use different on-screen tools to create multimedia compositions when they use programs such as *Kid Pix Deluxe 4* (2003–2005). This program allows students to move easily among artistic tools (e.g., paintbrushes, drawing pencils, clip art icons, background designs), multimedia tools (e.g., animation, photographs, slide show production, sound effects, music, narration) and word-processing tools (e.g., keyboard typing, letter stamps, pencil writing, cutting, pasting, erasing) to create a message.

As children explore using a software program, they develop insights into new literacies. They learn that they can use the computer socially when they exchange notes with classmates. They learn that they can use the computer to publish stories. They also learn that they can use the computer to create works of art. Children also learn that they can use the computer as a storehouse for their work in progress.

When children use digital cameras to create photographs that are imported into multimedia composing software, they learn many new literacies. This instructional procedure, the digital language experience approach (D-LEA), allows youngsters to take a photograph of an experience, import and arrange the photographs in chronological order, record an audio message for each photograph, write descriptive sentences, and produce an electronic slide show.

Steps for conducting a D-LEA presentation include the following:

Day 1

Step 1. Teachers take digital photographs of an experience with a small group of children (no more than five). For example, going for a walk in the playground provides occasions for trying out playground equipment, noticing plant or insect life, and seeing other people.

Step 2. Teachers import digital photographs from the camera to the computer. Many digital cameras come with software that provides specific programs and directions for importing photographs.

Day 2

Step 3. Teachers and students view, discuss, and select a series of photographs that best capture the experience. Children determine the order of the photographs. For example, a story about a walk through the school playground might be best told in chronological order. What happened first, second, and third? A digital photo essay about playing on the playground equipment could involve a focus on action words (verbs) or describing words (adjectives). The important component of this step is to elicit rich language as children describe what they see in the photographs.

Step 4. Teachers import the photographs into a presentation (e.g., *PowerPoint*) or creativity software (e.g., *Kidpix Deluxe*).

Day 3

Step 5. Children dictate, type, or stamp text to accompany each photograph. Editing and revising of the story is easy to accomplish at this stage with cutting and pasting software functions. Children may also record their voices narrating the story of each photograph.

Step 6. Teachers create a title page, include children's names as authors, and arrange the photographs into a slide show presentation. Children practice orally reading their parts of the D-LEA slide show.

Day 4

Step 7. Students present D-LEA stories/slide shows with other students or parents present. Teachers print out hard copies so students can take the stories home and extend the experience, and the opportunities to read aloud, with parents.

Day 5

Step 8. Children engage in follow-up activities that focus on word meanings, word recognition, and/or phonic elements of words. For example, print out on stock paper 5 to 10 words that have high utility (e.g., words that have similar meanings, word families, words with same onsets, words that rhyme, high-frequency words) so students can engage in word sorts. As indicated in the steps above, children learn many digital literacies that allow them to create multimedia presentations.

RESPONSE TO LITERATURE ACTIVITIES SUPPORTS YOUNG CHILDREN'S VOCABULARY DEVELOPMENT WHEN LEARNING *WITH* A COMPUTER

The most powerful use of computer technologies in the early grades occurs in learning environments that infuse programs and applications into the daily instructional routines of the classroom. Computers technologies should also be used to support the literacy development of children who sometimes struggle with oral language, vocabulary, and paper and pencil resources.

For example, recent research suggests that young children from low socioeconomic status (SES) backgrounds typically begin school with less vocabulary knowledge than their more affluent peers (Hart & Risley, 1992). This was the case in a predominately low SES school where I worked recently. Six primary grade teachers, the literacy coach, and I formed a research study group to design an instructional cycle to explore the potential of computer technologies to enhance 85 kindergarten through 2nd-grade children's vocabulary development. Early in our discussions of observational data (e.g., field notes, transcripts of classroom talk), we determined that we wanted to use technology to initiate a flood of vocabulary words into the classroom; thus we coined the phrase "a vocabulary flood." We also wanted to use children's literature, the resource that is used daily in millions of classrooms across the United States, because storybooks provide rich vocabulary words that are suitable for response activities. Another goal was to use the power of computer technologies to enhance literacy learning within the context of a warm, inviting, and supportive learning environment.

The first step in the vocabulary flood process involved focusing the talk of teachers and students on dozens of vocabulary terms encountered during read alouds of books that were connected thematically. This was a dramatic departure from the teachers' approaches to vocabulary instruction in the past. Prior to the project, teachers primarily mentioned a few important vocabulary words while in the context of reading a storybook aloud. During and after the project, the teachers stated that they were pleased with sharing the role of noticing vocabulary with their young students. They believed that if students generated the list of words they found the most interesting or the most important to understanding the story, they would more likely become invested in learning more about them.

The second step in the process involved highlighting, noticing, and using the words in children's oral language and in their writing after books were read. This step was also a departure from teachers' previous approaches to vocabulary instruction. For example, observational field notes suggested that the teachers were doing 90 percent of all of the talking about words during and after storybook reading sessions. The following transcript provides a brief scenario of a typical kindergarten teacher-student interaction during storybook reading before the vocabulary flood project.

TEACHER: (Reading a storybook aloud) "Mother turned her head." (Addressing students) "Do it.... turn your head," (Teacher turns her head to model the action.)

STUDENTS: (Turn their heads, mimicking the teacher's movement)

TEACHER: (Reading text aloud) "Grandma sucked in her cheeks." (Addressing students) "Show me how to suck in your cheeks."

STUDENTS: (Suck in their cheeks, puckering their lips, and smiling afterwards) (Researcher note—the students appear to be actively engaged—an important component of successful teacher/student interactions; however, students are doing very little talking. Indeed, once they've heard the words in the story, they never seem to deal with them again on any consistent basis.)

In this scenario, the teacher appropriately involved students with engaging and motivating activities related to phrases and words in the storybook; however, the children rarely talked about or used the words independently.

The third step in a vocabulary flood process involved students in using a digital camera during digital language experience approach (D-LEA) work, in order to use the vocabulary in personally meaningful ways. For example, if students read a text about how to make something (e.g., involving a recipe), they photographed and wrote about a follow-up activity that involved making the recipe. In one classroom, the children read a story about how to make a strawberry shortcake. The next day, the teacher brought in the ingredients and photographed students making and eating their own version of the dessert. If students read a fictional story, they created a photo essay of the reenactment. For example, one class of 1st graders heard a story about a little girl who didn't get along with anyone in the playground during recess time until she met a new student who challenged her bullying ways. The teacher photographed the students role playing the story events. Later, the students wrote their own list of playground rules.

The use of the photographs generated opportunities for children to use a high percentage of the words that they had noticed during the read alouds of the storybooks in their dictation or keyboarding of sentences to accompany photos. An analysis of scores on vocabulary tests indicated that many of the students improved their vocabulary knowledge. For example, only 7 percent of the students scored above average for expressive vocabulary, the ability to orally provide a label for a picture, before the "vocabulary flood" began. After four months of the intervention, 50 percent scored above average on expressive vocabulary.

It is important to note the theoretical underpinnings of the study, because the two theoretical perspectives underscore the importance of creating a warm, inviting, and supportive learning environment. The two perspectives draw from sociocognitive (Vygotsky, 1962) and multiple literacies perspectives (New London Group, 2000). Sociocognitive theories focus on understanding the nature and type of talk that students engage in during read alouds and D-LEA activities. The notion behind s sociocognitive perspectives is that children construct knowledge as they interact with others who support, challenge, or extend their thinking. The multiple literacies framework, which focuses on the role of multimedia as encountered on computer screens, was helpful in sorting out the nature and type of the audio and visual systems that students used in their D-LEA creations.

YOUNG CHILDREN BENEFIT FROM GUIDED INTERNET EXPLORATIONS

Children in the early grades also benefit from guided explorations of the Internet (Leu & Kinzer, 2003). Unfortunately, teachers of young children tend to be a bit skeptical of the appropriateness of the Internet for classroom activities.

There are many benefits of using the Internet in the classroom with early readers, however. The Internet provides quick communication with experts on topics of study, authors of wonderful works of children's literature (for example, see www.janbrett.com, www.eric-carle.com), other children in close or distant classrooms, and other teachers. The Internet provides possible collaborations with students around the world on projects of shared interest. For example, a 2nd-grade class in the United States exchanged stuffed animals with a class in Brisbane, Australia. Students in each country took turns taking the stuffed animals home and wrote about their adventures. Children were highly motivated to exchange e-mails and learn more about the similarities and differences between the two countries (Wepner, Valmont, & Thurlow, 2000).

Teachers can also find important electronic resources to use in lessons. Using the Internet in the early grades helps young children learn that the computer is an avenue of access to various types and forms of communication, such as rich graphics, video clips, animations, music, narrated passages, and interactive games that include instant, corrective feedback. Students learn they can assemble knowledge from various Internet and print-based resources as they attempt to answer questions related to topics of study.

Internet sites provide excellent resource materials for teachers of young children. Some Internet sites provide additional information about children's literature (see http://www.ucalgary.ca/~dkbrown/rteacher.html), or provide scripts to print out so children can practice fluency by reading plays aloud (see http://www.aaronshep.com/rt/). Teachers can also locate Internet locations for publishing students' creative compositions. Such sites include Global Children's Art (http://www.naturalchild.com/gallery/), Stone Soup (http://www.stonesoup.com; this requires a subscription; however, the site provides a free sample issue), or Giggle Poetry (http://www.gigglepoetry.com/).

Students in the intermediate and secondary grades frequently conduct individual or collaborative Internet projects called WebQuests.

A WebQuest is an inquiry-oriented activity in which most or all of the information used by learners is drawn from the Web. WebQuests are designed to use learners' time well, to focus on using information rather than looking for it, and to support learners' thinking at the levels of analysis, synthesis, and evaluation (see http://webquest.sdsu.edu/).

Adult-guided WebQuest inquiries can also be an appropriate literacy learning activities in the early grades. The Internet offers a wealth of virtual experiences and access to information that can be enriching to the early literacy curriculum if a few guidelines are followed.

Teachers may read aloud and summarize Internet information related to answering a question that leads to an inquiry during whole-group instruction. An Internet inquiry WebQuest might focus, for example, on learning more about life in different neighborhoods across the United States. In fact,

ZuZu, an online magazine by and for children (see http://www.zuzu.org), has a link called "Neighborhood Reports," which allows teachers to read aloud what children like or do not like about their hometowns. One child wrote the following report about life in California:

> Where I live it is very quiet some people in my neighborhood have chickens, which is funny because I live in the suburbs. I like to go to the beach out hear it is fun. I like California because you can go to the beach an snow on the same day. (http://www.zuzu.org/ncali.html, retrieved September 20, 2006)

Teachers may guide children to write their own neighborhood reports to post online in the magazine Teachers will need to read the reports aloud and also guide children to draw, take photographs, and write about the things they like or don't like in their own neighborhoods.

Teachers of young children should be extremely careful to provide safety for all children who have access to Internet resources. One primary way that teachers protect children from inadvertently accessing offensive or inappropriate material is to limit their interactions to previously bookmarked sites, selected by the teacher because they are developmentally appropriate and content specific. Many school districts provide filtering services (e.g., http://www.netnanny.com; http://www.cyberpatrol.com) that control access by blocking Internet resources that are meant for adults or mature audiences.

WHAT PRIMARY TEACHERS NEED TO KNOW ABOUT COMPUTER TECHNOLOGIES

It is imperative that primary teachers become knowledgeable about the National Educational Technology Standards for Teachers (International Society for Technology in Education, 2002)) that are appropriate for teachers at all grade levels. There are six key areas of focus that outline the relationship among instructional practices and computer technology strategies and skills:

1. Teachers should understand technology operations and concepts.
2. Teachers need to be able to plan and design learning environments and identify, evaluate, and manage technology resources.
3. Teachers must be able to address content standards and student technology standards to support student-centered strategies and to develop students' higher-order thinking skills.
4. Teachers must be able to use various assessment techniques, communicate findings, and apply multiple forms of evaluation.
5. Teachers should engage in ongoing professional development.
6. Teachers must model and teach ethical practices, empower learners, affirm diversity, facilitate equitable access, and promote the healthy use of technology resources.

Young children's ability to learn traditional literacies can be fostered by introducing them to developmentally appropriate computer-related activities and materials. Talking books, available on CD-ROM and on Internet sites, help primary grades children learn new vocabulary, hear models of fluent reading, and better understand how print functions. As youngsters interact with multimedia tools in digital environments, they also learn about new literacies that include learning how to navigate through Internet links. They may also learn how to make meaning from various types of multimedia modes such as animation, music, audio narration, and print. Clearly, children will learn both traditional and new literacies with computers when caring adults provide support, encouragement and guidance.

REFERENCES

Bailey's book house. (1996–2005). San Francisco: Edmark/Riverdeep/The Learning Company.

Bus, A. G., de Jong, M. T., & Verhallen, M. J. (in press). CD-ROM talking books: A way to enhance early literacy? In M. McKenna, L. D. Labbo, L. R. Kieffer, & D. Reinking (Eds.), *International handbook of literacy and technology* (2nd ed). Mahwah, NJ: Lawrence Erlbaum Associates.

Cuban, L. (2001). *Oversold and overused: Computers in the classroom.* Cambridge, MA: Harvard University Press.

Gilster, P. (1997). *Digital Literacy.* New York: John Wiley & Sons.

Goldberg, K., & Sherwood, R. D. (1983). *Microcomputers: A parent's guide.* New York: Wiley.

Flood, J., & Lapp, D. (1995). Broadening the lens: Toward an expanded conceptualization of literacy. In K. Hinchman, D. J. Leu, & C. K. Kinzer (Eds.), *Perspectives on literacy research and practice: Forty-fourth yearbook of the National Reading Conference* (pp. 1–16). Chicago, IL: National Reading Conference.

Hart, B., & Risley, T. R. (1992). American parenting of language-learning children: Persisting differences in family-child interactions observed in natural home environments. *Developmental Psychology, 26*(6), 1096–1105.

International Society for Technology in Education. (2002). *International Society for Technology in Education standards for students.* Retrieved November 7, 2006, from http://cnets.iste.org/.

Irwin, V. (2003). Hop, skip … and software? Educators debate whether computer use for young students makes them better learners or not. *Christian Science Monitor.* Retrieved August 15, 2006, from http://www.csmonitor.com/2003/0311/p11s02lecl.html.

Just grandma and me (1992). Novato, CA: Living Books.

Kid Pix deluxe 4 [Computer Software]. (2000–2005). Cambridge, MA: Broderbund/Riverdeep/The Learning Company.

Leu, D. J., & Kinzer, C. K. (2003). *Effective literacy instruction: Implementing best practices* (5th ed.). Upper Saddle River, NJ: Merrill Prentice Hall.

Little monster at school (1994). Novato, CA: Living Books.

McKenna, M. (1998). Electronic texts and the transformations of beginning reading. In D. Reinking, M. C. McKenna, L. D. Labbo, & R. D. Kieffer (Eds.), *Handbook of literacy and technology: Transformations in a post-typographic world* (pp. A45–59). Mahwah, NJ: Lawrence Erlbaum Associates.

National Association for the Education of Young Children. (1996). *Technology and young children—ages 3–8.* Washington, DC: Author. Retrieved September 5, 2006, from http://www.naeyc.org/resources/position_statements/pstech98.htm.

National Center for Educational Statistics (NCES). (1999). Internet access in public schools and classrooms: 1994–98. Retrieved December 14, 2005, from http://nces.ed.gov/surveys/frss/publications/1999017/

New London Group. (2000). A pedagogy of multiliteracies: designing social futures. In B. Cope & M. Kalantzis (Eds.), *Multiliteracies: Literacy learning and the design of social futures* (pp. 9–38). London: Routledge.

Richard Scarry's busy town (1995). New York: Pearson, Simon & Schuster Interactive.

The ugly duckling (version 1). (1993). San Francisco: Morgan Interactive.

Verhallen, M. J., Bus, A. G., & de Jong, M. T. (2003). *Elektronische Boeken in de Vroegschoolse Eductie.* Amsterdam: Schiting Lezen.

Vygotsky, L. (1962). *Thought and language.* Cambridge, MA. The MIT Press.

Wepner, S. B., Valmont, W. J., & Thurlow, R. (2000). *Linking literacy and technology: A guide for K–8 classrooms.* Newark, DE: International Reading Association.

Chapter Sixteen

INTERACTION, SOUND, AND SENSE: RESOURCES FOR EARLY LITERACY DEVELOPMENT

Ruth Alice Jurey

Literacy is skill with language in its written form, skill that is built upon the child's existing language development. From birth, language grows through *interaction* with other people, so interaction with caring adults is the child's greatest resource for learning language and building literacy. No video, audio, or computer program can compare with an abundance of language provided through give-and-take interactions with important adults in a child's life.

Most children do not simply grow from listening and speaking into reading and writing. Rather, literacy skills must be specifically developed. Like the foundation for a house, the child's language development needs to be solid if the literacy skills built upon it are to be strong.

The critical elements of language for building literacy are *sound* and *sense.* The *sounds* of language are its rhythms and melodies, speech sounds and sequences, rhymes and memories. Well-developed auditory skills, or sound skills, prepare children to learn to read and write well. The *sense* of language is the meaning of words and sentences, the way language expresses experiences, and the way that experiences can be imagined from language. Well-developed vocabularies and the skills of listening and of expressing their ideas in words prepare children to comprehend what they read and to express themselves in writing. The following resources will assist in developing and enhancing children's *language interaction, sound* and *sense* along the path from language to literacy.

NURTURING LANGUAGE THROUGH INTERACTION

Apel, K., & Masterson, J. (2001). *Beyond baby talk: From sounds to sentences—A parent's complete guide to language development.* New York: Three Rivers Press.

The premise of this book is that parents teach language to their children, and they do not need special equipment or extraordinary activities to do it well. This engaging book explains the components of language, children's stages of learning it, and natural ways to help them get the most out of each stage. The sample parent-child dialogs reflect the authors' expertise in interacting with children in effective, language-expanding ways: the child-directed speech modeled here is simple rather than wordy, and genuine rather than self-consciously didactic. The authors describe four broad stages of language development from infancy to written language, discuss gender, birth order, child care, cultural influences, and media influences; and provide guidance for suspected language problems. Well-written and authoritative, this book will be enjoyed by parents, grandparents, and teachers of children from birth through five years old.

American Speech-Language-Hearing Association. (n.d.). *Language and literacy development.* Retrieved September 17, 2006, from http://www.asha.org/public/speech/development/lang_lit.htm.

This is a concise year-by-year summary of children's progress into language and literacy from birth through age five, provided by the national association of language-learning professionals. Born out of this specialized expertise, the suggestions here describe the pathways from language to literacy in ways effective for each age. This accessible guide will be valuable for parents and caregivers of children from birth through five years.

National Association for the Education of Young Children. (2004). *Early years are learning years: Singing as a teaching tool.* Retrieved September 17, 2006. from http://www.naeyc.org/ece/2004/01.asp.

Parents and teachers do not need special talent or training to give children the benefits of singing. This page explains the memory boost that music offers, and encourages caregivers to sing to, and with, young children. By singing familiar tunes, either with their original lyrics or made-up words, children can develop their auditory and language skills.

Schwartz, S. (2004). *The new language of toys: Teaching communication skills to children with special needs* (3rd ed.). Bethesda, MD: Woodbine House.

The premise of this book is that play is the young child's work. This volume contains descriptions of about ninety toys, both commercial and homemade, organized by their appropriateness for babies and young children through the age of five years. A sample toy dialog for each toy gives ideas for language an adult might use while playing with the child. Each year is summarized by providing lists of typical vocabulary items and concepts to talk about, and a list of dozens of age-appropriate books with brief descriptions. Written specifically for use with young children with special needs, this book will be useful for teachers, parents, and grandparents of all children from birth through five years.

McGuiness, D. (2004). *Growing a reader from birth: Your child's path from language to literacy.* New York, W. W. Norton.

"All the evidence shows that the major predictor of becoming a good reader is the development of good language skills during the early years of life" (McGuiness, 2004, p. 9). Cognitive psychologist Diane McGuiness explains in detail how literacy begins with language, and provides parents with fascinating information about how children grow in language at each stage. Asserting that about half of children's language ability depends upon the richness of their language environment during the formative years, McGuiness provides a guide for expanding on what we are doing right, and avoiding what we may be doing wrong. Although McGuiness dismisses the need to enhance children's auditory skill in preparation for reading, and takes a wait-and-see approach to some speech and language problems that could be differentiated and should be treated early, this book is recommended for its clear illumination of the linguistic origin of reading ability.

READ ALOUD RESOURCES

Interaction, sound, and *sense,* the critical pathways from language to literacy, are all embodied in the read-aloud experience. Reading aloud to children is the single most valuable activity for helping them to become better and better readers. It should begin at birth and never stop.

The youngest listeners enjoy books with clear, uncomplicated pictures and very simple text. Books about baby's daily routines, or books that simply name the pictures, are examples. Wordless picture books encourage parents to tell the story, and books with flaps, holes, or things to feel encourage babies to participate. Baby's auditory skills are stimulated with rhyming books and Mother Goose poems, books with repetitive lines, and books with strong rhythm, such as "Stomp your feet! Clap your hands! Everybody ready for a Barnyard Dance!" Boynton, Sandra. (1998). *Barnyard dance.* New York: Workman Publishing Co.

Trelease, J. (2006). *The read-aloud handbook* (6th ed.). New York: Penguin Putnam.

In the first half of this outstanding resource for parents and teachers, Jim Trelease makes the case for spending a pleasurable 15 minutes a day reading to children. Trelease explains and documents how reading aloud improves children's reading, writing, speaking, and listening, concluding that reading aloud is more important than worksheets, drill, assessments, or homework. Here are both the prods and the inspiration to make reading aloud to children a priority. The second half of the book describes a "treasury" of recommended read alouds: wordless books, predictable books, reference books, picture books, short novels, full-length novels, poetry, anthologies, fairy tales, and folk tales. The books are well organized by suggested grade range, with descriptions. Trelease has a Web site with a useful sampling of the book's contents including some of the "treasury": *Trelease-on-reading.com.* (n.d.). Retrieved September 17, 2006, from http://www.trelease-on-reading.com.

New York Public Library. (n.d.). *"On-Lion" for kids! Recommended reading: Best books for children.* Retrieved September 17, 2006, from http://kids.nypl.org/reading/recommended.cfm.

This site has links to lists of wonderful books for children, with pictures of the covers and one-sentence descriptions. The visitor browses through lists of the 100 best children's books by year of publication, the 100 favorite children's books, the 100 picture books everyone should know, and more. This is an attractive resource that will appeal to children and adults alike, and encourage families to search their local library for their choices.

RESOURCES ON LEARNING TO READ

In today's world, literacy is not optional. Even children whose natural talents lie elsewhere need to learn to read and write. Fortunately, research points the way to literacy success for all children. One or more of the resources listed below should fit the needs of parents, caregivers, and teachers.

U.S. Department of Education. (2003). *Reading tips for parents (Consejos practicos para los padres sobre la lectura).* Retrieved September 17, 2006. from www.ed.gov/parents/read/resources/readingtips/edlite-index.html.

A few minutes' quick and easy reading of bulleted points, these tips are also available in PDF format for printing, or in PowerPoint presentation. This resource begins with true/false questions about reading, followed by the answers with explanations. Tips include "What Every Parent Should Look For in a Good Early Reading Program"; "Homework Tips" for reading time; and "Five Essential Components of Reading." Available in English and Spanish, this is vital, concise information for parents, provided in various formats to assist professionals to share it with them.

U.S. Department of Education. (2003). *My child's academic success: Helping your child become a reader, with activities for children from infancy through age 6.* Retrieved September 17, 2006, from http://www.ed.gov/parents/academic/help/reader/index.html.

This booklet, available in English and Spanish, presents the basics of children and adults talking and reading together, choosing books, being a good role model, children's learning about print, and their early writing efforts. In an encouraging tone, the text assures parents who may not be confident of their own reading skills that they can nevertheless be positive models of literacy for their children. Parents of children whose first language is not English are encouraged to support the first language also, as the child works toward the special accomplishment of speaking two languages. There are tips for talking with babies and with older children; for introducing books and the alphabet; for enjoying predictable books, rhymes, sound play, and dramatic play; and for storytelling and writing. To demonstrate how important the child's books are, parents are encouraged to provide a special "home" for them and to include bookstore, gift, used, and homemade books in the child's library. Finally, parents are guided to take advantage of the public library's books, CDs and tapes, movies, computers, and other resources, as well as the librarian and library programs for children and families. The encouraging conversational style and sound advice in this work makes it an outstanding choice for explaining the vital contribution parents make at home, even before children begin formal instruction at school.

Lee Pesky Learning Center. (2004). *Every child ready to read: Literacy tips for parents.* New York: Random House.

This is a succinct and readable book from a highly regarded nonprofit learning center that combines introductory background, activities, and recommended books and musical resources in one handy package. Research-based, the book presents resources for infants to 18 months, toddlers to 36 months, and preschoolers aged three to four; resources for children with learning disabilities; and further resources for parents. The authors' expertise in working with real children is evident in the advice to help insure children's engagement and participation, such as following a baby's lead and expressing heightened enthusiasm. This resource is recommended as a guide that parents can keep on hand and refer to again and again.

Partnership for Reading, National Institute for Literacy, National Institute of Child Health and Human Development, U.S. Department of Education. (2003). *A child becomes*

a reader: Proven ideas from research for parents. Retrieved September 17, 2006, from http://www.nifl.gov/partnershipforreading/publications/html/parent_guides.
Based upon more than 460 studies, the Partnership for Reading has extracted the essential findings about what has been scientifically proven to work for children's literacy. Divided into two booklets, one for birth through preschool, and one for kindergarten through grade 3, this resource provides a short summary of what research says about how children learn to read and write, activities to do at each age to nurture that process, and a glossary of helpful terms. Suggested books to read and organizations to contact are provided for more information. The booklets are clearly written, thorough, accurate, and well designed; and they are highly recommended for parents, grandparents, and teachers. Printable PDF versions are available:

A child becomes a reader: Proven ideas from research for parents, birth through preschool. Retrieved September 17, 2006. from http://www.nifl.gov/partnershipforreading/publications/pdf/low_res_child_reader_B-K.pdf.

A child becomes a reader: Proven ideas from research for parents, kindergarten through grade 3. Retrieved September 17, 2006, from http://www.nifl.gov/partnershipforreading/publications/pdf/low_res_child_reader_K-3.pdf.

Copies can also be ordered from the National Institute for Literacy at EdPubs, P.O. Box 1398, Jessup, MD 20794; by calling 800 / 228–8813; or by sending an e-mail message to edpubs@inet.ed.gov.

National Association for the Education of Young Children. (2005). *Early years are learning years: Raising a reader.* Retrieved September 17, 2006, from http://naeyc.org/ece/1998/19.asp,
This Web page of practical information is valuable for its important guidance on motivating children to participate in literacy activities. There are tips on making time for reading, tolerance of children's preferences, appealing read-aloud styles, and more.

Paulu, N. (1993). *Helping your child get ready for school, with activities for children from birth through age 5.* Retrieved September 17, 2006, from http://readyweb.crc.uiuc.edu/library/1992/getready/getready.html,
This resource contains explanations of the foundations that help children prepare for kindergarten, and presents a concise developmental guide from birth to five years, with practical suggestions for easy activities and encouragement of the preschool child. This is a broad guide encompassing the child's physical, mental, social, and emotional preparation for the important learning tasks ahead. Clearly written, wise, and to the point, this book will assist parents and others in helping children to get ready for school.

National Association for the Education of Young Children. (2005). *Learning to read and write: Developmentally appropriate practices for young children.* Retrieved September 17, 2006, from http://www.naeyc.org/about/positions/pdf/PSREAD98.PDF,
This printable document is the joint position statement of the International Reading Association and the National Association for the Education of Young Children. Their position is endorsed by numerous other national organizations including the American Speech-Language-Hearing Association, the Association for Childhood Education International, the National Association of Elementary School Principals, the American Academy of Pediatrics, the National Head Start Association, and others. This readable 16-page report presents rationales and recommended teaching

practices for each stage of life, and provides guidance and support for teachers, parents, and others who want to insure that young children through age eight receive the instruction and support they need, whether individually or school- or district-wide.

Neuman, S. and Copple, S. (2000). *Learning to read and write: Developmentally appropriate practices for young children.* Washington, DC: National Association for the Education of Young Children.

This book includes the joint position statement of the International Reading Association and the National Association for the Education of Young Children, and effective teaching practices and ways that teachers can turn their classrooms into environments that promote literacy. In addition, the authors answer frequently asked questions and provides a glossary of terms. Teachers can improve their understanding of what is expected at various levels, and can reflect on their own literacy practices with a self-inventory, "Taking stock of what you do to promote children's literacy." This book is recommended for teachers of preschool through the primary grades.

Burns, S., & Snow, C. (Eds.). (1999). *Starting out right: A guide to promoting children's reading success.* Washington, DC: The National Academies Press.

Based upon extensive research and focusing on the child from birth through the early school years, this book from the National Academy of Sciences is an authoritative guide for parents, caregivers, teachers, and policy makers. It helps to answer questions such as how to support children's growth from language to literacy; and what to look for in preschool, child care, kindergarten, and the early grades; and it includes questions to ask about whether children are making progress and how to determine whether they are doing so. Key aspects of language and literacy for birth through age four and kindergarten through grade 3 are presented and accompanied by suggestions and activities to enhance literacy development at those ages. A section on the prevention of reading difficulties details activities to equalize opportunities for children at risk, the participation of early childhood health care professionals, and early intervention opportunities. The narrative sections of this text provide snapshots of everyday literacy-promoting interactions. Especially recommended, with links to the pages' printable versions, are the following:

"Everyday literacy: One family home." Retrieved September 17, 2006, from http://newton.nap.edu/pdf/0309064104/pdf_image/17.pdf.

"Everyday narrative and dinner conversations." Retrieved September 17, 2006, from http://newton.nap.edu/pdf/0309064104/pdf_image/27.pdf.

"Connecting to books." Retrieved September 17, 2006, from http://newton.nap.edu/pdf/0309064104/pdf_image/75.pdf.

Parents and especially teachers will benefit from this resource, which contains principles and a wealth of activities for promoting literacy for all children. Single chapters or entire book can also be purchased in PDF format and are entirely viewable and searchable online, courtesy of the publisher at the link below:

Starting out right: A guide to promoting children's reading success. Retrieved September 17, 2006, from http://darwin.nap.edu/books/0309064104/html.

Jurey, R. (2005). *AdvanceAbility: The reading treehouse.* Retrieved September 17, 2006, from http://www.aability.com.

Based on detailed task analyses by a speech and language pathologist, and intended to convey the complex language-literacy continuum in concrete fashion, *The reading treehouse* illustrates the process of learning to read via examples and simulated experiences. This resource will be useful for teachers and parents who want to understand how the elements of literacy come together, find out what specific reading difficulties may occur, and learn some approaches to ameliorating those problems.

WETA Public Television Station, Washington, DC. (2006). *Reading rockets.* Retrieved August 11, 2006, from http://www.readingrockets.org.

"Reading Rockets is a national multimedia project offering information and resources on how young kids learn to read, why so many struggle, and how caring adults can help" (http://www.readingrockets.org/about). This resource provides an overview of and links to the extensive multimedia resources that the project makes available, which are funded by the U.S. Department of Education, Office of Special Education Programs. Included are links to PBS television programs, available on tape and DVD with some streamed online; professional development resources; information for teachers; and more. Of particular interest to teachers and policy makers working on research-based practices is the link to:

"Research & reports," retrieved September 17, 2006, from http://www.readingrockets.org/research.

Reading Rockets is a recommended portal for parents, teachers, and others who want accessible, authoritative information about reading, and resources for both adults and children.

SPECIAL SKILL WITH SOUND: PHONEMIC AWARENESS

The special mental *sound* skills critical to fluent success in phonics are known as phonemic awareness, or PA. Distinct from phonics, these auditory skills are teachable within reasonable amounts of time and benefit students including those whom teachers may think of as visual learners only.

Jurey, R. (2005). *The reading treehouse: The floor.* Retrieved September 17, 2006, from http://www.aability.com/papreface.htm.

A speech and language pathologist explains in bullet points, examples, and simulated experiences the critical area of phonemic awareness. She gives a hierarchical list of the essential skills, and emphasizes that children need to learn to play with sound without the crutches of letters at first, relying only on the "mind's ear" in order to develop the auditory power that leads to success in reading; she also provides a comprehensive selection of PA skill-building games. These include "Games to go," which can be played in short segments of time during pauses in daily activities; and "Block challenges," puzzles for the table or floor. Accompanying the games are lists of the easiest words for beginners to manipulate, task analyzed to maximize the child's early success. This material is recommended for parents and teachers of children from preschool age through the early grades, and parents and teachers of older struggling readers.

Sound Reading Solutions. (2003). *Hop, skip and jump into reading* [software on CD]. Retrieved September 17, 2006, from http://www.soundreading.com/srs_new/product/cd-hsj-2.cfm.

This software, available for purchase on CD, is designed to help children ages four to seven to strengthen phonemic awareness and other connections between speech and print. The games are simple to learn, but children may need help from time to time with new learning tasks. A child can play these games with a parent alongside. As children learn to focus and work with sound, their parents will learn accurate pronunciation of the speech sounds for phonics, which are clearly modeled here. (Older children and parents can use the primary grade CD.) These games are recommended for young children to develop auditory phonemic awareness power at home or at school.

Adams, M., Foorman, B., Lundberg, I., & Beeler, T. (1998). *Phonemic awareness in young children: A classroom curriculum.* Baltimore, MD: Paul H. Brookes Publishing Co.

This resource includes listening games and activities to develop skills of phonemic awareness for preschool, kindergarten, and 1st grade children. Specifically designed for classroom use for 15 or 20 minutes a day, this authoritative book includes teaching objectives and lesson plans, as well as a discussion of the nature and importance of phonemic awareness, why this kind of learning can be tricky for children, and information from research.

FUN FOR KIDS

Kids learn most easily when they are having fun, and they love the special attention of the adults in their lives. The following resources are useful for this purpose:

Hauser, J. (2000). *Wow! I'm reading! Fun activities to make reading happen.* Charlotte, VT: Williamson Publishing Co.

This is an accessible book of crafts, games, and activities for fun and learning. Grouped according to language comprehension and expression, auditory skill, print and alphabet familiarity, phonics, early writing, and working with stories, each of 48 themes has several activities. This easy-to-browse resource will be valued by parents and teachers, and make the learning personal and memorable for children from preschool through kindergarten.

Schiller, P. (2001). *Creating readers: Over 1000 games, activities, tongue twisters, fingerplays, songs and stories to get children excited about reading.* Beltsville, MD: Gryphon House.

Beginning with a brief introduction to children's development from language to literacy, Pam Schiller then presents a wealth of excellent, engaging activities for children's growth in listening, auditory skill, in-depth experience with stories, and more. A large section of phonological awareness activities details songs, poems, fingerplays, and more, organized by speech sounds through the alphabet (omitting the "sh," "ch," and "th" speech sounds). Reproducible pages at the back of the book provide materials for the activities, wordless picture stories, and phonemic awareness card games. This is an inclusive resource that will be appreciated by teachers of preschool to early-grade students.

West, S., & Cox, A. (2004). *Literacy play: Over 300 dramatic play activities that teach prereading skills.* Beltsville, MD: Gryphon House.

This resource for early childhood education exploits children's love of dramatic play to extend the language skills basic to reading. The authors offer 40 interesting dramatic play areas with materials, props, and directions for setup, songs, poems and fingerplays, book-making ideas, and related resources for follow-up. The book specifically highlights vocabulary and literacy objectives. An organized resource to simplify the planning of imaginative learning centers, this book is recommended for teachers of young children.

Wordwindow LLC. (2005). *Word window.* Retrieved September 17, 2006, from http://www.wordwindow.com.

This resource is a unique, colorful, audiovisual alphabet for purchase on DVD or video. A letter appears stroke by stroke, each stroke accompanied by silly vocal sounds, then the name of the letter is given, followed by its associated speech sound. The speech-sound quality is well exaggerated, assisting auditory discrimination. After some variations on this sequence, the segment ends with an example syllable and example word, each beginning with the relevant letter-sound, and finally a video clip illustrating the example word. Think-time between the speech stimuli is enlivened by more silly nonverbal sounds in synchronization with equally nonmeaningful animated elements. The strangely captivating presentation can be sampled at the Word Window web site, for which see above. Word Window will be useful for young children who need a boost for engaging with the alphabet, or extra rehearsal to learn it.

INDEX

ABOUT THE CONTRIBUTORS

BARBARA J. GUZZETTI is a professor of language and literacy at Arizona State University in the Mary Lou Fulton College of Education. She is also an affiliated faculty member in the College of Liberal Arts and Sciences in women's and gender studies. Her research interests include gender and literacy, science education and literacy, adolescent literacy, popular culture, and the new literacies, including digital literacies.

BENITA A. BLACHMAN is the Trustee Professor of Education and Psychology at Syracuse University. She has published extensively on early reading, focusing her research on early intervention to prevent reading failure. Her research has been funded by the National Institute of Child Health and Human Development, the U.S. Department of Education, and the National Center for Learning Disabilities.

MARIO CASTRO is a PhD student in educational leadership and policy studies at Arizona State University. He has a master of public affairs degree from the Lyndon B. Johnson School of Public Affairs at the University of Texas at Austin and a bachelor of science degree in industrial engineering from Texas A & M. He is currently working on his dissertation, investigating the validity of various assumptions about the Spanish language in the United States related to economic implications, with specific reference to Mexican origin/ancestry populations.

JAMES CHRISTIE is a professor in the Division of Curriculum and Instruction at Arizona State University, where he teaches courses in language, literacy, and early childhood education. His research interests include early literacy development and children's play. James is a member of the Early Literacy Development Commission of the International Reading Association and a past president of the Association for the Study of Play.

JEANNE GILLIAM FAIN is a senior lecturer and multilingual/multicultural initial teacher certification coordinator in the Division of Curriculum and Instruction at Arizona State University. She earned her PhD in language, reading, and culture from the University of Arizona. Her areas of interest include children's talk about children's literature, family-led literature discussions, biliteracy, bilingualism, early literacy, linguistic diversity, and critical literacy.

TERRI FAUTSCH-PATRIDGE is an instructor and doctoral student in the Department of Educational Psychology at the University of Minnesota. Her research interests include reading fluency and reading acquisition in special populations, particularly in children with cognitive disabilities.

LEE GALDA, PhD, is a professor of children's and adolescent literature at the University of Minnesota. She has written 11 books, many book chapters, and articles in journals such as *Reading Research Quarterly, Research in the Teaching of English, The Reading Teacher, Language Arts,* and *The New Advocate.* She was the children's books department editor for *The Reading Teacher,* coauthored the Professional Resources column for *The New Advocate,* was a contributing editor for *The Riverbank Review,* and served as a member of the 2003 Newbery Award Selection Committee.

LINDA B. GAMBRELL is professor in the Eugene T. Moore School of Education at Clemson University and is a past president of the International Reading Association. She has written extensively in the areas of literacy motivation, comprehension strategy instruction, and the role of discussion in teaching and learning. In 2004 she was elected to the Reading Hall of Fame.

DONNA J. GRACE is an associate professor in the Institute for Teacher Education at the University of Hawaii at Manoa. She teaches and conducts research in the areas of early literacy, critical literacy, and media literacy.

CAROLINE L. HILK is currently a doctoral student specializing in educational psychology and serves as an instructional technology fellow at the

University of Minnesota, Twin Cities. She has worked as a literacy program coordinator for the Minnesota Literacy Council and the America Reads program. Her research interests include the psychology of learning and cognition, cooperative problem-solving, and evaluation of educational programs.

RUTH ALICE JUREY is a speech and language pathologist for Horizon Charter School in Lincoln, California. She has a long-standing interest in the language-literacy continuum and has presented on auditory and language issues affecting reading and writing to school districts, private schools, and parent groups. She is the author of the Web site *AdvanceAbility: Positive Principles in Speech, Language and Learning* at http://www.aability.com.

LINDA D. LABBO, PhD, professor of language and literacy education, University of Georgia, Athens, conducts research and teaches courses on digital literacies and early childhood literacy courses. Her recent awards include an American Library Association Award for an Outstanding Academic Book, the National Reading Conference Edward Fry Book Award, the Phi Delta Kappa Faculty Research Award, and the Ira Aaron Award for Teaching Excellence. She received the Computers in Reading Research Award from the Technology in Literacy Education International Reading Special Interest Group.

LAUREN AIMONETTE LIANG, PhD, is an assistant professor of literacy education at the University of Utah, where she researches and teaches courses on comprehension instruction and children's and adolescent literature. Published in journals such as *Reading Research Quarterly, Research in the Teaching of English, The Reading Teacher,* and *Reading Psychology,* Dr. Liang also serves on committees and editorial boards for local, national, and international reading organizations and reviews children's literature for *The Horn Book Guide, The Five Owls,* and other publications.

BARBARA A. MARINAK is assistant professor of elementary and early childhood education at Pennsylvania State University at Harrisburg. She has written in the areas of comprehension instruction, motivation, and the observation of reading and writing.

CARMEN M. MARTÍNEZ-ROLDÁN is an assistant professor of language and literacy in the Mary Lou Fulton College of Education at Arizona State University. Her work examines Latino/a children's reading and interpretations of narrative and expository texts and the contexts that mediate students' literate thinking. Her work focuses on the intersection of literacy/biliteracy, learning, and identity.

KATHLEEN M. MCCOY is an associate professor in the Department of Curriculum and Instruction at Arizona State University, where she teaches methods of instruction and evaluation with special emphasis on inclusion. As director of Arizona State University's Special Education Clinic and member of the graduate faculty for the Interdisciplinary Doctoral Program, she is responsible for the preparation and implementation of the Fast Track Special Education Master of Education Program at Arizona State University. Also founder and director of the Renaissance Institute for Children and Adults, an academically focused learning program, she has written numerous articles, presented papers at many national conferences, and published educational texts.

LESLEY MANDEL MORROW holds the rank of professor II at Rutgers University's Graduate School of Education, where she is chair of the Department of Learning and Teaching. She has more than 250 publications, which have appeared as journal articles, chapters in books, monographs, and books. Most recently, she served as president of the International Reading Association (IRA), an organization of 80,000 educators in a hundred countries, and was elected to the Reading Hall of Fame.

SUSAN B. NEUMAN is a professor in educational studies at the University of Michigan. Prior to coming to Michigan she was the assistant secretary for elementary and secondary education under President George W. Bush. She has written or edited eight books and over a hundred articles on early literacy for economically disadvantaged children.

LYNNE HEBERT REMSON, PhD, CCC-SLP, is a speech-language pathologist specializing in language and literacy disorders and fluency disorders (stuttering). She was a clinical associate professor at Arizona State University and an assistant professor at California State University, Los Angeles, for a combined 12 years before returning to Scottsdale, Arizona. She currently maintains a private practice and evaluates preschool children for the Scottsdale Unified School District.

KATHLEEN ROSKOS teaches courses in reading instruction and reading diagnosis at John Carroll University. For two years she served in state government as the director of the Ohio Literacy Initiative at the Ohio Department of Education, providing leadership in P–12 literacy policy and programs. She studies early literacy development, teacher cognition, and the design of professional education for teachers.

TERRY SALINGER is managing director and chief scientist for reading research at the American Institutes for Research. Currently the project director for an Institute of Education Sciences (IES) study of the effectiveness of reading interventions for adolescent struggling readers, her specific areas of focus are reading and literacy research and assessment. Additionally, she provides content expertise on studies investigating preservice teachers' preparation to teach beginning reading, developing a curriculum for adult ESL learners, and monitoring the implementation of the Reading First program.

S. JAY SAMUELS holds the International Reading Association Wm. S. Gray Research Award, the National Reading Conference Oscar Causey Research Award, and the College of Education Distinguished Teaching Award from the University of Minnesota. He is a member of the National Reading Panel and is in the Reading Hall of Fame.

DIANE H. TRACEY is an associate professor of education at Kean University, where she teaches graduate classes to students pursuing their master's degrees as reading specialists. She has written widely on topics related to literacy achievement, has received many grant awards, and is an active presenter at national conferences. She has served on editorial review boards for the *Journal of Literacy Research*, *The Reading Teacher*, and the *National Reading Conference Yearbook* and is past chair of the International Reading Association's Technology Committee.

CHRISTINE WALSH is an assistant professor in the Department of Curriculum and Instruction at the State University of New York at Oswego, teaching courses in literacy, methods of instruction, and critical thinking about parenting. In addition to her teaching, she has written several publications, made presentations at national and international conferences, secured substantial national grants for preservice and in-service teachers, and serves as a professional development school leader.